THIS IS GRAMMAR 고급 2

지은이 넥서스영어교육연구소
펴낸이 임상진
펴낸곳 (주)넥서스

출판신고 1992년 4월 3일 제311-2002-2호 2-8
10880 경기도 파주시 지목로 5
Tel (02)330-5500 Fax (02)330-5555

ISBN 979-11-6165-099-9 54740
       979-11-5752-362-7 (SET)

www.nexusEDU.kr

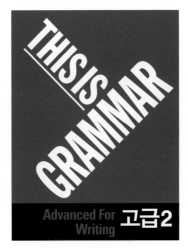

THIS IS GRAMMAR

Advanced For Writing 고급**2**

넥서스영어교육연구소 지음

NEXUS Edu

Preface

To Teachers and Students,

This brand new edition of *This Is Grammar* contains a wide range of engaging exercises designed to improve students' English grammar skills in the areas of speaking and writing. In Korea, middle and high school students have traditionally learned English grammar through rote memorization. We believe, however, that grammar learning is more effectively realized when explicit explanation is paired with practice. *This Is Grammar*(Updated version) provides Korean students with opportunities to practice using English while learning more about the world around them.

The exercises in the workbooks have been specially redesigned to give students more practice producing the target structures in a wide range of natural contexts. The teacher's guide includes additional grammar explanations and notes, comments on usage, and classroom presentation tips.

In sum, *This Is Grammar* provides teachers in Korea with a comprehensive set of materials to help them teach their students English grammar more effectively and with greater ease. It will help beginner to advanced level students improve their English skills in the areas of speaking and writing. We trust you will enjoy using *This Is Grammar* as a classroom textbook or by itself as a self-study aid.

- Christopher Douloff

This Is Grammar 최신개정판은 무조건 외우면서 학습하던 과거의 방법과는 달리, 현실에서 많이 쓰이는 진정성 있는 문장들을 토대로 핵심 문법을 체계적으로 설명하고 있다. 또한, 자연스러운 문맥 안에서 영어의 문장구조가 습득될 수 있도록 단계별 연습문제와 활동들을 제공하고 있어 초급부터 고급까지의 학습자들이 문법 지식을 바탕으로 말하기와 쓰기 등의 영어 실력을 향상시키는 데 큰 도움을 줄 수 있으리라 기대한다. *This Is Grammar*(최신개정판)가 강의용뿐만 아니라 자습서로서도 훌륭히 그 역할을 해 낼 수 있으리라 믿으며, 학습자들의 영어 실력 향상에 큰 다리 역할을 할 수 있기를 기대한다.

- 집필진 Christopher Douloff, McKathy, Rachel S. L

Series of features
시리즈의 특징

초급 1, 2

기초 문법 강화 + 내신 대비

영어의 기본 구조인 형태(form)와 의미(meaning), 용법(usage) 등을 설명하여 기초적인 문법 지식을 강화할 수 있도록 하였습니다. 다양한 유형의 연습문제를 단계별로 구성하였습니다. 또한, 시험에 자주 등장하는 문법 문제를 Review 및 Review Plus에서 다루고 있어 기본 실력을 강화하고 내신에 대비할 수 있도록 구성하였습니다.

중급 1, 2

문법 요약(Key Point) + 체계적인 문법 설명

Key Point 부분에 도식화·도표화하여 한눈에 보기 쉽게 문법을 요약해 놓았습니다. Key Point 에는 문법의 기본적인 내용을, FOCUS에는 문법의 상세한 설명을 수록해 놓았습니다. 이를 통해 기초 문법부터 심화 문법까지 체계적으로 습득할 수 있습니다. 또한, 문법 오류 확인 문제부터 문장 완성하기와 문장 바꿔 쓰기 등의 다양한 유형의 연습문제들로 문법 지식을 확실히 다질 수 있도록 구성하였습니다.

고급 1, 2

핵심 문법 설명 + 각종 수험 대비

중·고급 영어 학습자들을 대상으로 수능, 텝스, 토플, 토익 등 각종 시험을 완벽하게 대비할 수 있도록 핵심적인 문법 포인트를 분석, 정리하였습니다. 다양하고 진정성 있는 지문들을 통해 풍부한 배경지식을 함께 쌓을 수 있도록 하였습니다. 고급 1권으로는 일목요연하게 정리된 문법으로 수험 완벽 대비를 할 수 있도록 하였고, 그리고 고급 2권으로는 문장 쓰기에서 에세이 쓰기까지의 영작 연습을 통해 기본적인 작문 실력을 향상시킬 수 있도록 구성하였습니다.

Workbook

초급 1, 2, 중급 1, 2, 고급 1 총 5권

별책으로 구성된 Workbook은 원어민이 직접 집필하여 생생한 실생활 영어 표현으로 문장을 구성하였으며, Unit별 2페이지씩 연습문제를 수록하여 학습한 내용을 다시 한 번 점검하고 확실한 본인의 실력을 쌓을 수 있도록 구성하였습니다.

Composition and Features
구성과 특징

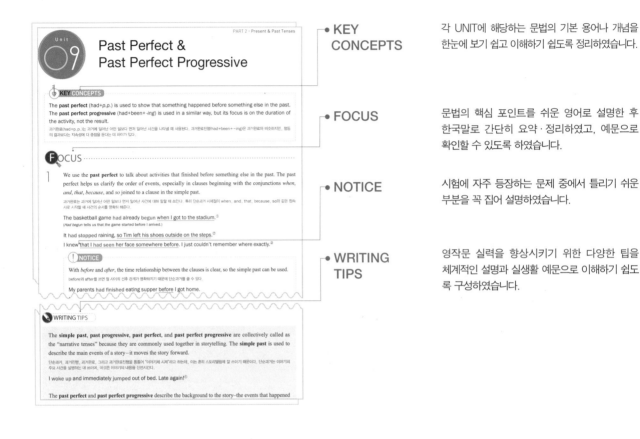

● KEY CONCEPTS

각 UNIT에 해당하는 문법의 기본 용어나 개념을 한눈에 보기 쉽고 이해하기 쉽도록 정리하였습니다.

● FOCUS

문법의 핵심 포인트를 쉬운 영어로 설명한 후 한국말로 간단히 요약·정리하였고, 예문으로 확인할 수 있도록 하였습니다.

● NOTICE

시험에 자주 등장하는 문제 중에서 틀리기 쉬운 부분을 꼭 집어 설명하였습니다.

● WRITING TIPS

영작문 실력을 향상시키기 위한 다양한 팁을 체계적인 설명과 실생활 예문으로 이해하기 쉽도록 구성하였습니다.

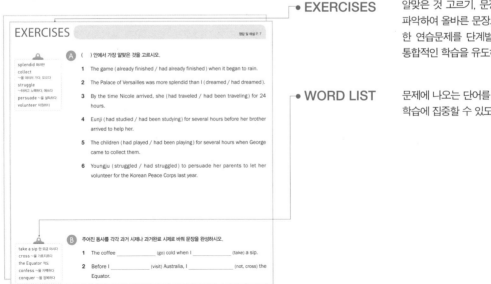

● EXERCISES

알맞은 것 고르기, 문장 완성하기, 틀린 부분을 파악하여 올바른 문장으로 다시 쓰기 등의 다양한 연습문제를 단계별로 제시하여 체계적이고 통합적인 학습을 유도하였습니다.

● WORD LIST

문제에 나오는 단어를 뜻과 함께 정리하여 문법 학습에 집중할 수 있도록 도움을 줍니다.

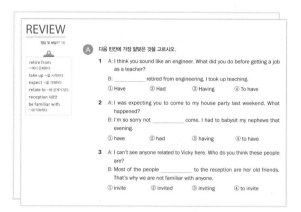

• REVIEW
대화를 통해 앞서 학습한 문법 포인트를 재확인하고, 문법적으로 부족한 문장을 완벽히 완성할 수 있도록 리뷰문제를 구성하였습니다.

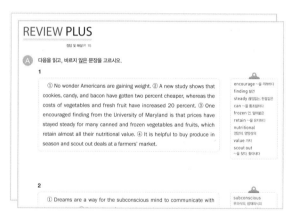

• REVIEW PLUS
중문 → 장문의 순으로 구성된 지문을 통해, 학습한 문법 포인트를 전체적으로 학습할 수 있습니다. 내신뿐만 아니라 수능 및 텝스 유형의 문제와 실제 수능 기출, 모의 기출 문제까지 응용·수록하여 실전 시험에 대비할 수 있도록 구성하였습니다.

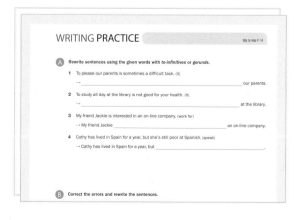

• WRITING PRACTICE
파트에서 학습한 문법 사항들을 활용하여 학습자 스스로 문장을 고쳐 보고 다시 써 볼 수 있는 학습 코너를 마련하였습니다. 또한 중요 표현을 활용하여 직접 문장을 만들어 보고, 전체적인 맥락 속에서 틀린 부분을 스스로 찾아내고 고쳐 가면서 작문 실력을 향상 시킬 수 있도록 구성하였습니다.

Contents 차례

Contents 차례

PART 1

Sentence Types, Coordination & Subordination

Unit 01 Simple Sentences

KEY CONCEPTS

A **simple sentence** consists of a subject and a verb, and it expresses a complete thought. Simple sentences are often expanded to include additional or extra information.

단문은 주어와 동사로 이루어지며, 하나의 완결된 생각을 표현한다. 단문은 종종 부가적인 정보 또는 추가 정보를 포함하기 위해 확장된다.

FOCUS

1   *A **main clause**—or independent clause—contains a subject and a verb, and it expresses a **complete thought**. A sentence with one main clause is called a **simple sentence**.*

주절(독립절)은 주어와 동사로 이루어지며, 하나의 완결된 생각을 표현한다. 하나의 주절로 이루어진 문장을 '단문'이라고 한다.

a   *With be or linking verbs* be동사나 연결 동사가 쓰인 경우

Jiyoung's father **is** a Thai Airlines pilot.[1] (subject＋be＋complement)

The rehearsal **will be** tomorrow afternoon.[2] (subject＋be＋complement)

Polar bears **seem** gentle.[3] (subject＋linking verb＋complement)

b   *With transitive or intransitive verbs* 타동사나 자동사가 쓰인 경우

Susan's new dress **glimmered**.[1] (subject＋intransitive verb)

Industrial activity **has muddied** the river.[2] (subject＋transitive verb＋direct object)

Jennifer **will send** you an email.[3] (subject＋transitive verb＋indirect object＋direct object)

The teacher **called** his students brilliant.[4] (subject＋transitive verb＋object＋complement)

The governor **declared** New Orleans a disaster area.[5] (subject＋transitive verb＋object＋complement)

2   *Simple sentences often contain adjuncts or additional structures which show "how," "when," "where," or "why" something happened. (NOTE: Removing the adjunct(s) will still leave the sentence grammatically complete.)* 단문은 어떤 일이 '어떻게', '언제', '어디서', '왜' 일어났는지 보여주는 부가어나 부가적인 구조를 포함한다. (주의: 부가어를 제거하더라도 문장은 문법적으로 완전하다.)

The rehearsal will be tomorrow afternoon <u>in the school's main auditorium</u>.[1] (tells "where")

Susan's new dress glimmered <u>brightly under the glowing lights</u>.[2] (tells "how")

<u>Tomorrow</u>, Jennifer will send you an email <u>about our plans to hold an English speech contest</u>.[3]
(tells "when" and "why")

---

1 a ① 지영이의 아버지는 타이 항공사의 조종사이다. ② 리허설은 내일 오후에 있을 것이다. ③ 북극곰은 온순해 보인다.   b ① 수잔의 새 드레스는 반짝거렸다. ② 산업 활동으로 인해 그 강이 더러워졌다. ③ 제니퍼가 너에게 이메일을 보낼 것이다. ④ 선생님은 자신의 학생들이 명석하다고 했다. ⑤ 주지사는 뉴올리언스를 재난 지역으로 선포했다.   2 ① 리허설이 내일 오후에 학교 본 강당에서 있을 것이다. ② 수잔의 새 드레스는 휘황찬란한 불빛 아래에서 밝게 반짝거렸다. ③ 내일 제니퍼가 영어 말하기 대회를 개최하려는 우리의 계획에 대해 너에게 이메일을 보낼 것이다.

EXERCISES

 A 문장을 읽고, 부가어(*adjuncts*)에 밑줄을 그으시오.

1 Interest will accrue on this bond at a rate of 7%.

2 Most of the adventure scenes were filmed on location in the Swiss Alps.

3 The tiles that I bought from your store the other day did not adhere properly.

4 The rocket fuel spontaneously ignited because of the high temperature and pressure.

5 The interview with the president will air tomorrow morning at 10:15 a.m. Eastern Standard Time.

6 The taxi driver accelerated quickly to overtake the driver of the slow moving vehicle in front of him.

interest 이자
accrue
(이자, 세금 등이) 붙다, 증가하다
bond 채권
at a[the] rate of
~의 비율로
film ~을 촬영하다
adhere 들러붙다, 부착하다
properly 제대로
rocket fuel 로켓 연료
spontaneously
자발적으로, 자연스럽게
ignite 불붙다, 발화하다
temperature 온도
pressure 압력
air 방송되다
accelerate 가속하다
overtake
~을 따라잡다, 추월하다

 B 우리말과 같은 뜻이 되도록 주어진 단어를 배열하시오.

1 가위와 색종이를 나에게 가져다주겠니?
(me, fetch, a pair of scissors, and some colored paper, could you)
→ _____

2 공항에서 출입국 관리관이 나에게 비자를 교부해 주었다.
(me, granted, an immigration officer at the airport, an entry visa)
→ _____

3 우리 스터디 그룹 모임은 도서관 3층에 있는 자료실에서 있다.
(is, in the resource room, on the third floor of the library, our study group meeting)
→ _____

4 이 최근의 국경을 넘어선 공격은 기존에 있었던 양국 간의 긴장 관계를 악화시킬 것이다.
(will exacerbate, the already tense relations between the two countries, this latest cross-border attack)
→ _____
_____

5 선발 절차를 감독하는 위원회는 레이놀즈 박사님을 물리학과 학과장으로 선출했다.
(elected, Chair of the Physics Department, the committee overseeing the selection process, Dr. Reynolds)
→ _____
_____

fetch ~을 가서 가지고 오다
colored paper 색종이
grant
~을 수여하다, 교부하다
immigration officer
출입국 관리관
entry visa 입국 비자
resource room 자료실
exacerbate
~을 악화시키다
tense 긴박한, 긴장한
relation 관계
cross-border
국경을 넘는
attack 공격
oversee ~을 감독하다
selection process
선발 절차

Coordination Conjunctions

 **KEY CONCEPTS**

Conjunctions are words that compound — or join — sentences and their parts. The coordinating conjunctions (e.g.: *and, but, or, for, yet, so, nor*) join two similar grammatical constructions of equal importance; for example, **words, phrases,** or **clauses.**
접속사는 문장과 문장의 일부분을 연결하는 단어이다. 등위 접속사 and, but, or, for, yet, so, nor는 동등한 문법 구조를 취하는 단어, 구, 절을 연결한다.

 FOCUS ....

1   *The most commonly used coordinating conjunctions are **and**, **but**, and **or**. These conjunctions are used to join subjects, verb phrases, objects, and main clauses. Two main clauses connected by a coordinating conjunction make a **compound sentence.***

가장 일반적으로 사용되는 등위 접속사는 and, but, or로 주어, 동사구, 목적어, 주절을 연결하는 데 사용되며, 등위 접속사로 연결된 두 개의 주절은 중문을 만든다.

General Electric **and** Ford were two of America's most iconic companies of the 1950s.① (two subjects)

My mom cooks breakfast in the morning **and** prepares dinner in the afternoon.② (two verb phrases)

Canada is famous for the beauty of its landscape **and** the hospitality of its people.③
(two objects of the preposition)

Call me old-fashioned, **but** I like handwritten letters better than emails.④
(joins two main clauses to make a compound sentence)

> **!NOTICE**
>
> *A comma (,) is used before the coordinating conjunction only when it joins two independent clauses.*
> 등위 접속사가 두 개의 독립절을 연결할 때에만 등위 접속사 앞에 콤마(,)를 쓴다.

2   *Other coordinating conjunctions include **for**, **yet**, **so**, and **nor**. These conjunctions are used mainly to join two main clauses.* for, yet, so, nor와 같은 등위 접속사는 주로 두 개의 주절을 연결하는 데 사용된다.

a   *When **for** is used as a coordinating conjunction, it means "because" or "as." It is a little old-fashioned, so because is preferred. (NOTE: For is also used as a preposition. e.g.: I gave him a card for his birthday.)*

for가 등위 접속사로 쓰일 때는 because 또는 as의 뜻을 가진다. 이는 약간 구식 표현이므로 because를 쓰는 편이 좋다. (주의: for는 전치사로도 사용된다. 예: 나는 그의 생일에 그에게 카드를 주었다.)

Jessica remained silent, **for** she knew that she had disappointed her father.①

I woke up early in the morning, **for** I knew it was going to be a long day.②

b *When* **yet** *is used as a coordinating conjunction, it means "nevertheless" or "but." It contains the idea of surprise. (NOTE: Yet is also used as an adverb. e.g.: Are you finished yet?)*

yet이 등위 접속사로 쓰일 때 nevertheless 또는 but의 뜻을 가지며, 놀라움의 뜻을 포함한다. (주의: yet은 부사로도 쓰인다. 예: 벌써 끝났니?)

Jeffery doesn't usually enjoy playing with other children, **yet** he looks happy now, doesn't he?[①]

Salt-water crocodiles are among the most feared creatures in Australia, yet they are amazingly gentle with their young.[②]

c *When* **so** *is used as a coordinating conjunction, it means "therefore."*

so가 등위 접속사로 쓰일 때 therefore의 뜻으로 쓰인다.

Mark was busy talking with Professor Larry, **so** I waited for him in the library.[①]

The nurse was still bandaging my arm, **so** I tried in vain to look brave.[②]

d ***Nor*** *has a negative meaning, and it is often used with not. (NOTE: When nor is used as a coordinating conjunction, the subject and verb reverse order.)*

nor는 부정적인 뜻을 가지며, 종종 not과 같이 쓰인다. (주의: nor가 등위 접속사로 쓰이면 주어와 동사의 순서가 바뀐다.)

Jennifer doesn't like to eat meat, **nor** <u>does</u> <u>she</u> like dairy products like eggs, milk, or cheese.[①]

I didn't hear the speeding train approach, **nor** <u>did</u> <u>my</u> <u>friends</u>.[②]

---

1 ① 제너럴 일렉트릭사와 포드사는 1950년대 미국을 상징하는 두 회사였다. ② 우리 엄마는 아침에 아침 식사를 요리하시고, 오후에 저녁 식사를 준비하신다. ③ 캐나다는 아름다운 풍경과 국민들의 친절함으로 유명하다. ④ 나를 구식이라고 해도 좋아. 하지만 나는 이메일보다 손으로 쓴 편지가 좋아. 2 a ① 제시카는 자신이 아버지를 실망시켰다는 것을 알았기 때문에 조용히 있었다. ② 긴 하루가 될 것이라는 것을 알았기에, 나는 아침에 일찍 일어났다. b ① 제프리는 보통 다른 어린이들과 노는 것을 즐기지는 않지만 지금은 행복해 보여, 그렇지 않니? ② 인도악어는 호주에서 가장 무서운 동물 중 하나이지만, 자신들의 새끼들에게는 놀랍게도 온화하다. c ① 마크는 래리 교수와 이야기하느라 바빠서 나는 도서관에서 그를 기다렸다. ② 간호사가 여전히 내 팔에 붕대를 감고 있었고, 나는 용감해 보이려고 했지만 잘 안 됐다. d ① 제니퍼는 고기 먹는 것을 좋아하지 않고, 계란, 우유, 치즈와 같은 유제품도 좋아하지 않는다. ② 나는 고속철이 다가오는 소리를 듣지 못했고, 내 친구들도 듣지 못했다.

EXERCISES

farmhand 농장 노동자
lead ~을 이끌다
a flight of stairs 층계
참(층계와 층계를 잇는 부분)
chemicals 화학 약품
with care
신중히, 주의 깊게
prompt
프롬프트(상기시켜 주는 것)
brainstorm
~을 브레인스토밍하다
abandon ~을 버리다
run out of ~이 떨어지다
dashboard
(자동차의) 계기판

 A ( ) 안에서 가장 알맞은 것을 고르시오.

1 Most farmhands know that it is possible to lead a cow up a flight of stairs, (and / or / but) not back down again.

2 Have you seen (for / or / but) heard from Scott this week? I haven't, and I'm starting to get a little worried.

3 In the science lab, dangerous chemicals should be handled with care (and / or / but) put back in the cabinet after use.

4 Miya read the writing prompt, brainstormed a list of ideas, (and / or / but) wrote her response in less than forty-five minutes.

5 We abandoned the car when it ran out of gas, (for / or / but) we made sure to leave a note on the dashboard explaining what had happened.

6 Mr. Kim told me that I could use the computer in the lab (for / or / but) this computer here. He said that he didn't mind either way as long as I finished my report by noon.

lullaby 자장가
drift off 잠이 들다
hearty (식사의 양이)
풍부한, 영양가 있는

B 〈보기〉에서 가장 알맞은 것을 골라 문장을 완성하시오.

보기	so	for	yet	nor

1 Helen won't speak to me, _____ will her sister.

2 Craig sang the beautiful lullabies to the babies, _____ they drifted off to sleep.

3 My younger brother, Gary, hates exercising, _____ does he like spending time outdoors.

4 Soojin had not known her new co-worker, Hoon, very long, _____ she felt very close to him.

5 We packed a hearty lunch, _____ we knew we would be hungry after a day trekking in the Everglades.

6 Shakey's Restaurant has the worst food and the most expensive prices in town, _____ you always want to go there for lunch. Why?

C 〈보기〉에서 가장 알맞은 것을 골라 문장을 완성하시오.

보기	for	yet	nor	and

1 Colin works hard, _____ he wants to buy a new computer on his own.

2 We will no longer be supplying our customers with plastic grocery bags, _____ will we be validating parking tickets.

3 The Hubble Space Telescope weighs 12 tons _____ is 43 feet long, and it cost $2.1 billion to build and put into orbit above the earth.

4 I knew that times were tough, _____ I was shocked to see Mr. Mitchell, formerly the plant manager, applying for unemployment benefits along with his former line workers.

validate
~을 유효하게 하다
weigh 무게가 ~이다
put into orbit
궤도에 올리다
formerly 이전에, 예전에
apply for ~을 신청하다
unemployment
benefit 실업 수당
along with ~와 함께

D 문장을 읽고, 밑줄 친 부분을 바르게 고치시오.

1 Someone rang for Helen earlier, <u>and</u> they wouldn't leave a message.

2 I can't remember his name right now, <u>so</u> I definitely know his face from somewhere.

3 Leslie and I are going to go shopping on Sunday <u>yet</u> buy some new summer clothes.

4 Advertising is a fast-paced, high-pressure industry, <u>or</u> there is a constant need for creative ideas.

5 A powerful beam of light radiated from the lighthouse, <u>nor</u> the ship's captain was unable to steer his craft away from the rocky shore.

6 Being a carpenter by trade, John could easily have renovated the cottage himself, <u>for</u> he hired an out-of-work friend to do the work instead.

7 It is commonly held that no piece of paper can be folded in half more than seven times, <u>for</u> on several occasions this fact has been exposed to the myth.

ring for ~에게 전화하다
fast-paced
여러 가지 일이 빨리 일어나는
high-pressure
고압적인, 강요하는
constant
일정한, 끊임없는
beam (등대 등의) 빛
radiate from
~에서 발산되다
lighthouse 등대
steer away from
~에서 떠나다, ~을 피하다
craft 배
carpenter 목수
by trade 직업으로, 직업상
renovate ~을 개조하다
out-of-work 실직한
it is commonly held
that ~라는 통념이다
fold in half
~을 반으로 접다
be exposed 드러나다

Unit

Correlative Conjunctions

 KEY CONCEPTS

Correlative conjunctions work in pairs to connect sentence elements of the same kind: nouns, adjectives, verbs. The most commonly used correlative conjunctions are *both ... and*, *either ... or*, *neither ... nor*, and *not only ... but also*.

상관 접속사는 동일한 문장 성분(명사, 형용사, 동사)을 연결할 때 짝을 이루어 쓰인다. both ... and, either ... or, neither ... nor, not only ... but also가 가장 일반적으로 쓰이는 상관 접속사이다.

 FOCUS ···

1 *Correlative conjunctions are used in pairs. They show the relationship between the ideas expressed in different parts of a sentence.*

상관 접속사는 짝을 이뤄 쓰이고 문장의 서로 다른 부분에서 표현된 사고 간의 관계를 나타낸다.

McKathy is **both** intelligent **and** good-natured.①

Ruddin is **not only** clever **but also** hard-working.②

We will go to **either** the Met **or** the Guggenheim.③

Mr. Leach is **neither** rich **nor** famous, but he is content.④

2 *We use **both ... and** to show "addition." When joining two subjects with **both ... and**, use a plural verb.*

추가의 의미를 나타내기 위해 both ... and를 사용하며, 두 개의 주어를 연결할 때는 동사의 복수형을 사용한다.

Both my younger sister **and** my older brother <u>are</u> majoring in chemical engineering.①

(*both ... and* links the two noun phrases that act as the compound subject of the sentence)

I found Dave's collection of antique dolls **both** fascinating **and** creepy at the same time.②

(*both ... and* links the two adjectives that act as complements of the object *collection*)

(!) NOTICE

Both ... and cannot connect two independent clauses.

both ... and는 두 개의 독립절을 연결하지 못한다.

3 *We also use **not only ... but also** to show "addition." When joining two subjects with any of the remaining correlative conjunctions (not only ... but also, either ... or, and neither ... nor), the subject closer to the verb will determine whether it is singular or plural.*

not only ... but also도 추가의 뜻을 나타내며, 두 개의 주어가 상관 접속사 not only ... but also, either ... or, neither ... nor로 연결된 경우에는 동사에 가까운 주어에 따라 동사의 수가 결정된다.

Jacob **not only** lost his keys **but also** misplaced his homework assignment.①
(*not only ... but also* links two verb phrases)

Not only Mr. Kim **but also** <u>his two sons</u> <u>were</u> aboard the airplane when it mysteriously vanished.②
(*not only ... but also* links two noun phrases)

4 *We use **either** ... **or** to talk about a "choice" between two possibilities.*
either ... or는 두 개의 가능성 중에서 하나를 선택할 때 쓴다.

You must **either** follow me up the mountain **or** go back down yourself.①
(*either ... or* links two verb phrases)

Either I'll go snowboarding with my brother, Greg, **or** I'll play hockey with my cousin, Steve.②
(*either ... or* links two complete sentences)

> *A comma is used to join two full sentences.*
> 두 개의 완전한 문장을 연결할 때는 콤마를 사용한다.
> **Either** you can go now, **or** you can leave later.③

5 *We use **neither** ... **nor** to join two negative ideas. It is the opposite of both ... and.*
두 개의 부정적인 생각을 연결할 때는 neither ... nor를 사용하며, both ... and와 반대의 의미를 가진다.

Neither my triceps **nor** my chest has developed much since I started this new exercise routine.①
(*neither ... nor* links two noun phrases)

At the golf range this afternoon, I hit **neither** the 500 yard mark **nor** the 400 yard mark.②
(*neither ... nor* links the two noun phrases that act as objects of the verb *hit*)

6 *Other correlative conjunctions include **hardly ... when, no sooner ... than**, and **whether ... or**.*
그 외 상관 접속사에는 hardly ... when, no sooner ... than, whether ... or가 있다.

Mr. Richard had **hardly** begun to eat **when** he was rudely interrupted by the doorbell.①
No sooner <u>had</u> <u>Stacey</u> sat down **than** the phone began to ring again.② (부정어구+동사+주어: 도치 문장)
Have you decided **whether** you will come **or** not?③

---

1 ① 맥캐시는 지적이고 마음씨도 착하다. ② 루딘은 영리할 뿐만 아니라 성실하다. ③ 우리는 메트로폴리탄 미술관이나 구겐하임 미술관에 갈 것이다. ④ 리치 씨는 부자도 아니고 유명하지도 않지만, 만족하고 있다. 2 ① 내 여동생과 오빠 둘 다 화학 공학을 전공하고 있다. ② 나는 데이브가 수집한 골동품 인형들이 매혹적이면서도 섬뜩하다고 생각했다. 3 ① 제이콥은 열쇠를 잃어버렸을 뿐만 아니라 숙제를 놓아둔 장소를 잊어버렸다. ② 김 씨뿐만 아니라 그의 두 아들도 비행기가 불가사의하게 사라졌을 때 그곳에 탑승해 있었다. 4 ① 너는 나와 같이 산 위로 가든지, 아니면 너 혼자 내려가야 한다. ② 나는 형 그레그와 스노보드를 타러 가든지, 아니면 내 사촌 스티브와 하키를 할 것이다. ③ 너는 지금 가든지, 아니면 나중에 떠나도 된다. 5 ① 내가 이 새 운동 일정을 시작한 이후로 삼두박근도 가슴근육도 많이 발달하지 않았다. ② 오늘 오후 골프장에서 나는 500야드도, 400야드 마크도 찍지 못했다. 6 ① 리차드 씨가 음식을 먹기 시작하자마자 갑작스럽게 초인종이 울려 그를 방해했다. ② 스테이시가 앉자마자 전화가 다시 울리기 시작했다. ③ 너는 올지 말지 결정했니?

EXERCISES

bank teller 은행원
signal for
~에게 신호로 알리다
step forward
앞으로 나가다
generously
관대하게, 아낌없이
stock 주식
bond 채권
underperform 기대
이하로 행하다, 실적을 못 내다
feature 상영 작품
announce
~을 알리다, 발표하다

 ( ) 안에서 가장 알맞은 것을 고르시오.

1 Hardly had I stood up (when / while) the bank teller signaled for the next customer in line to step forward.

2 Not only does Catherine volunteer at the local library, (and / but) she also gives generously to several children's charities.

3 Both stocks (and / also) bonds are underperforming this year. It's the perfect time to invest your money for the future.

4 Tonight's feature movie is either *Madagascar* (or / nor) *Charlie and the Chocolate Factory*. Why don't you check the listing for times?

5 No sooner had I bought my new computer (than / for) the company announced a newer, faster model would be available in the coming weeks.

glue 접착제
clamp 죔쇠(죄는 기구)
require ~을 요구하다
complete ~을 완성하다
columnist
칼럼니스트, 특별 기고가
go on strike 파업하다
stimulus 자극
priority 우선 사항

 ( ) 안에서 가장 알맞은 것을 고르시오.

1 Either you or Jennifer (is / are) to finish this project.

2 Both glue and clamps (is / are) required to complete the model.

3 Both the newspaper's columnists and its editor (is / are) going on strike.

4 Either the environment or economic stimulus (have to / has to) be our priority.

5 Neither the library nor the bookstores in town (have / has) the novel I want to read.

crowd 군중
enthusiastic 열광적인
bumble bee 땅벌
fly into
~ 안으로 날아들어 오다

 문장을 읽고, 밑줄 친 부분을 바르게 고치시오.

1 We should either walk more quickly <u>and</u> take a taxi.

2 It was not only a beautiful day <u>yet</u> the first day of winter.

3 I don't know <u>no sooner</u> Sam has seen that movie before or not.

4 The crowd waiting outside the hotel was neither large <u>or</u> very enthusiastic.

5 No sooner <u>I had</u> opened the window than a giant bumble bee flew into the room.

16

D 〈보기〉에서 알맞은 것을 골라 문장을 완성하시오.

| 보기 | and | but | or | nor |

1 My cousin Nicole will either attend UC Berkeley _____ Harvard in the fall.

2 Neither the manager _____ any of the waiters milling about seem willing to take our order.

3 Both individuals _____ nations will have to rethink how they use energy if they are to have any hope of staving off environmental ruin.

4 A well-designed tourist map should not only tell you how to get from A to B, _____ it should also point out places of interest along the way.

E 주어진 상관 접속사를 이용하여 문장을 완성하시오.

1 Raising a pet develops a child's curiosity. It also fosters a sense of responsibility. (not only A but also B)
→ Raising a pet _____.

2 Help us put up these posters for the school dance, or stop pestering us and let us finish before we run out of time. (either A or B)
→ _____
_____

3 In his lifetime, Alexander Graham Bell invented the telephone. He also set a world water-speed record of over seventy miles an hour. (both A and B)
→ In his lifetime, Alexander Graham _____
_____.

4 Before undergoing extensive training, these dogs are not smart enough to perform complex operations. They are not disciplined enough to remain focused on the task at hand, either. (neither A nor B)
→ Before undergoing extensive training, these dogs are _____
_____.

Unit 04

Subordination & Complex Sentences

 KEY CONCEPTS

Coordinating conjunctions link words, phrases, and clauses of equal importance. **Subordinating conjunctions**, however, connect only clauses. A subordinate—or dependent clause—is one that adds more information to a full sentence, the main clause. On their own, **dependent clauses** are **incomplete**.

등위 접속사는 단어, 구, 절을 연결하지만 종속 접속사는 절과 절을 연결한다. 이때 주절은 하나의 완결된 문장인 반면, 종속절은 주절에 정보를 추가해 줄 뿐 그 자체로는 불완전하다.

FOCUS ....

1

*A **subordinate clause**—or dependent clause—contains a subject and a verb, but it **does not** express a **complete thought**. A sentence with at least one subordinate clause is called a "complex sentence." Common subordinating conjunctions include after, because, even though, since, unless, when, and whereas.*

종속절은 주어와 동사로 이루어지지만, 완전한 생각을 표현하지 못한다. 최소한 하나의 종속절을 가진 문장을 복문이라고 한다. 일반적인 종속 접속사로 *after, because, even though, since, unless, when, whereas*가 있다.

They are essential for winter hiking. (a complete main clause)

(×) Because sunglasses filter harmful UV rays. (an incomplete dependent clause)

→ Because sunglasses filter harmful UV rays, they are essential for winter hiking.[1]
(a complex sentence: a dependent clause+a main clause)

! NOTICE

A comma is always used if the dependent clause comes first. A comma is usually not used if the dependent clause follows the main clause. However, for words like while and whereas, which show direct contrast, a comma may be used.

종속절이 먼저 나오면 항상 콤마를 사용한다. 종속절이 주절 다음에 오면 일반적으로 콤마를 사용하지 않지만, *while*이나 *whereas*처럼 직접적인 대조를 나타내는 콤마를 사용하기도 한다.

Before it became an independent nation in 1947, India was a colony of the UK.

→ India was a colony of the UK before it became an independent nation in 1947.[2]

While his daughter looks only about sixteen, Mr. Stevens' eldest son must be about thirty.

→ Mr. Stevens' eldest son must be about thirty, while his daughter looks only about sixteen.[3]

2

There are three kinds of subordinate clauses: **adverb clauses, adjective clauses,** *and* **noun clauses.**

종속절에는 부사절, 형용사절, 명사절 세 가지가 있다.

I had never even heard of *ssireum* before I moved to Korea.[1] (an adverb clause: tells "when")

Jake is a man who takes great pride in everything he does.[2] (an adjective clause: describes *Jake*)

Who Sally resembles most in her family is her mother.[3] (a noun clause: acts as the "subject")

3

Coordinating conjunctions join two main clauses of equal importance. **Subordinating conjunctions** *however,* **emphasize** *the idea expressed in the* **main clause.**

등위 접속사는 동등한 중요성을 지닌 두 개의 주절을 연결하는 반면, 종속 접속사는 주절에서 표현된 생각을 강조한다.

Leslie spent all morning finishing her homework and doing her chores. **Since** she had nothing left to do, she was able to enjoy the rest of her day with friends at the mall.[1]

4

A **compound-complex sentence** *contains at least one dependent clause and two (or more) independent clauses.*

중복문은 최소한 한 개의 종속절과 두 개 이상의 독립절로 이루어져 있다.

Even if you fail, at least you tried, **and** you're a better person for it.[1]

---

1 ① 선글라스는 해로운 UV 광선을 차단해주기 때문에 겨울 하이킹에 필수적이다. ② 인도는 1947년에 독립 국가가 되기 전에 영국의 식민지였다. ③ 스티븐스 씨의 맏아들은 서른 살 정도인 것이 틀림없는데 반면에 그의 딸은 열여섯 살쯤으로 보인다. 2 ① 나는 한국으로 이사 오기 전에는 씨름에 대해 들어 본 적이 없었다. ② 제이크는 자신이 하는 모든 것에 강한 자부심을 느끼는 사람이다. ③ 샐리가 가족 중에서 가장 많이 닮은 사람은 엄마이다. 3 ① 레슬리는 숙제를 끝마치고, 허드렛일을 하느라 오전을 다 보냈다. 그녀는 할 것이 아무것도 남아 있지 않아서 나머지 시간에 쇼핑몰에서 친구들과 즐겁게 보낼 수 있었다. 4 ① 실패하더라도 적어도 노력은 했으니, 너는 그런 면에서 더 나은 사람인 거야.

EXERCISES

electronic passport
전자 여권

recognize ~을 알아보다

coin
(새로운 말을) 만들어 내다

crumbling
산산이 조각난

medieval 중세의

stoically 의연하게, 냉정하
게, 감정을 드러내지 않고

atop ~의 정상에

overlook ~을 내려다보다

industrial 산업의

A 문장에서 종속절을 찾아 밑줄을 긋고, 그 종속절이 부사절(*adverse clause*), 형용사절(*adjective clause*), 명사절(*noun clause*) 중 어떤 역할을 하는지 〈보기〉에서 골라 그 기호를 쓰시오.

> 보기   ⓐ adverb clause   ⓑ adjective clause   ⓒ noun clause

1 Mr. Park needs to find out how he can get one of those new electronic passports. _____

2 The two brothers recognized each other at once even though they had not seen each other for many years. _____

3 In today's class, we learned that International Business Machines (IBM) coined the term word processor in 1964. _____

4 The crumbling medieval castle, which stands stoically atop a small hill overlooking the village, can still be seen for miles. _____

5 The firm whose new product won the industrial design competition held last month in Geneva is celebrating the event with a special dinner for its employees. _____

dive 다이빙하다

earn one's degree
학위를 따다

geography 지리학

B 주어진 접속사를 이용하여 두 문장을 한 문장으로 연결하시오. [필요하면 콤마(,)를 사용할 것]

1 You would not believe me. I told you the truth. (even if)

→ _____

2 Do you know? Are the stores at the mall open today? (whether)

→ _____

3 You cannot become an expert diver. You dive professionally for several years. (until)

→ _____

4 It was well past 2:00 a.m. Neither Mark nor his wife, Kate, felt the least bit tired. (although)

→ _____

5 She earned her degree in education. Ms. Mills started teaching high school geography at Centennial Collegiate. (after)

→ _____

20

Conjunctive Adverbs

Conjunctive adverbs are used to connect ideas and provide smooth flow between sentences. And because they are adverbs, they are movable.

접속 부사는 생각을 연결하고 문장 간의 윤활유 역할을 하는 부사로 이동이 자유롭다.

1 **Conjunctive adverbs** *are used as* **transitions** *between two main clauses. They provide a link back to information discussed earlier. (NOTE: Conjunctive adverbs are weak connectors; therefore, a* **semicolon** *is required when connecting two independent clauses.)*

접속 부사는 두 개의 주절을 연결하는 데 사용되며 앞서 언급된 정보에 대한 연결 고리를 제공한다. (주의: 접속 부사는 등위 접속사와는 달리, 문법적인 기능이 약하므로 두 개의 독립절을 연결할 때는 세미콜론(;)을 사용해야 한다.)

That is one possible solution to the problem; **however**, there are others.[1]

→ That is one possible solution to the problem. **However**, there are others.

→ That is one possible solution to the problem. **There are**, however, others.

→ That is one possible solution to the problem. There are others, **however**.

Conjunctive adverbs lose their connective power the farther away they appear in the sentence.

접속 부사는 문장에서 뒤에 위치할수록 연결력이 약해진다.

2 *Conjunctive adverbs that show "addition" include* **also, besides, furthermore, in addition, likewise,** *and* **moreover.** *These conjunctive adverbs have a meaning similar to the coordinating conjunction and.*

위에 나열된 접속 부사는 추가의 의미를 나타내며, 등위 접속사 and와 비슷한 의미를 가진다.

You should start exercising; **furthermore**, you should do it at once! (more formal)

→ You should start exercising, **and** you should do it at once![1] (less formal)

Your essay is wonderfully written. **Moreover**, it contains some interesting insights.

→ Your essay is wonderfully written, **and** it contains some interesting insights.[2]

3

*Conjunctive adverbs that show "contrast" include **however**, **in contrast**, **instead**, **nevertheless**, **nonetheless**, **on the contrary**, **on the other hand**, and **still**. These conjunctive adverbs have a meaning similar to the coordinating conjunction but.*

위에 나열된 접속 부사는 대조를 나타내며, 등위 접속사 but과 비슷한 의미를 가진다.

CCTV cameras do deter crime; they are an invasion of privacy, **however**.

→ CCTV cameras do deter crime; **however**, they are an invasion of privacy. (adverbs are movable)

CCTV cameras do deter crime, **but** they are an invasion of privacy.①

(✕) CCTV cameras do deter crime, they are an invasion of privacy, ~~but~~. (conjunctions are not movable)

> **On the contrary** and **on the other hand** have different meanings.
>
> on the contrary와 on the other hand는 다른 의미를 가진다.
>
> The risk of infection hasn't decreased. **On the contrary**, it has increased.②
> (*on the contrary* means "No, it isn't.")
>
> Earth isn't the biggest planet in our solar system. **On the other hand**, it isn't the smallest either.③
> (*on the other hand* means "one point of view")

4

*Conjunctive adverbs that show "result" include **accordingly**, **as a result**, **consequently**, **hence**, **therefore**, and **thus**. These conjunctive adverbs have a meaning similar to the coordinating conjunction so.*

위에 나열된 접속 부사는 결과를 나타내며, 등위 접속사 so와 비슷한 뜻을 가진다.

Ms. Lim is an expert in her field; **accordingly**, we paid her 10% over the going rate.

→ Ms. Lim is an expert in her field, **so** we paid her 10% over the going rate.①

Liam's math grades have slipped this semester. **As a result**, he'll have to attend summer school.

→ Liam's math grades have slipped this semester, **so** he'll have to attend summer school.②

---

1 ① 그것은 그 문제에 대한 하나의 해결책이지만, 다른 해결책들도 있다.   2 ① 너는 운동을 시작해야 해, 당장 해야 해! ② 네 논설문은 훌륭하게 써졌고, 그것은 몇 가지 흥미로운 통찰력도 포함하고 있다.   3 ① CCTV 카메라는 범죄를 방지하지만, 사생활 침해이다. ② 감염의 위험이 줄어들지 않았다. 반대로 증가했다. ③ 지구는 태양계에서 가장 큰 행성이 아니다. 반면에, 가장 작은 행성도 아니다.   4 ① 임 선생님은 자신의 분야에서 전문가이기에 우리는 그녀에게 시세보다 10% 더 지불하였다. ② 이번 학기에 리암은 수학 성적이 떨어져서 여름학교에 다녀야 할 것이다.

EXERCISES

정답 및 해설 P. 3

 A ( ) 안에서 가장 알맞은 것을 고르시오.

1 Matt Damon is a talented American actor; (moreover / thus), he is intelligent.

2 The food was delicious. (Likewise / Nevertheless), the service was outstanding.

3 Jane's new office assistant is kind. (Consequently / However), she is rather forgetful.

4 My grandfather is almost ninety. (Nonetheless / Therefore), his mind is still active, and he has the carefree spirit of a man half his age.

5 It was another typically cloudy day at Everest Base Camp. (Hence / However), we weren't able to get a clear view of the mountain.

6 The kind of work Mr. Smith wanted Christine to do was completely new to her. (Accordingly / Nevertheless), it didn't seem that difficult.

> outstanding
> 우수한, 뛰어난
> rather 다소
> forgetful
> 잘 잊는, 건망증이 있는
> carefree 느긋한, 태평한
> typically 전형적으로

B 문장을 읽고, 주어진 접속 부사를 이용하여 두 문장으로 나눠 쓰시오.

1 Maria studied for many months, so she knew the material thoroughly. (consequently)

→ _____

2 I would rather travel to Canterbury by train, but the bus leaves earlier, and it's cheaper. (however)

→ _____

3 This smartphone has more storage capacity, and it also comes with a built-in Bluetooth headset. (moreover)

→ _____

4 Nell applied herself conscientiously during practice, so she performed well at the recital. (as a result)

→ _____

_____

5 Namhee is well-educated, and she has very good manners. (besides)

→ _____

> thoroughly 완전히
> storage capacity
> 저장 용량
> apply oneself 전념하다
> conscientiously
> 공들여
> well-educated
> 잘 교육받은

REVIEW

정답 및 해설 P. 3

engineering 공학
highlight 하이라이트,
가장 흥미 있는 부분
fuel 연료
rise 오르다, 상승하다

 A 다음 빈칸에 가장 알맞은 것을 고르시오.

1 A: What would you like to do _____ you finish your studies?

B: I would like to go abroad and study engineering in the UK or Australia.

① and   ② for   ③ after   ④ because of

2 A: Did you visit the Louvre Museum _____ you were in Paris last month?

B: I did! Seeing Leonardo da Vinci's *Mona Lisa* was the highlight of my trip.

① since   ② before   ③ after   ④ while

3 A: Is bicycle riding popular where you live?

B: It is! Nowadays, many people ride bikes to work _____ the price of fuel has risen so high.

① and   ② because   ③ whether   ④ that

policy 정책
be due back
돌아오게 되어 있다
check out ~을 대출하다
new release 신간
condiment 조미료, 양념
draft 초안을 작성하다
revise ~을 수정하다

B 다음 대화를 읽고, 바르지 <u>않은</u> 문장을 고르시오.

1 ① A: Excuse me, but for how long may I borrow these DVDs?

② B: The library's policy is that they are due back in seven days.

③ A: Only seven days? That's not very long. Well, I'll check out just these two.

④ B: I'm terribly sorry, but neither new releases or e-learning DVDs are allowed to be checked out.

2 ① A: Did you pack up everything for the picnic like I asked you to do?

② B: I sure did. Everything you asked for is in the basket on the kitchen table.

③ A: Jerry! Both the condiments for the burgers or the soft drinks for the kids are missing.

④ B: Oh, I packed those away in the cooler and put them in the car already.

3 ① A: I'm sorry that I have to tell you this, but Mr. Thomas is not satisfied with the proposal you drafted.

② B: Oh, no! What am I going to do? Have you got any spare time to help me revise it?

③ A: Well, either I can stay late after work this week, also I can come in on the weekend.

④ B: I can't come in on the weekend because my son is visiting. Would you mind staying late this week?

24

REVIEW PLUS

정답 및 해설 P. 4

A 다음을 읽고, 바르지 <u>않은</u> 문장을 고르시오.

1

① Freeze-drying is the process of removing moisture from foods by using a vacuum. ② There are many benefits to freeze-drying food. For example, when perishables such as meat, vegetables, or fruits are freeze-dried, they may be stored at room temperature without refrigeration. ③ Moreover, freeze-dried food weighs 70 to 90 percent less. ④ These twin advantages make freeze-dried products perfect for campers and hikers, who often have either a way to keep their rations cold nor enough space to store them.

freeze-drying
동결 건조; 동결 건조의
vacuum 진공
perishable
부패하기 쉬운 (것)
store ~을 저장하다
room temperature
실내 온도, 상온
refrigeration
냉동, 냉각
weigh 무게가 ~ 나가다
ration 식량; 배급

2

① Much has changed in the United States in the last one hundred years. ② For example, a century ago less than 15% of homes had a bathtub. ③ Most women washed their hair only once a month, but they used a detergent called borax, or sometimes even egg yolks, for shampoo. ④ In another example, there were fewer than 8,000 cars and 144 miles of paved road in the entire country, and the maximum speed limit in most cities was a mere 10 mph.

detergent 세제
egg yolk 달걀노른자
paved road 포장도로

3

① Another important difference between speaking and writing is that speaking occurs in real time. ② As a result, speakers almost always have the opportunity to clarify themselves if they feel that a point has been either misunderstood and misinterpreted. ③ In contrast, writers are afforded no such luxury; ④ they must take great care to encode their messages as accurately and precisely as possible the very first time, for the careful writer knows that he or she will be afforded no such second chance.

as a result 그 결과
clarify ~을 명백히 하다
misunderstand
~을 오해하다
misinterpret
~을 잘못 해석하다
in contrast 대조적으로
take care
주의하다, 조심하다
encode ~을 표현하다
accurately 정확하게
precisely 명확하게

B 다음 (A), (B), (C)에서 어법에 맞는 표현으로 가장 적절한 것을 고르시오. [기출 응용]

willow 버드나무
bark 껍질
chemist 화학자
ingredient 성분, 요소
lining (위장의) 속, 내장
conduct ~을 시행하다
effective 효과적인
side effect 부작용
trademark 상표를 붙이다

About 2,400 years ago, Hippocrates prescribed willow bark, (A) _____ contains a natural form of aspirin. It wasn't until the early nineteenth century, (B) _____, that chemists created a simpler version of that ingredient. Unfortunately, it ate the lining of the stomach. In the late 1880s, a chemist, Felix Hoffmann, conducted further experiments. He created an effective fever and pain medicine with fewer side effects. In January 1899, a German company (C) _____ Bayer trademarked "Aspirin" for this new drug.

	(A)		(B)		(C)
①	what	…	whatever	…	named
②	what	…	whatever	…	naming
③	what	…	however	…	named
④	which	…	however	…	named
⑤	which	…	however	…	naming

C 다음 글의 밑줄 친 부분 중, 바르지 않은 것을 고르시오. [기출 응용]

fall out of
~에서 떨어지다
flock of ~의 떼, 무리
eagerly 열심히, 간절히
grownup 성인

① When I was growing up, one of the places I enjoyed most was the cherry tree in the backyard. Every summer ② when the cherries began to ripen, I would spend hours high in the tree picking and eating the sweet, sun-warmed cherries. My mother always worried about my falling out of the tree, but I never did. ③ But I had some competition for the cherries. Flocks of birds enjoyed them ④ as much as I did and would gather together in the tree, eating the fruit quickly and eagerly whenever I wasn't there. I used to wonder ⑤ how the grownups never ate any of the cherries.

A **Correct the errors and rewrite the sentences.**

1 The bola is a rope which is used to catch animals, <u>but</u> it has weights on the end of it.

→ _____

2 The young boy who is playing the piano is my cousin from Canada, <u>yet</u> he will be staying with us for the whole summer.

→ _____

3 After the tornado moved on, my house was gone; <u>in addition</u>, my neighbor's house remained as it was—seemingly oblivious to the maelstrom that had passed.

→ _____

_____

4 <u>Because</u> Jill and her sister searched the entire neighborhood, their pet Dachshund, Doxie, was nowhere to be found, and the girls couldn't help but feel that she was lost forever.

→ _____

_____

B **Correct the errors and rewrite the sentences.**

1 <u>Before</u> the long hike through Lynn Canyon, the kids were hot, sweaty, and a bit cranky.

→ _____

2 Neither Susan <u>or</u> her husband will be able to attend the family reunion next month.

→ _____

3 Miley wasn't in the backyard, <u>and</u> was she upstairs. Honestly, I don't have a clue where she's gotten to.

→ _____ Honestly, I don't have a clue where she's gotten to.

4 As the lions <u>approaching</u> the dead elk, the jackals and buzzards retreated to a safe distance to wait.

→ _____

5 The fox ran into a hole or behind those rocks. I can't be sure <u>because of</u> I was trying to find my camera.

→ The fox ran into a hole or behind those rocks. _____

Rearrange the words. Use commas where necessary. Follow the example.

> (do / Michael's email address / or telephone number / you / know)? I urgently need to reach him.
> → ___Do you know Michael's email address or telephone number___ ? I urgently need to reach him.

1 (I didn't get to see / did / the end of the game / nor / anyone else). It was called on account of rain.

→ _____

It was called on account of rain.

2 (has / will come to see / decided / she / whether / Jessie / us) this summer or not?

→ _____

this summer or not?

3 (John and his friend Larry / toward the summit / set off / scarcely had) when it started to snow fiercely.

→ _____

when it started to snow fiercely.

4 (is / but also more fuel efficient / this new model / more powerful / not only), making it the perfect city car.

→ _____ ,

making it the perfect city car.

5 (was / rich / neither / my great grandfather / nor famous), but by all means, he thoroughly enjoyed his life all the same.

→ _____ ,

but by all means, he thoroughly enjoyed his life all the same.

6 Since the early 1970s, (in the previous 5,000 years / humans / have created and stored / more information than).

→ Since the early 1970s, _____ .

7 Nowadays, delivering a baby in the relative comfort and safety of a hospital is commonplace, yet it was (that / took place / 95% of births / only one hundred years ago / at home).

→ Nowadays, delivering a baby in the relative comfort and safety of a hospital is commonplace, yet it was _____ .

PART 2

Present & Past Tenses

Unit

Simple Present & Present Progressive

The **simple present** (base form+ -*(e)s*) is used to express actions that happen regularly, or to describe things that we see as being permanent. The **present progressive** (am/are/is+ -*ing*) is used to express actions that we see as being temporary and happening over a limited period of time.

단순현재 시제(동사원형+ -(e)s)는 정기적으로 일어나는 행동이나 영구적인 것을 나타낸다. 현재진행(am/are/is+ -ing)은 일시적인 행동이나 제한된 시간 내에 일어나는 행동을 나타낸다.

1
*We use the **simple present** to talk about actions and habits that are repeated—things we do regularly. We often say precisely when using **expressions of repeated time** and **adverbs of frequency**.*

단순현재 시제는 반복적으로 일어나는 행동이나 습관을 나타낼 때, 종종 반복되는 시간 표현과 빈도부사와 함께 쓰인다.

> *Expressions of repeated time: on Mondays, once a month, every winter ...*

> *Adverbs of frequency: always, often, frequently, seldom, rarely, never ...*

Aunt May **accompanies** her nephew to church <u>most Sundays</u>.①
My best friend Kelly **flies** home to Ireland <u>once a year</u>.②
I <u>often</u> **practice** speaking English with my father.③

2
*The simple present is also used to talk about **general truths**, or to introduce permanent and unchanging **facts** about the world.*

단순현재 시제는 일반적인 사실을 말하거나 불변의 진리를 나타낼 때 사용한다.

The earth **revolves** around the sun once per year.①
Coffee beans **grow** on small bushes in hot climates.②
February 29th **comes** only once every four years.③

3
*Sometimes, we use the simple present with **stative verbs** to describe states—conditions or situations that exist and stay the same.*

단순현재 시제가 상태동사와 함께 쓰이면 같은 상황이나 상태가 지속되는 것을 나타낸다.

> *Stative verbs: be, believe, belong to, dislike, look, own, prefer, seem, understand ...*

Aaron **wants** to be a sports announcer when he grows up.①
I **understand** what you're saying; I just don't agree.②
My cousin Darren still **believes** in UFOs.③

4 *We use the* **present progressive** *to talk about temporary actions happening now. These actions can be* **continuous** *or* **periodic**.

현재진행 시제는 말하는 시점에 일어나고 있는 지속적이거나 주기적인 행동을 나타낸다.

I can't come to the door because I'm curling my hair.[1] (a continuous action)

Terrific news! Dad's cooking dinner again this week.[2] (a periodic action)

5 *We also use the present progressive to talk about* **temporary actions** *happening around the moment of speaking. We often say when using* **time expressions**.

현재진행 시제는 말하는 시점에서 일어나고 있는 일시적인 행동에 대해 설명하며, 시간을 나타내는 표현과 함께 자주 쓰인다.

> *Time expressions: at the moment, now, these days, this week, today ...*

A: What are you doing to get in shape for the summer?

B: Me? Well, I'm taking yoga classes these days.[1] (*NOT* at the moment of speaking)

6 *The present progressive is also used to describe* **changing** *or* **developing states**, *especially with verbs like become, decrease, develop, get, increase, and slow.*

현재진행 시제는 변화 또는 진행되는 상황을 설명한다. 특히, *become, decrease, develop, get, increase, slow*와 같은 동사와 쓰인다.

The environment is becoming more and more polluted.[1]

The economy is getting worse. In fact, GDP is expected to fall by 5%.[2]

7 *We don't normally use verbs that have a stative meaning to talk about ongoing, temporary actions in the present progressive.*

상태동사는 일반적으로 진행형으로 사용하지 않는다.

> *Verbs that have a stative meaning: consist of, envy, fear, know, love, need, owe, possess ...*

Quickly! I need some help over here.[1] (~~I'm needing~~)

John fears heights more than anything else.[2] (~~John is fearing~~)

Michael owes a lot of money on his credit card.[3] (~~Michael is owing~~)

 NOTICE

However, some verbs have both a dynamic and a stative meaning.

하지만 예외적으로 동작 및 상태의 의미 둘 다 가지고 있는 동사는 진행형으로 사용 가능하다.

> *Verbs that have both a dynamic and a stative meaning*
> *: cost, feel, forget, have, include, look, remember, see, taste, think, want ...*

Call an ambulance. This man is having a heart attack![4] (dynamic)

You have a beautiful room. What a great view of the river![5] (stative)

We are thinking about buying our son a car for his graduation.[6] (dynamic)

I think I'll stay in tonight. I have a lot of work to do.[7] (stative)

8

The present progressive can also be used—like the simple present—to talk about habits with certain time expressions.

단순현재 시제처럼 현재 진행 시제는 시간을 나타내는 특정 표현과 함께 쓰여 습관을 나타낼 수 있다.

> *Time expressions to talk about habits: all the time, always, constantly, continually, forever ...*

a *We do this to stress repetition* 반복되는 행동을 강조할 때

The Kims **are always saying** nice things about Korea. We should visit there someday.①

b *or annoyance.* 불평을 강조할 때

I **am always doing** my little brother's laundry. I really wish he would do it himself.①

Vs. Simple Past & Past Perfect 단순과거 & 과거완료

*We use the **simple present** to talk about actions and habits that are repeated—things we do regularly.*
*We also use the **present progressive** to talk about temporary actions happening now.*

단순현재 시제는 반복적으로 일어나는 행동이나 습관을 나타낸다. 또한 현재진행 시제는 말하는 시점에 일어나고 있는 행동을 나타낸다.

Mark **works out** at the gym on Tuesdays and Wednesdays.① (a regular habit)

I'm **working out** right now. Call me back later.② (an action happening now)

I don't usually **prepare** breakfast in the mornings.③ ([not] a regular habit)

I'm not **preparing** dinner this week.④ (something [not] happening around now)

---

1 ① 메이 고모는 거의 일요일마다 자신의 조카와 함께 교회에 간다. ② 나의 가장 친한 친구인 켈리는 일 년에 한 번씩 아일랜드의 집으로 비행기 타고 간다. ③ 나는 자주 아버지와 영어로 말하는 연습을 한다. 2 ① 지구는 일 년에 한 번씩 태양 주위를 공전한다. ② 커피콩은 기후가 더운 지방의 작은 덤불에서 자란다. ③ 2월 29일은 4년에 한 번씩만 온다. 3 ① 애론은 커서 스포츠 아나운서가 되고 싶어 한다. ② 나는 네가 하는 말은 이해하지만, 단지 동의하지 않을 뿐이다. ③ 내 사촌 대런은 여전히 UFO를 믿는다. 4 ① 나는 머리를 말고 있어서 문을 열어줄 수가 없다. ② 정말 좋은 소식이야! 아빠가 이번 주에 또 저녁을 요리하셔. 5 ① A: 여름을 위한 몸매 관리로 무엇을 하고 있니? B: 나? 음, 나는 요즘 요가 수업을 받고 있어. 6 ① 환경이 점점 더 오염되고 있다. ② 경제가 점점 더 나빠지고 있다. 사실상, GDP가 5% 하락할 것으로 예상된다. 7 ① 빨리! 여기 도움이 좀 필요해. ② 존은 그 무엇보다도 높은 곳을 무서워한다. ③ 마이클은 신용카드 빚이 많다. ④ 구급차를 불러요. 이 남자 분 심장마비가 왔어요! ⑤ 방이 아름답네요. 강 전망이 정말 좋아요! ⑥ 우리는 우리 아들 졸업 선물로 차를 사주려고 생각하고 있어요. ⑦ 오늘은 그냥 집에 있을 게. 할 일이 많거든. 8 ① 김 씨 가족은 한국에 대해 항상 좋은 이야기를 한다. 언젠가 그곳을 한 번 방문해 봐야겠다. ② 나는 항상 내 남동생의 빨래를 한다. 그가 스스로 했으면 정말로 좋겠다. VS. ① 마크는 화요일과 수요일에 체육관에서 운동한다. ② 저는 지금 운동 중입니다. 나중에 다시 전화 주세요. ③ 나는 아침에 아침 식사 준비를 거의 하지 않는다. ④ 나는 이번 주에 저녁을 준비하지 않는다.

EXERCISES

정답 및 해설 P. 5

 A ( ) 안에서 가장 알맞은 것을 고르시오.

> cram school 입시 학원
> disturb ~을 방해하다
> connect ~을 연결하다

1 It (is taking / takes) 8.3 minutes for light to travel from the sun to the earth.

2 You can't go into the bathroom just now. Jessica (is taking / takes) a shower.

3 Phillip (is going / goes) to cram school every Monday, Wednesday, and Friday.

4 Jisu (is preparing / prepares) for her big job interview tomorrow. Don't disturb her.

5 The Brooklyn Bridge (is connecting / connects) the island of Manhattan to Brooklyn.

6 Catherine plans to go to Italy in August. Nowadays, she (is learning / learns) some Italian.

7 I usually take the bus to school. But this month I (am walking / walk) to get some exercise.

B 주어진 단어를 현재 시제나 현재진행 시제로 바꿔 문장을 완성하시오.

> economy class 일반석
> upgrade
> 상향, 개선; 등급 격상
> business class
> 비즈니스석
> landline 유선 전화

1 Sarah _____ (often, wear) jeans, but she _____ (wear) a dress for the party today.

2 I'm so surprised my cat _____ (eat) carrots. He _____ (never, eat) vegetables.

3 They _____ (often, meet) for lunch, but they _____ (meet) for dinner these days because of longer working hours.

4 Orlando _____ (always, travel) in economy class, but today he received an upgrade, so he _____ (travel) business class.

5 Patrick _____ (always, have) fruit for breakfast, but this morning he _____ (have) toast because he forgot to go shopping.

6 It _____ (usually, snow) for the first time at the end of November, but it is only the end of October, and it _____ (snow) outside.

7 Craig _____ (often, call) his friends in the U.S. from his cell phone, but because of the cost he _____ (call) from a landline this month.

cause ~을 야기하다
clinic 병원, 진료소
pocket money 용돈
Muslim
이슬람교도; 이슬람교의
prophet 예언자
tornado 토네이도, 폭풍
millions of 수백만의
damage 피해, 손상

C 〈보기〉에서 알맞은 동사를 골라 현재 시제나 현재진행 시제로 바꿔 문장을 완성하시오.

> **보기** believe   sleep   fish   take   cause   spend

1 Look! Justin _____ in the river with his friends.

2 I'll be late for work today. I _____ my sister to the clinic.

3 This week my brother _____ very little because of exams.

4 Every week, Peter _____ all his pocket money before Friday.

5 Muslims _____ that God spoke through the prophet Mohammed.

6 Tornadoes _____ millions of dollars of damage in the U.S. every year.

weigh
~의 무게를 달다, 무게가 ~이다
salesperson 판매원
lift ~을 들어 올리다
perfume 향수
smell up
~을 냄새로 채우다
make a decision
결정하다
raise ~을 올리다
charge 요금
self-portrait 자화상
landscape 풍경화, 풍경
see
~을 이해하다, 조사하다
judge 심사 위원; 판사
tough 엄격한; 강인한; 힘든
competitor 경쟁자

D 주어진 단어를 문맥에 맞게 현재 시제나 현재진행 시제로 바꿔 문장을 완성하시오.

1 (weigh) ① The salesperson _____ the bananas for me now.
② This piano is too heavy for me to lift. It _____ too much.

2 (smell) ① Whenever I enter my brother's room, it _____ a bit strange.
② Nicole's perfume _____ up the whole room; it's making me sick.

3 (think) ① I _____ I need a little more time before I make a decision.
② These days, ABC Bank _____ of raising service charges when customers use the ATM after office hours.

4 (feel) ① There was something wrong with the food we ate because all of us _____ a bit sick.
② The self-portrait was great, but I _____ that the landscape should have won.

5 (see) ① I _____ what you mean when you said the movie was not all that exciting.
② The judges this year are tough; they _____ all of the mistakes the competitors make.

34

Simple Past & Past Progressive

Unit 07

KEY CONCEPTS

The **simple past** (base form+ -*(e)d*, irregular verbs without -*(e)d*) is used to express completed actions or states in the past. The **past progressive** (was/were+ -*ing*) is used to express actions that were happening in the past, or that we see as incomplete.

과저 시제(기본형+ −ed 또는 불규칙 동사)는 이미 완료된 행동이나 과거의 상태를 나타낸다. 과거진행(was/were+ −ing)은 과거 어느 특정한 시점에서 진행되고 있었던 행동을 나타낼 때 사용한다.

FOCUS

1   *We use the **simple past** to talk about **actions**, **events**, or **states** that have ended. And like the simple present, we often say precisely when, using **expressions of finished time**.*

단순과거 시제는 과거에 끝난 행동, 사건 또는 상태를 나타내며, 시간 표현을 사용해서 정확한 때를 나타낸다.

> *Expressions of finished time: yesterday, last week [month/year], three years ago, in the 90s ...*

It **snowed** up in the mountains <u>yesterday</u>.①
Jim **lived** in Seoul <u>last year</u>. He **taught** English.②
My father **studied** accounting at the University of Sydney <u>in the 1970s</u>.③

Actions can be short or long, single or repeated. 행동은 짧거나 길 수 있고 단발적이거나 반복적일 수 있다.

The twig **snapped** under my foot.④ (a short, single action)
My grandfather **walked** to work every day of his life.⑤ (a long-term, repeated action)

2   *We also use the simple past with the word **when** to talk about actions and states in the past.*

단순과거 시제는 when과 함께 쓰여 과거의 행동이나 상태를 나타낸다.

I **envied** my sister <u>when</u> I saw her win the prize.①
<u>When</u> I was an elementary school student, I **loved** gym class.②
Jiyoung **didn't learn** much Italian <u>when</u> she lived in Milan two years ago.③

3   *A few pairs of English verbs are tricky to use and are often confused:* **lay/lie, raise/rise, set/sit**.

과거형을 혼동하기 쉬운 동사들이 있다.

   a   ***Lay** (lay-laid-laid) is a transitive verb (it can take an <u>object</u>), whereas **lie** (lie-lay-lain) is intransitive (it does not take an object)* lay는 타동사(목적어를 취할 수 있음)이고, lie는 자동사(목적어를 취하지 않음)이다.

      Jacob **is laying** <u>the table</u>.①

The jeweler **laid** <u>the ring</u> on the counter.②

The alligator **has laid** <u>her eggs</u>, which she will now guard carefully.③

Marie **is lying** on the sofa.④

We **lay** on the beach in the sun.⑤

Marvin **has lain** in bed at the hospital for a week.⑥

On the sofa, on the beach, and in bed are prepositional phrases, not objects.
이때 on the sofa, on the beach, in bed는 목적어가 아닌 전치사구이다.

b *Similarly, **raise** (raise-raised-raised) is a transitive verb, and **rise** (rise-rose-risen) is intransitive.*
raise는 타동사이고, rise는 자동사이다.

My neighbor **is raising** <u>exotic fish</u> in his apartment.①

Susan **raised** <u>the window</u> to let in some fresh air.②

The moon **is rising** in the east.③

The temperature **has risen** by five degrees.④

c **Set** *(set-set-set) is a transitive verb;* **sit** *(sit-sat-sat) is intransitive.*
set은 타동사이고, sit은 자동사이다.

Have you **set** <u>the date</u> for your wedding yet?①

He **sat** in the park after school yesterday.②

*In addition to the simple past, we can also use **used to** or **would** to talk about past habits. **Used to** is used to describe past habits, actions, and situations which are now finished.*
단순과거 시제뿐만 아니라, used to 또는 would도 과거의 습관적인 행동을 나타낸다. used to는 이미 완료된 과거의 습관, 행동, 상황을 설명할 때 쓴다.

My father **used to** smoke.①

I **used to** weigh over 90 kilos.②

*But when we are telling a story or describing events from our past, we often prefer to use **would**. (Note: **Used to** is also possible.)* 이야기 또는 과거의 사건을 설명할 때에는 would를 더 자주 사용한다. (주의: used to도 사용 가능하다.)

When I was a boy, my father **would** throw me up in the air.③ *(throw ... up is an action)*

My mother **would** rub my tummy when I was sick.④ *(rub is an action)*

Would *is more limited: it cannot be used to refer to past states.*
would는 더 제한적으로 쓰이며, 과거의 상태를 나타낼 때는 사용할 수 없다.

There **used to** be a cabin here.⑤

(×) ~~There would be a cabin here.~~

4   *We use the **past progressive** to talk about **temporary actions** happening in the past. And like the simple past, we often say when, using words like this morning, yesterday afternoon, at seven o'clock, and then.*

과거진행 시제는 과거에 일어난 일시적인 행동을 나타내며, 시간을 나타내는 표현과 함께 사용하여 행위가 일어난 시점을 나타낸다.

I **was playing** basketball <u>yesterday afternoon</u>.①

Stacey **was visiting** her cousin in New York <u>then</u>.②

Peter **was chopping** wood in the backyard earlier <u>this morning</u>.③

*Sometimes, the past action is interrupted. In this case, we can use **when** or **while**.*

진행되고 있었던 과거 행동이 다른 행동에 의해 중단된 경우 when 또는 while을 사용할 수 있다.

I **was drying** my hair <u>when</u> the blow drier suddenly shorted out.④

<u>While</u> I **was organizing** my desk this morning, I spilled water all over my keyboard.⑤

NOTICE

Use be + -ing in the part of the sentence that happened first.

먼저 일어난 일에 과거진행형 동사가 쓰인다.

First this happened ...	And then this happened ...
I **was drying** my hair	when the blow drier suddenly <u>shorted</u> out.
While I **was organizing** my desk this morning,	I <u>spilled</u> water all over my keyboard.

*If both past actions were happening at the same time, use **while**.*

과거의 행동이 동시에 일어날 때는 while을 쓴다.

<u>While</u> Kenneth **was chopping** the onions, Sam **was washing** the peppers.⑥

I **was relaxing** on the couch while my sister **was scrubbing** the floors.⑦

<u>While</u> my wife **was packing** our bags, I **was looking for** our passports.⑧

---

1 ① 어제 산 위에 눈이 내렸다. ② 짐은 작년에 서울에서 살았다. 그는 영어를 가르쳤다. ③ 우리 아버지는 1970년대에 시드니 대학에서 회계를 공부하셨다. ④ 발밑에서 나뭇가지가 부러졌다. ⑤ 우리 할아버지는 평생을 걸어서 출근하셨다.   2 ① 나는 언니가 상을 타는 것을 보자 샘이 났다. ② 나는 초등학교 학생이었을 때, 체육 시간을 좋아했다. ③ 지영이는 2년 전 밀라노에서 살 때, 이탈리아어를 별로 배우지 않았다.   3 a ① 제이콥이 식탁을 차리고 있다. ② 보석상이 판매대에 반지를 놓았다. ③ 악어는 알을 낳았고, 이제는 그것을 조심스럽게 지킬 것이다. ④ 마리가 소파에 누워 있다. ⑤ 우리는 태양이 내리쬐는 해변에 누웠다. ⑥ 마빈은 일주일간 병원에 누워 있었다. b ① 내 이웃은 자신의 아파트에서 이국적인 물고기를 키우고 있다. ② 수잔은 신선한 공기가 들어오도록 창문을 올렸다. ③ 달이 동쪽에서 떠오르고 있다. ④ 기온이 5도 올랐다. c ① 너는 벌써 결혼 날짜를 잡았니? ② 그는 방과 후에 공원에 앉아 있었다. WT ① 우리 아버지는 담배를 피우곤 하셨다. ② 나는 90kg이 넘게 나갔었다. ③ 내가 소년이었을 때, 우리 아버지가 나를 공중으로 던져주시곤 했다. ④ 우리 어머니는 내가 아플 때 배를 문질러주시곤 하셨다. ⑤ 여기에 오두막집이 있었다.   4 ① 나는 어제 오후에 농구를 하고 있었다. ② 스테이시는 그때 뉴욕에 있는 사촌을 방문하고 있었다. ③ 피터는 오늘 아침 일찍 뒷마당에서 장작을 패고 있었다. ④ 내가 머리를 말리고 있는데 드라이어기가 갑자기 합선되었다. ⑤ 나는 오늘 아침에 책상 정리를 하다가 키보드에 물을 엎질렀다. ⑥ 케네스가 양파를 써는 동안, 샘은 고추를 씻었다. ⑦ 내 여동생이 바닥을 닦는 동안, 나는 소파에서 쉬고 있었다. ⑧ 내 아내가 우리의 짐을 싸는 동안, 나는 여권을 찾고 있었다.

EXERCISES

run into ~을 우연히 만나다
discover ~을 발견하다
gravity 중력
axis 축; 중심선
create
~을 만들어 내다, 창조하다

 A ( ) 안에서 가장 알맞은 것을 고르시오.

1 While Mary (jogged / was jogging) this morning, she ran into her high school friend.

2 Isaac Newton was sitting under an apple tree when he (discovered / was discovering) gravity.

3 The earth (rotates / rotated) on its axis once every 24 hours. This (creates / created) our 24-hour day.

4 Eric (already had / was already having) a bad day when he (found / was finding) out he had failed the test.

heat
~을 따뜻하게 하다, 데우다
lay
~을 놓다, 두다; 눕히다; (식탁 등을) 차리다
increase
(가격이) 증가하다, 상승하다
pray
~을 기도하다, 바라다
government 정부
standard 기준
production 생산품, 생산
complain 불평하다

 B ( ) 안에서 가장 알맞은 것을 고르시오.

1 While he was heating the chicken soup, I (laid / lay) the table.

2 The shop owner (rose / raised) his prices because the price of oil had increased.

3 As Janice (set / sat) to take the exam, her mother prayed that she would pass.

4 When the sun (raised / rose), many people had already (raised / risen) to start work.

5 The government (set / sat) a new standard for food production because people were complaining.

spinach 시금치
greasy 기름진
regularly 정기적으로
at least 적어도

 C would 또는 used to 중 알맞은 것을 골라 빈칸에 쓰시오.

1 Carrie _____ never eat spinach. She _____ always feed it to her dog when her mother wasn't watching.

2 Before I came to Korea, I _____ eat a lot of greasy fast food for lunch. I _____ eat hamburgers and French fries regularly.

3 Ken's brother _____ read to himself on his way home from school. He _____ visit the library at least three times a week.

4 When my sister was young, she _____ be a fan of Marvin Williams. She _____ be one of the first people in line to buy his concert tickets.

〈보기〉에서 알맞은 동사를 골라 과거 시제나 과거진행 시제로 바꿔 문장을 완성하시오.

| 보기 | become | belong to | create | exist | prefer | look |

belong to ～에 속하다
exist 존재하다
prefer A to B
B보다 A를 더 좋아하다
dinosaur 공룡
rule ～을 통치하다, 지배하다
governor 주지사
accurate 정확한

1 When I was a child, I _____ oranges to grapes.

2 Dinosaurs _____ long before they came to rule the earth.

3 Before it became part of the United States, Texas _____ Mexico.

4 Thomas _____ for his cell phone when he heard it ring in the other room.

5 Arnold Schwarzenegger was famous long before he _____ governor of California.

6 The Mayas _____ an accurate calendar long before Columbus arrived in the New World.

E 주어진 단어를 과거 시제나 과거진행 시제로 바꿔 대화를 완성하시오.

decorate ～을 장식하다
in ages 오랫동안
vacuum
진공청소기로 청소하다
return
～을 반환하다, 환불하다
hurry 서두르다

1 A: Where did you get all these storybooks?

B: While my father _____ (travel) in London, he bought them for me.

2 A: What were you two doing when I called you at noon?

B: While I _____ (bake) Dad's birthday cake, Ralph _____ (decorate) the living room.

3 A: When _____ (be) the last time you _____ (speak) to Jenny? I got a call from her last night.

B: Oh! That's surprising! I haven't spoken to her in ages. Why did she call you?

4 A: Weren't you at home last night? I knocked on the door several times, but no one answered.

B: I was at home. Maybe I _____ (vacuum) the carpet when you knocked on the door.

5 A: I saw you in the store yesterday, but I don't think you saw me.

B: Oh, really? I _____ (return) a jacket that I had bought, and I was hurrying to meet my mother.

Unit 08

Present Perfect & Present Perfect Progressive

KEY CONCEPTS

The **present perfect** (have/has+*p.p.*) is used to express actions that happened at an indefinite time in the past or that started in the past and continue to the present. The **present perfect progressive** (have/has+been+-*ing*) is used to express actions that started in the past and continue to the present.

현재완료(have/has+p.p.)는 과거의 불특정한 시간에 일어난 행동을 표현할 때나 과거에 시작된 행동이 현재에도 계속됨을 표현할 때 사용된다. 현재완료진행(have/has+been+−ing)은 과거에 시작해서 현재까지 지속되고 있는 행동을 나타낼 때 사용된다.

FOCUS

1
*We use the **present perfect** to talk about **completed actions**, **events**, or **states** in the past. The event or action is finished, but the time period is unfinished. We commonly use **time expressions** to highlight the fact that the period of time is unfinished.* 현재완료는 과거에 완료된 행동, 사건, 또는 상태를 나타낼 때 쓰인다. 이때 사건이나 행동은 끝났지만, (현재까지 영향이 미치는) 시간은 아직 끝나지 않았음을 의미한다. 시간이 완료되지 않음을 강조하기 위해 다음과 같은 시간 표현을 흔히 사용한다.

> Time expressions: today, this week [month/year], in my life, up to now, recently, lately ...

It **has rained** three times this week.[1] (*this week* is an unfinished period of time)
Bret Easton Ellis **has written** several novels in his life.[2] (*his life* is an unfinished period of time)
Your work on this project **has been** great up to now.[3] (*up to now* suggests the project is ongoing)

2
*The present perfect is also used to stress the idea of **repetition** in the past.* 현재완료는 과거에 반복된 일을 강조하기 위해 쓰인다.

Our team **has won** every game so far.[1]
I **haven't met** anyone interesting for ages.[2]
Alexis **has flown** many times, but never first class.[3]

3
*With **for** and **since**, the present perfect describes a situation that began in the past and continues to the present.* 현재완료는 for, since와 함께 쓰여 과거에 시작해서 현재까지 계속되고 있는 상황을 설명한다.

My father has owned this car **since 1985**.[1]
Jiyoung and her sister have lived in Toronto **for two years**.[2]
I have appreciated your commitment to the company **for a long time**.[3]

NOTICE

Since is used with a particular time. For is used with a duration of time.
since는 특정 시점을 나타내는 표현과 함께 쓰이고, for는 일정 기간을 나타내는 표현과 함께 쓰인다.

> Since+last week/1985/the early 90s ...   For+an hour/two years/a long time ...

4 *We use the **present perfect progressive** to talk about **activities** that started in the past and continue to the present, often with words like all morning [day/week], for, and since.*

현재완료진행은 과거에 시작된 행동이 현재에도 계속되고 있음을 나타내며, all morning[day/week], for, since와 함께 자주 쓰인다.

We've **been cleaning** the house all morning. I need a break!①

Stacey **has been studying** for the chemistry final for over twelve hours.②

Without any mention of time, the present perfect progressive refers to a general activity happening around the time of speaking or writing.

시간에 대한 특별한 언급이 없으면, 현재완료진행은 말을 하거나 글을 쓰는 시점 무렵에 일어나는 일반적인 행동들을 나타낸다.

Have you **been dieting**? You look like you've lost a few pounds.③

Stative verbs are not used in the present perfect progressive. Use the present perfect instead.

상태동사는 현재완료진행에서는 사용되지 않기 때문에 현재완료를 사용한다.

I've **known** Jessica since she was only a child.④

(×) I've ~~been knowing~~ Jessica since she was only a child.

Simple Tenses & Perfect Tenses

Simple Past VS. *Present Perfect*

A: **Have** you ever **driven** a car with a stick shift? (an action in the past)

B: Sure. My father has an old Lincoln. I **drove** it last week.① (an action ended with an expression of finished time)

Present Perfect VS. *Present Perfect Progressive*

Peter **has locked** himself out of his house again.② (a completed action in the past in an unfinished period of time)

That poor man **has been trying** to unlock his car door for over an hour now.③
(an activity that started in the past and continues to the present)

<At the Venice Film Festival>

A: I've **seen** over eight films this week. How about you? (a completed action in the past in an unfinished period of time)

B: I've **been watching** films all week, but I haven't seen quite that many.④
 (an activity that started in the past and continues to the present)

---

1 ① 이번 주에 비가 세 번 왔다. ② 브렛 이스턴 엘리스는 평생 몇 편의 소설을 썼다. ③ 이 프로젝트에서 지금까지 당신의 작업은 훌륭했어요. 2 ① 지금까지 우리 팀은 모든 경기에서 이겼다. ② 나는 오랫동안 관심이 가는 사람을 만나지 못했다. ③ 알렉시스는 비행기를 많이 타봤지만, 일등석을 타본 적은 없다. 3 ① 우리 아버지는 1985년부터 이 차를 소장해 오셨다. ② 지영이와 그녀의 여동생은 토론토에서 2년 동안 살고 있다. ③ 나는 당신이 오랜 기간 회사에 헌신해온 것을 고맙게 생각합니다. 4 ① 우리는 아침 내내 집을 치우고 있어. 나는 좀 쉬어야겠어! ② 스테이시는 열두 시간 넘게 화학 기말 시험공부를 하고 있다. ③ 다이어트하고 있니? 너 몇 파운드는 빠진 것 같아 보여. ④ 나는 제시카가 어렸을 때부터 그녀를 알아왔다. VS. ① A: 수동 변속 레버 차(수동으로 기어를 넣는 차)를 운전해 본 적 있니? B: 물론. 우리 아버지는 낡은 링컨을 소유하고 계셔. 지난주에 그것을 운전했어. ② 피터는 또 열쇠를 집에 두고 집 문을 잠갔다. ③ 저 불쌍한 남자는 한 시간 넘도록 자동차 문을 열려고 하고 있다. ④ A: 나는 이번 주에 영화를 8개도 넘게 봤어. 너는? B: 나는 이번 주 내내 영화를 보고 있지만, 그렇게 많이는 못 봤어.

EXERCISES

anymore 더 이상
entire 전체의
deserve ~할 만하다
allowance 용돈
conflict 투쟁, 충돌
rage
광란하다, 맹렬히 계속되다
return to ~으로 돌아가다

A 주어진 단어를 현재완료 시제로 바꿔 문장을 완성하시오.

1 Lisa _____ (work) on her project for three hours. She is still in the library.

2 I _____ (wear) these shoes since 2015. It is hard to find this style anymore.

3 Hoon _____ (clean) the entire house. Now that he is finished, he deserves a good long rest.

4 The children are at the park. They _____ (play) on the same baseball team for the last two seasons.

5 Paul _____ (spend) his entire allowance on comic books. Now he doesn't even have enough money to take the bus.

6 The conflict in Syria _____ (rage) for more than seven years. No one can say right now when peace will return to the country.

column 칼럼
decade 10년
be due for
~하게 되어 있다, ~할 예정이다
promotion 승진
throw a party
파티를 열다
transportation
운송, 교통
strike 파업

B 주어진 단어를 현재완료진행 시제로 바꿔 문장을 완성하시오.

1 I _____ (study) Korean for several years, but it is very difficult.

2 For two hours, Glenn _____ (play) basketball with his friends.

3 Carrie _____ (write) a column for the newspaper for two years.

4 They _____ (build) the Victoria Dam for more than a decade.

5 Sarah _____ (work) at her company for five years. She's due for a promotion.

6 Sangwoo _____ (clean) the house all day because he's throwing a party tomorrow.

7 This transportation strike is beginning to cause serious problems. We _____ (wait) for more than an hour, and the train has still not come.

〈보기〉에서 알맞은 것을 골라 빈칸에 써넣으시오.

보기	have started	have been waiting	has been studying
	has eaten	already bought	

1 A: John, where have you been? We _____ for hours.

B: Really? I didn't know you were still here. I'm so sorry.

2 A: Look, Nelson! This laptop computer is on sale. Didn't you want to buy one?

B: Oh, no. I _____ one yesterday, but I paid much more.

3 A: Who _____ my tuna sandwich? I was saving it for lunch.

B: Sorry, Dan. I had no idea you were going to eat it.

4 A: I _____ taking driving lessons. I cannot believe how exciting it is!

B: Wow! Are you going to buy a car? I really envy you.

5 A: John _____ Japanese for years, but he still has difficulty with Kanji.

B: I totally understand his situation. I am not good at Japanese, either.

D 〈보기〉에서 알맞은 동사를 골라 현재완료나 현재완료진행으로 바꿔 문장을 완성하시오.
[둘 다 가능한 경우도 있음]

보기	not / taste	help	not / visit	be	watch	look for

1 I _____ Canada since the Christmas of 2015.

2 Peter _____ president of our class for three months.

3 Edmond _____ kimchi since he left Korea in November.

4 Insu _____ me with my work for as long as I can remember.

5 Oscar _____ his puppy for almost two hours, but he cannot find it.

6 _____ you _____ TV since I left? You shouldn't sit in front of the TV all day.

Past Perfect &
Past Perfect Progressive

The **past perfect** (had+*p.p.*) is used to show that something happened before something else in the past. The **past perfect progressive** (had+been+ -*ing*) is used in a similar way, but its focus is on the duration of the activity, not the result.

과거완료(had+p.p.)는 과거에 일어난 어떤 일보다 먼저 일어난 사건을 나타낼 때 사용된다. 과거완료진행(had+been+ -ing)은 과거완료와 비슷하지만, 행동의 결과보다는 지속성에 더 중점을 둔다는 데 차이가 있다.

1 *We use the **past perfect** to talk about activities that finished before something else in the past. The past perfect helps us clarify the order of events, especially in clauses beginning with the conjunctions when, and, that, because, and so joined to a clause in the simple past.*

과거완료는 과거에 일어난 어떤 일보다 먼저 일어난 사건에 대해 말할 때 쓰인다. 특히 단순과거 시제절이 when, and, that, because, so와 같은 접속사로 시작할 때 사건의 순서를 명확히 해준다.

The basketball game **had** already **begun** when I got to the stadium.①
(*Had begun* tells us that the game started before I arrived.)

It **had stopped** raining, so Tim left his shoes outside on the steps.②

I knew that I **had seen** her face somewhere before. I just couldn't remember where exactly.③

> **! NOTICE**
>
> *With before and after, the time relationship between the clauses is clear, so the simple past can be used.*
> before와 after를 쓰면 절 사이의 선후 관계가 명확해지기 때문에 단순과거를 쓸 수 있다.
>
> My parents **had finished** eating supper before I got home.
> My parents **finished** eating supper before I got home.④
>
> After I **had jumped** in the pool, I realized that my wallet was still in my pocket.
> After I **jumped** in the pool, I realized that my wallet was still in my pocket.⑤

2 *We use the **past perfect progressive** to emphasize the duration of an activity or event—one that took place before a particular point in the past.*

과거완료진행은 과거의 한 시점 이전에 일어난 행동이나 사건의 진행을 강조하기 위해 사용한다.

a *The activity or event may stop at that particular point.* 행동이나 사건이 바로 그 시점에서 끝났을 수도 있다.

Tina finally showed up at six o'clock. I'd **been waiting** for almost two hours.①
(I stopped waiting at six o'clock.)

44

b *The activity or event may continue beyond that point.* 행동이나 사건이 그 시점을 지나 계속될 수도 있다.

I'**d been living** with John for two months before I realized what a great cook he was.①
(I'm still living with John.)

c *The activity or event may stop sometime before that point.* 행동이나 사건이 그 시점 이전에 끝났을 수 있다.

Tim was up, but his hair was tussled. I could tell that he'**d been sleeping**, not **studying**.①
(Tim woke up just before I saw him.)

 Simple Past & Past Perfect 단순과거 & 과거완료

Yesterday, I **went** to a Chinese medical clinic to get acupuncture. I **had** never **been** to a Chinese medical clinic before in my life.① (This had never happened before yesterday.)

The apartment was too quiet when I **got** home, so I **turned on** the TV for company.②
(I turned on the TV after I got home, not before.)

By the time my roommate **came** home, I **had** already **finished** arranging the furniture.③
(First I finished arranging the furniture, and then my roommate came home.)

 WRITING TIPS

The **simple past**, **past progressive**, **past perfect**, *and* **past perfect progressive** *are collectively called as the "narrative tenses" because they are commonly used together in storytelling. The* **simple past** *is used to describe the main events of a story – it moves the story forward.*
단순과거, 과거진행, 과거완료, 그리고 과거완료진행을 통틀어 "이야기체 시제"라고 하는데, 이는 흔히 스토리텔링에 잘 쓰이기 때문이다. 단순과거는 이야기의 주요 사건을 설명하는 데 쓰이며, 이것은 이야기의 내용을 진전시킨다.

I **woke up** and immediately **jumped** out of bed. Late again!①

The **past perfect** *and* **past perfect progressive** *describe the background to the story – the events that happened before the main narrative.* 과거완료와 과거완료진행은 이야기의 배경을 설명하는 데 쓰인다. 즉, 주요 사건 이전에 일어난 이야기들을 설명할 때 쓰인다.

But I **had been having** such a wonderful dream. I dreamed that I **had landed** on a beautiful desert island in the middle of the ocean...②

The **past progressive** *is used to describe the actions taking place at or around the time the main events happened.* 과거진행은 주요 사건이 일어난 시점이나 그 주변 시간에 일어난 행동들을 설명할 때 사용된다.

When I finally got downstairs, my mother **was waiting** for me in the kitchen. She scolded me and warned me not to oversleep again. I ate my breakfast quickly and rushed out the door to catch my bus.③

---

1 ① 내가 경기장에 도착했을 때 농구 경기는 이미 시작해 있었다. ② 비가 그쳐서 팀은 바깥 계단에 신발을 놔두었다. ③ 내가 그녀를 예전에 어디선가 본 것은 분명한데, 어디인지 정확히 기억이 안 나. ④ 우리 부모님은 내가 집에 도착하기 전에 저녁 식사를 마치셨다. ⑤ 나는 풀장에 뛰어들고 나서, 내 주머니에 지갑이 있다는 것을 깨달았다. 2 a ① 티나는 결국 여섯 시가 되어서야 나타났다. 나는 거의 두 시간이나 기다렸다. b ① 나는 존과 두 달이나 살고 나서 그가 훌륭한 요리사라는 것을 알았다. c ① 팀은 깨어 있었지만, 머리는 헝클어져 있었다. 나는 그가 공부한 것이 아니라, 잠을 잤다는 것을 알 수 있었다. VS. ① 나는 어제 침을 맞으려고 한의원에 갔다. 나는 평생 한 번도 한의원에 가본 적이 없었다. ② 나는 집에 왔을 때 아파트가 너무 조용해서 적적함을 없애려고 TV를 켰다. ③ 내 룸메이트가 집에 왔을 때 나는 이미 가구 배치를 끝냈다. WT ① 나는 일어나자마자 즉시 침대에서 튀어나왔다. 또 늦었다! ② 하지만, 나는 너무나도 황홀한 꿈을 꾸고 있었다. 나는 내가 바다 한 가운데에 있는 아름다운 무인도에 떨어진 꿈을 꾸었는데… ③ 내가 마침내 아래층에 갔을 때 우리 어머니는 부엌에서 나를 기다리고 계셨다. 어머니는 나를 혼내시면서 다시는 늦잠을 자지 말라고 하셨다. 나는 아침을 빨리 먹고 버스를 잡으려고 문을 뛰쳐나갔다.

EXERCISES

splendid 화려한
collect
~을 데리러 가다, 모으다
struggle
~하려고 노력하다, 애쓰다
persuade ~을 설득하다
volunteer 자원하다

 ( ) 안에서 가장 알맞은 것을 고르시오.

1 The game (already finished / had already finished) when it began to rain.

2 The Palace of Versailles was more splendid than I (dreamed / had dreamed).

3 By the time Nicole arrived, she (had traveled / had been traveling) for 24 hours.

4 Eunji (had studied / had been studying) for several hours before her brother arrived to help her.

5 The children (had played / had been playing) for several hours when George came to collect them.

6 Youngju (struggled / had struggled) to persuade her parents to let her volunteer for the Korean Peace Corps last year.

take a sip 한 모금 마시다
cross ~을 가로지르다
the Equator 적도
confess ~을 자백하다
conquer ~을 정복하다

B 주어진 동사를 각각 과거 시제나 과거완료 시제로 바꿔 문장을 완성하시오.

1 The coffee _____ (go) cold when I _____ (take) a sip.

2 Before I _____ (visit) Australia, I _____ (not, cross) the Equator.

3 Jillian _____ (be) very excited to go to Jejudo. She _____ (not, take) a vacation for several years.

4 Joyce _____ (confess) to her mother that she _____ (receive) a poor score on the science exam.

5 The Great Pyramid of Giza _____ (exist) for two thousand years when Rome _____ (conquer) Egypt.

6 I _____ (get) sick yesterday because of the blueberry cheesecake that I _____ (eat) on my birthday the day before.

7 Marvin _____ (miss) the bus because he _____ (forget) to set his alarm. He ran all the way to school, but class had already begun.

Verb Tense Review

1   *Simple Past & Present Perfect* 단순과거 & 현재완료

President Obama **addressed** world leaders at the G20 summit in London yesterday.①

Donors **have pledged** $4.5 billion over the next five years to help eliminate world hunger.②

A: You've **been** to Europe before, haven't you? I **saw** photos of you last summer in Portugal and Spain.

B: Yes, but neither of my parents **has been** abroad yet. They're looking forward to it.③

2   *Simple Past & Past Perfect* 단순과거 & 과거완료

I **met** an old friend today who I **hadn't seen** in ages. We **were** so close in grade 6.①

The Smiths **lived** a normal life until they **won** the lottery last month. In fact, they **had struggled** to make ends meet and pay for their children's college tuition. But now all of their worries are over; the Smith family now has enough money to live comfortably.②

Yesterday in Costa Rica, a group of animal rights activists **rescued** several rare species of animals. Mysteriously, the captured animals **had disappeared** back into the jungle when the hunters **returned** to their traps.③

3   *Simple Present & Present Progressive* 단순현재 & 현재진행

You shouldn't snoop in your sister's room, Billy. It **isn't** polite.①

I **think** that man **is eavesdropping** on our conversation. How rude!②

I usually **take** a short nap in the afternoon after class. I **find** it quite refreshing.③

If your father **is** still **snoozing** on the couch, wake him up and tell him dinner is ready.④

4   *Present Perfect & Present Perfect Progressive* 현재완료 & 현재완료진행

I've never **driven** from one side of the country to the other, so I suspect I'm in for an adventure.①

You've **been driving** for almost five hours straight. Don't you think it's time we took a break?②

A: I've **noticed** you looking at a lot of electronics ads lately. Are you in the market for a new computer?

B: Actually, I've **been waiting** for TIG Electronics to introduce their new line-up of flat-screen TVs.③

---

1 ① 오바마 대통령이 어제 런던 G20 정상회담에서 세계의 지도자들에게 연설했다.   ② 기부자들은 세계 기근 근절을 위해 앞으로 5년 동안 45억 달러를 약속하였다.   ③ A: 너는 예전에 유럽에 가본 적이 있지, 그렇지 않니? 네가 작년 여름에 포르투갈과 스페인에서 찍은 사진을 보았어. B: 응, 하지만 우리 부모님은 아직 외국에 못 가보셨어. 두 분 모두 (외국에 가기를) 고대하고 계셔.   2 ① 나는 오늘 오랫동안 보지 못했던 옛날 친구를 만났다. 6학년 때 우리는 정말 친했다.   ② 스미스 가족은 지난달에 로또에 당첨되기 전까지 평범한 삶을 살았다. 사실 그들은 생계를 꾸려가고 아이들의 등록금 을 대느라 애썼다. 하지만, 이제 그들의 걱정거리들이 모두 끝났다. 스미스 가족은 편안하게 살 수 있을 만큼 충분한 돈이 있다.   ③ 동물 권리 운동가들이 어제 코스타리카에서 몇 종의 희귀 동물들을 구 조했다. 신기하게도 사냥꾼들이 덫을 확인하러 돌아왔을 때 포획되었던 동물들은 이미 정글로 사라지고 없었다.   3 ① 빌리, 네 여동생의 방에 기웃거리면 안 돼. 그것은 예의 바르지 않은 거야.   ② 저 남자가 우리의 대화를 엿듣는 것 같아. 정말 무례해!   ③ 나는 수업이 끝나고 오후에 주로 잠깐 낮잠을 자. 그것은 꽤 상쾌해.   ④ 너희 아버지가 아직도 소파에서 주무시고 계시면 아빠를 깨우고 저녁 준 비가 다 됐다고 말하렴.   4 ① 나는 한 번도 나라를 횡단해서 운전해 본 적이 없어서 모험이 될 것 같다.   ② 너는 거의 다섯 시간 동안 계속 운전했어. 좀 쉬어야 한다고 생각하지 않니?   ③ A: 최근에 네 가 전자제품 광고를 자주 보는 것을 봤어. 새 컴퓨터를 사려는 거니? B: 사실 나는 TIG전자에서 새로운 평면 TV 시리즈가 출시되기를 기다리고 있어.

EXERCISES

정답 및 해설 P. 8

earn ~을 벌다
part-time job
아르바이트
national
국가의, 국가적인
sour 신, 시큼한
sparerib
살이 붙은 돼지갈비
tragic 비극의
Briton 영국 사람
mourn
~을 슬퍼하다, 애도하다
passing 죽음
hiccup 딸꾹질
cure ~을 치료하다

 A ( ) 안에서 가장 알맞은 것을 고르시오.

1 My sister called yesterday evening while we (had been eating / were eating) dinner.

2 In order to earn a little extra money, Kate (has decided / has been deciding) to take a part-time job.

3 The Scots (had been playing / have been playing) golf in Scotland for centuries. It's their national sport.

4 When we arrived in London, it looked as if it (has been raining / had been raining). The streets were still wet.

5 Yoonmi wants to have sweet and sour spareribs for dinner tomorrow. She (hasn't eaten / hadn't eaten) Chinese food for weeks.

6 Princess Diana (died / has died) in a tragic car accident in the summer of 1997. Many Britons (came / have come) out to mourn her passing.

7 Wendy just got back from the doctor's office. She (has had / had had) the hiccups for three days. But the doctor cured her, and now her hiccups are gone.

post ~을 게시하다
folktale 설화, 전설
pull out 출발하다
attend ~에 참석하다
neighborhood
근처, 이웃
get around 돌아다니다

B 주어진 단어를 적절한 완료 시제를 바꿔 문장을 완성하시오.

1 More than a hundred messages _____ (be posted) to my blog this week alone.

2 Native Americans _____ (tell) folktales about their culture for centuries now.

3 We're too late. The train for Melbourne _____ (pull out, already) of the station.

4 Jina _____ (attend) English classes at a neighborhood institute since last month.

5 I _____ (talk) about going to Africa for years, and I finally got around to it last winter.

6 When Christopher Columbus discovered America in 1492, Native Americans _____ (live) there for thousands of years.

REVIEW

정답 및 해설 P. 8

A 다음 빈칸에 가장 알맞은 것을 고르시오.

> familiar 낯익은
> ride ~을 타다
> give a presentation 발표하다

1 A: _____ before? You look very familiar to me.

B: Maybe, but I'm not sure. Which university did you go to?

① Haven't we met   ② Have we meet

③ Do we meet   ④ Had we met

2 A: Did you hear about Somi's good luck?

B: Yes, she found $10 on the street while she _____ her bike to school. I wish I had that kind of luck.

① rides   ② has ridden

③ had ridden   ④ was riding

3 A: Where have you been, Darren? I have been trying to call you for hours.

B: I was giving a presentation at work, and it took longer than I _____.

① was expecting   ② had been expecting

③ had expected   ④ had been expected

B 다음 대화를 읽고, 바르지 <u>않은</u> 문장을 고르시오.

>
> matinee 마티네(낮 공연)
> exhibition 전시회
> be supposed to ~하기로 되어 있다
> discuss ~에 대해 논의하다

1 ① A: Hello, Jason. Don't you have any plans for tomorrow?

② B: I am not having any plans yet. Would you like to do something together? How about going to a movie?

③ A: I would like to see the new comedy film. What time does the matinee start?

④ B: I am not sure. It usually starts around two o'clock.

2 ① A: Hi, Carl. Have you seen the new European art exhibition at the Arts Center?

② B: No, I haven't. Yesterday I read a review about it. It's supposed to be really good.

③ A: It is! Do you want to go tomorrow morning? The Arts Center usually opens at 9 a.m.

④ B: Oh, no! At 9 a.m. on Mondays I am always meeting my professor to discuss my research project.

3 ① A: Hey, Minsu! What a small world! I didn't expect to see you here.

② B: Scott, what a nice surprise! What are you doing here at the airport?

③ A: Well, I was deciding to take a vacation. I'm off to Australia this afternoon.

④ B: Oh, really? I've just come from Australia. I hope you enjoy it.

REVIEW PLUS

정답 및 해설 P. 9

 다음을 읽고, 바르지 <u>않은</u> 문장을 고르시오.

1

current 현재의, 지금의
The United Nations
Secretariat 유엔 사무국
Foreign Minister
외무 장관
Secretary-General
사무총장
particularly 특히
Darfur
다르푸르(수단 서부의 주)

Ban Ki-moon is a role model for many young Koreans. ① Ban Ki-moon had worked hard all of his life until he became the head of the United Nations Secretariat. ② He has been Foreign Minister of Korea from 2004 to 2006. ③ In February 2006, he began to campaign for the office of Secretary-General. ④ Since elected, he had taken particularly strong views on global warming and Darfur.

2

organization 조직, 기구
biodiversity
생물학적 다양성
endangered
멸종 위기에 처한
species 종
habitat 서식지
destruction 파괴
pollution 오염
extinction 멸종
in harmony with
~와 조화롭게

WWF is a non-governmental organization that supports global biodiversity. ① From its start in 1961, WWF has been working to protect endangered species. ② It is trying to make sure that the world of the future will contain elephants, whales, giant pandas, and other wildlife. ③ Habitat destruction and pollution are pushing many animals to extinction these days. ④ For decades, WWF is building a future where human needs are met in harmony with nature.

3

naturalist 동식물학자
establish
~을 자리 잡게 하다
respected 존경받는
intriguing
흥미를 돋우는, 흥미로운
World Heritage
세계 유산
preserve ~을 보호하다
generation 세대
legislation 법률
poacher 밀렵꾼

Charles Darwin was a British naturalist of the 19th century. His five-year voyage on HMS Beagle established him as a respected scientist. ① In September of 1835, Darwin arrived on the islands that most greatly affected his thoughts, the Galapagos. ② These islands remain very intriguing to scientists even today. ③ In addition, thousands of tourists has been visiting the Galapagos Islands every year. ④ In 2007, UNESCO placed these islands on the World Heritage in Danger List. In order to preserve these islands for future generations, Ecuador will introduce legislation that protects the animals of the Galapagos from poachers and tourists alike.

B 다음 (A), (B), (C)에서 어법에 맞는 표현으로 가장 적절한 것을 고르시오. [기출 응용]

sideline
(축구 경기장의) 사이드라인
attentively 주의 깊게
show up 나타나다
bend ~을 구부리다
respond to
~에 반응하다
comment 의견, 논평

Dad came to football games whenever I played. He (A) _____ on the sidelines and watched the game attentively. I never told him how to get to a game; he just showed up. When I left the field at the end of a quarter, he would call me over. Not quite sure what he (B) _____ about, he always said the same thing: "You (C)_____ well, Ron. Bend your knees a little more." I would respond to his comments by bending my knees more and running faster when I got back into the game.

	(A)		(B)		(C)
①	had stood	···	talked	···	are playing
②	stood	···	talked	···	are playing
③	was standing	···	was talking	···	are playing
④	stood	···	was talking	···	are playing
⑤	had stood	···	was talking	···	are playing

C 다음 글의 밑줄 친 부분 중, 바르지 <u>않은</u> 것을 고르시오. [기출 응용]

spread ~을 퍼뜨리다
throughout ~ 도처에
slave 노예
attempt 시도
translation 번역
linguist 언어학자
recognize ~을 인정하다
material 자료
switch to ~으로 바꾸다

Gullah began as a trade language in West Africa. Later, it was spread throughout the Caribbean and America by slaves ① <u>brought</u> from Africa. Although Gullah ② <u>has spoken</u> for hundreds of years, until recently there were few attempts to write it down. The Sea Island Translation Team is now working ③ <u>to preserve</u> this language. In the past, Gullah speakers were often told that Gullah was poor English. They felt ④ <u>ashamed for</u> speaking it. Linguists now recognize Gullah as a true language. The team wants to develop classroom materials in Gullah to give children a better understanding of their own language and to make ⑤ <u>it</u> easier to switch to English later.

WRITING PRACTICE

 A Correct the errors and rewrite the sentences.

1 Hojun <u>has drunk</u> coffee when I saw him at the cafe.

→ _____

2 By the time Timothy came home, we <u>has finished</u> the laundry.

→ _____

3 We <u>aren't able to</u> afford a new car since last year.

→ _____

4 While I <u>laid</u> on the couch watching TV, someone kept buzzing the intercom.

→ _____

5 Most of Europe was experiencing the Dark Ages when the Aztecs <u>build</u> the Pyramid of the Sun.

→ _____

B Rearrange the words to make sentences. Follow the example.

「One's experiences have shown that + S + V ~」 ~의 경험으로 미루어 보건대 …이다
have shown / the best policy / my experiences / that / honesty is
→ _____ My experiences have shown that honesty is the best policy. _____

1 have shown that / wearing protective eyewear / scientists' experiences / is necessary in the laboratory

→ _____

2 taking adequate rest / the dancer's experiences / is needed / before a performance / have shown that

→ _____

3 a passport / Daniel's recent experience / has shown that / should be photocopied / when you travel

→ _____

PART 3

The Future & Voice

Unit

11

Simple Future

KEY CONCEPTS

We use a number of different forms to talk about the future: *will*, *be going to*, the simple present, and the present progressive. The form we choose depends on whether we are making a prediction, talking about a plan or an arrangement, or expressing willingness.

will, be going to, 단순현재, 현재진행을 사용하여 미래를 나타낼 수 있다. 예측, 계획, 예정 또는 의지 등 말하고자 하는 바에 따라 그 형태가 달라진다.

FOCUS ···

1 ***Will*** *is used to talk about* **unplanned future events** *(spontaneous decisions made at the moment of speaking) and to make* **general predictions** *about the future (e.g.: based on past behavior).*

will은 말하는 순간에 결정된 미래의 일이나 미래에 대한 일반적인 예측을 나타낸다.

A: Oh no! I've spilled sauce all over the front of my pants.

B: Stay here. I'll **get** you a napkin.[①] (Getting the napkin was an unplanned event; it was made at the moment of speaking.)

A: Do you think the Celtics will win this weekend?

B: I doubt it. They'll probably **lose**.[②] (a general prediction based on past behavior)

2 ***Be going to*** *is used to talk about* **planned future events** *and to make* **predictions** *based on present or past evidence.*

be going to는 이미 계획된 일정이나 근거가 있는 미래의 일에 대한 추측을 나타낸다.

A: Do you want to come over for dinner tonight?

B: I'm sorry, but I can't. I'm **going to work** late.[①](Working late was planned.)

Timmy, don't scrub the baby's back so hard. You're **going to hurt** her.[②]

(present evidence = watching Timmy scrub the baby's back)

3 *We can use the* **simple present** *to talk about the future with schedules, timetables, travel arrangements, and planned public events. This use is only possible with certain verbs: come, go, arrive, leave (depart), start (begin), and finish (end). We usually specify a precise time (e.g.: at 6:00 p.m.).*

come, go, arrive, leave, start, finish 등의 동사가 스케줄, 시간표, 여행 계획, 이미 확정된 공공의 행사에 쓰이면 현재 시제로 미래를 나타낸다.

The performance **starts** at 8:15 sharp, so please don't be late.[①]

What time does your train **leave**? I can take you to the terminal if you need a lift.[②]

My parents **arrive** from holidays tomorrow, so I want to clean up the apartment today.[③]

4 *We also use the **present progressive** to talk about the future when **arrangements** have been made.*
For example, when we've bought a ticket to travel, or when someone is expecting us to be somewhere.

현재진행은 예정된 경우, 미래에 대해 이야기 할 때 사용한다. 예를 들어, 여행 티켓을 산 경우 또는 누군가가 우리가 어떤 장소에 있을 거라고 예상할 때 쓰인다.

A: I heard you're going to Alex's wedding in Hamilton this weekend. Are you going to drive?

B: No, I'm **taking** the train from Union Station tomorrow morning.① (B has already bought a ticket.)

A: I heard you're going to Alex's wedding in Hamilton this weekend. Are you going to drive?

B: No, I'm **going to take** the train, if I can get a ticket.②
(B has planned to take the train, but B hasn't made a definite arrangement; for example, B hasn't bought a ticket.)

A: What **are** you **doing** this weekend?

B: I'm **playing** tennis with Gary.③ (B has arranged this with Gary.)

A: My roommate and I **are having** a party this Saturday. Can you come?

B: I'd love to! I'm **meeting** Sara later this afternoon at the mall. Can I invite her too?④

A: The 5th of May is a national holiday. Isn't that great?

B: I know. I'm **taking** an extra day off and **flying** to Bali with my family.⑤

! NOTICE

In the sentences above, be going to may also be possible. Still, the present progressive is more commonly used for arrangements, and will should not be used.

위의 문장에서는 be going to도 가능하다. 하지만 예정된 일에는 현재진행이 더 흔히 쓰이고, will로는 바꿔 쓸 수 없다. (계획(plan)이나 예정 (arrangement)된 일에는 will을 사용하지 않으므로 위의 문장들의 be −ing는 be going to로는 대체할 수 있으나, will로 대체할 수 없다.)

A: Do you want to have lunch with me tomorrow?

B: Sorry, I can't. I'm **having** lunch with Greg tomorrow at Cracker Barrel.⑥ (I have already arranged this.)

(×) Sorry, I can't. I'll have lunch with Greg tomorrow at Cracker Barrel.

---

1 ① A: 오, 이런! 바지 앞부분 전체에 소스를 쏟았어. B: 여기 있어. 내가 냅킨을 가져다줄게. ② A: 이번 주말 경기에 셀틱스팀이 이길 것 같니? B: 글쎄. 질지도 몰라. 2 ① A: 오늘 밤에 저녁 먹으러 올래? B: 미안하지만, 안 돼. 늦게까지 일을 할 거야. ② 티미, 아기의 등을 너무 세게 밀지 마. 아기를 다치게 할 거야. 3 ① 공연이 여덟 시 십오 분 정각에 시작하니까 늦지 마세요. ② 네 기차가 몇 시에 출발하니? 태워다 줄 사람이 필요하면 내가 터미널까지 데려다 줄 수 있어. ③ 우리 부모님이 내일 휴가에서 돌아오시니까 오늘 아파트를 청소해야겠다. 4 ① A: 나는 네가 이번 주말에 해밀턴 에서 하는 알렉스의 결혼식에 간다고 들었어. 운전해서 갈 거니? B: 아니. 내일 아침에 유니언 역에서 기차를 탈 거야. ② A: 나는 네가 이번 주말에 해밀턴에서 하는 알렉스의 결혼식에 간다고 들었어. 운전해서 갈 거니? B: 아니. 기차표를 구할 수 있으면 기차를 탈 거야. ③ A: 이번 주말에 무엇을 할 거니? B: 나는 개리와 테니스를 칠 거야. ④ A: 내 룸메이트와 나는 이번 토요일에 파티를 열 거야. 올 수 있니? B: 좋지! 오늘 오후에 쇼핑몰에서 사라를 만날 건데, 그녀를 초대해도 되니? ⑤ A: 5월 5일은 국경일이야. 정말 좋지 않니? B: 맞아. 난 휴가를 더 내서 가족들과 발리에 갈 거야. ⑥ A: 내 일 나와 점심 먹을래? B: 미안하지만, 그럴 수 없어. 내일 크래커 배럴에서 그레그와 점심을 먹기로 했어.

EXERCISES

roll in 나타나다
copy machine 복사기
be down 고장 나다
repairman 수리기사
fix 수리하다
industrial design
산업디자인
no doubt
의심의 여지없이, 확실히
be exhausted 지치다
rest 쉬다

A ( ) 안에서 가장 알맞은 것을 고르시오.

1 Look at those dark clouds rolling in! I think it (is going to rain / will rain). We'd better bring in the laundry. ·

2 Jasmine had a car accident this morning. I (am going to visit / will visit) her tonight. (Are you going to join / Will you join) me?

3 This copy machine is down again. I called the service center already. The repairman (is going to come / will come) and fix tomorrow.

4 Jinhee is really excited these days because she (is going to start / will start) college in the fall. She has decided to study industrial design.

5 Next week, Gretta (is going to fly / will fly) in from Switzerland. No doubt she (will be exhausted / is going to be exhausted) from the trip, so let's let her rest before taking her out to see the sights.

pale 창백한
nervous 긴장한
encouragement 격려
be supposed to
~하게 되어 있다
make it
(시간에) 대다, 성공하다

B will과 be going to 중 가장 알맞은 것을 고르고, 주어진 단어를 이용하여 대화를 완성하시오.

1 A: What's wrong, Aaron? You look a little pale.

B: I _____ (give) a presentation later today.

A: Try not to be so nervous. I'm sure you _____ (do) fine.

B: Thanks for the encouragement. I'll let you know how it went tomorrow.

2 A: Good afternoon. I'm Travis, and I _____ (be) your server today.

B: Hello, Travis. I think I _____ (have) the prime rib and a garden salad.

A: That's fine, sir. Will there be anything else?

B: Not just now, thanks.

3 A: Casey, are you going to the basketball game on Saturday?

B: I'd like to go, but I don't think I'll have time. I _____ (visit) my grandmother on Saturday.

A: It's supposed to be a really good game. It starts at noon. You should try to make it.

B: OK. I _____ (do) my best. I hope to see you there.

Unit 12

Future Progressive, Future Perfect & Future Perfect Progressive

KEY CONCEPTS

The **future progressive** (will+be+-*ing*) is used to show that something will be happening at a point in the future. The **future perfect** (will+have+*p.p.*) is used to talk about actions that will be finished before some point in the future. The **future perfect progressive** (will+have+been+-*ing*) is used to talk about actions that will be in progress at some point in the future.

미래진행은 미래의 한 시점에서 어떠한 일이 일어나고 있을 것이라는 것을 예측할 때 사용한다. 미래완료는 미래의 어느 한 시점이 되면 끝날 행동을 나타내며, 미래완료진행은 미래의 어느 한 시점에서 진행되고 있을 행동을 의미한다.

FOCUS

1 *We use the future progressive to talk about things that are predicted or likely to be happening at some time in the future.*

미래진행은 미래의 어느 한 시점에서 일어나고 있거나 예측 가능한 일을 나타낸다.

Don't call Ally between 10:00 and 11:00 p.m. She'll **be taking** an online test then.[1]

Mark and Alex **will be waiting** for us at the airport check-in counter tomorrow morning.[2]

My older sister **will be arriving** next week, and I still don't know how I'm going to entertain her.[3]

c.f. *<At an expensive restaurant>*

A: Excuse me. **Will** you **be needing** an English menu to order?

B: No, thank you. I **won't be needing one**. I can read Korean well enough.[4]

2 *We use the **future perfect** to talk about an activity that will be finished before another event or time in the future. We often use this form with by and before.*

미래완료는 미래의 또 다른 사건이나 시간 전에 끝날 행동을 나타내며 종종 by, before와 함께 쓴다.

You can call Ally after 11:00; she **will have finished** the test <u>by then</u>.[1]

Will our new clients **have received** the design plans <u>before the next meeting</u>?[2]

Megan is saving up to buy her own car. <u>By this time next year</u>, she **will have saved** enough money to buy a second-hand SUV.[3]

A: **Will** you **have found** a new apartment <u>by then</u>? You are more than welcome to stay with us.

B: That's very kind of you, but I'm sure I **will have found** one <u>by then</u>.[4]

3

*We use the **future perfect progressive** to emphasize a continuous, ongoing action—one that will be happening before another event or time in the future.*

미래완료진행은 미래에 진행 중인 동작을 강조할 쓴다.

A: How long will you have been learning English next year?

B: Five years.①

By this time next month, we will have been living here for one year.②

Mr. Kim will have been teaching there for over thirty years when he retires.③

A: How long have you and James been dating now?

B: Well, next month we will have been seeing each other for a year.

A: That's fantastic! Any plans to tie the knot soon?④

NOTICE

As with other progressive tenses, we don't use stative verbs with either the future progressive or the future perfect progressive.

다른 진행 시제처럼 미래진행 또는 미래완료진행에도 상태동사를 사용하지 않는다.

Steve will have known Sally for two years when they get married next month.⑤

(✗) Steve ~~will have been knowing~~ Sally for two years when they get married next month.

---

① 밤 열 시에서 열한 시 사이에 앨리에게 전화하지 마. 그녀는 그때 인터넷으로 시험을 보고 있을 거야. ② 마크와 알렉스가 내일 아침 공항 수속 카운터에서 우리를 기다리고 있을 것이다. ③ 우리 언니가 다음 주에 도착하는데, 나는 아직도 어떻게 그녀를 즐겁게 해 줘야 할지 모르겠다. ④ 〈고급 레스토랑에서〉 A: 실례합니다. 주문하시게 영문 메뉴판 가져다 드릴까요? B: 아니요. 됐어요. 필요 없을 것 같아요. 저는 한글을 잘 읽을 수 있어요. 2 ① 열한 시 이후에는 앨리에게 전화해도 돼. 그때쯤이면 시험을 끝마쳤을 거야. ② 저희의 새 고객들이 다음 회의 전에 디자인안을 받을 수 있을까요? ③ 메건은 차를 사려고 돈을 모으고 있다. 내년 이맘때쯤이면 중고 SUV를 살 정도의 돈을 모으게 될 것이다. ④ A: 그때쯤 되면 새 아파트를 구하겠니? 우리랑 같이 있어도 전혀 문제 되지 않아. B: 정말 고마워. 하지만, 그때까지면 구하게 될 거라 확신해. 3 ① A: 내년이면 얼마나 오래 영어를 공부해온 건가요? B: 5년이요. ② 다음 달 이맘때쯤이면 우리는 여기에서 일 년을 산 것이 된다. ③ 김 선생님이 은퇴할 때쯤 되면 그곳에서 30년 넘게 가르친 것이 된다. ④ A: 너와 제임스는 지금 사귄 지 얼마나 됐니? B: 음, 다음 달이면 사귄 지 1년이 돼. A: 멋진데! 곧 결혼할 계획은 없어? ⑤ 스티브와 샐리가 다음 달에 결혼하면 스티브는 샐리를 2년 동안 알고 지낸 것이 될 것이다.

EXERCISES

 ( ) 안에서 가장 알맞은 것을 고르시오.

act 연기하다
award (상을) 수여하다; 상

1 In June, I (will be living / will have been living) in Seoul for eight years.

2 By this time next week, Chris (will arrive / will have arrived) from Toronto.

3 Yoojin (will have been acting / will be acting) on Broadway for ten years in October.

4 Heeju (will be finishing / will have finished) her project by seven o'clock this evening.

5 Tomorrow, my parents (will have been / will have been being) married for twenty five years.

6 When he is awarded an Oscar, he (will have won / will have been winning) more film awards than any other actor.

B 주어진 단어를 이용하여 대화를 완성하시오.

clarinet 클라리넷(악기)
dedicated
몰두하는, 헌신적인
perfect
~을 완전하게 하다
tune 곡
recital 연주회, 발표회
disturb ~을 방해하다
land 도착하다
Johannesburg
요하네스버그(남아프리카 공
화국 북부의 도시)
complete ~을 끝내다

1 A: Is Liz practicing her clarinet again? She's really dedicated.
B: Yes. I'm sure she _____ _____ _____ (perfect) that tune by next week's recital.

2 A: Gary, can I call you later to ask about tomorrow's math test?
B: Of course, that'll be fine. But please don't call me between six and seven.
I _____ _____ _____ (eat) dinner then.

3 A: Julie, please be quiet when you get home. Your brother _____ _____ _____ (study) for his exams.
B: Sure, Mom. I promise not to disturb him.

4 A: Thomas, do you think we'll be landing soon?
B: I hope so, Sue. We _____ _____ _____ _____ (travel) for nearly 24 hours by the time we reach Johannesburg.

5 A: Jinju, would you like to go to the movies this weekend? Do you have time?
B: Sure. That'd be great. I _____ _____ _____ (complete) preparations for my presentation by Saturday.

Using Time Clauses to Express the Future

Unit **13**

KEY CONCEPTS

A **time clause** is a dependent clause. It contains both a subject and a verb, but it must be joined to a full sentence—the main clause. Time clauses clarify the time relationship between the two clauses.

시간절은 종속절이다. 주어와 동사를 포함하지만, 완전한 문장인 주절과 함께 와야 한다. 시간절은 주절과 종속절의 시간 관계를 명확히 해준다.

FOCUS

1 *Time clauses that refer to the future begin with when, before, after, as soon as, until[till], and by the time. Importantly, future forms (will, be going to) are not used in time clauses, even though the clauses may refer to the future.*

미래를 나타내는 시간절은 when, before, after, as soon as, until[till], by the time으로 시작한다. 시간절이 미래를 나타내더라도 미래형(will, be going to)은 사용하지 않는다.

a **When** *means "at that time."* when은 "~할 때"라는 의미

Let's go to the new fusion restaurant down the street **when** Rachel <u>comes</u> to visit.[①] (will come)

When my brother <u>graduates</u> next spring, he is going to travel to South America.[②] (will graduate)

b **Before** *means "earlier than."* before는 "~전에"라는 의미

She will have already left for the airport **before** I <u>get</u> a chance to say goodbye.

c **After** *means "following that moment."* after는 "~후에"라는 의미

I'll take the dog out for a walk **after** I <u>change</u> into a pair of jeans and <u>have</u> a snack.

d **As soon as** *means "right after."* as soon as는 "바로 직후 / ~하자마자"라는 의미

The judges will make their decision **as soon as** they <u>hear</u> from everyone in the contest.

e **Until[Till]** *means "up to that time."* until[till]은 "~할 때까지"라는 의미

These photos will be on display **until** the exhibition <u>changes</u> at the end of the month.

2 *Occasionally, we use the **present progressive** in time clauses to refer to the future.*

미래를 나타내기 위해 시간절에 현재진행을 쓰기도 한다.

<u>While</u> Veronica **is studying** social welfare at Duke next year, she is going to work part-time at the university library.

---

1 a ① 레이첼이 오면 길 아래쪽에 새로 생긴 퓨전 레스토랑에 가자. ② 내 남동생은 내년 봄에 졸업하면 남미로 여행을 갈 것이다. b 내가 작별 인사를 하기도 전에 그녀는 이미 공항으로 떠나 버리고 없을 것이다. c 나는 청바지로 갈아입고 간식을 먹고 나서 개를 데리고 산책하러 나갈 것이다. d 심사위원들은 경연대회의 참가자 모두의 노래를 들으면 바로 결정을 내릴 것이다. e 이 사진들은 이번 달 말에 전시회가 바뀔 때까지 진열될 것이다. 2 베로니카는 내년에 듀크 대학에서 사회 복지를 공부하면서 대학교 도서관에서 아르바이트를 할 것이다.

EXERCISES

정답 및 해설 P. 10

A ( ) 안에서 가장 알맞은 것을 고르시오.

> blackout 정전
> power station 발전소
> yeast 효모, 이스트
> dough 반죽
> allow ~을 허락하다
> rise 부풀다

1 Billy will visit Korea (until / when) he saves enough money for the trip.

2 Yongjun will return from Japan (while / when) the baseball season is over.

3 (Until / As soon as) we get home, I want you to go straight up stairs and take a shower.

4 Blackouts will continue to be a problem (until / after) the new power station is finished.

5 (While / As soon as) we get to the theater, we will have to find our seats. We're almost late.

6 Be sure to go to the toilet (before / after) we get into the car. We have a long trip ahead of us.

7 (Before / After) we mix the water, flour, and yeast together, the dough will be allowed to rise for 30 minutes.

B 주어진 단어를 이용하여 문장을 완성하시오.

> pollute ~을 오염시키다
> atmosphere 대기
> retire 은퇴하다
> golden years 노후

1 Jimin will be taking care of her brother's dog until he _____ (get) back from Jejudo next week.

2 As soon as the watermelons _____ (grow) big enough, the farmer will take them to the market to sell.

3 Until we _____ (stop) polluting the atmosphere, global temperatures will continue to rise every year.

4 My father will retire after he _____ (save) enough money to support himself during his golden years.

5 While you _____ _____ (enjoy) this beautiful spring weather, I will be preparing for my science test. Life is so unfair.

6 Before you _____ (leave) for Hawaii, you should be sure to buy a new swimsuit. The beaches there are amazing.

Unit 14

Passive Voice

KEY CONCEPTS

We use the **passive voice** when the "agent"—the person performing the action expressed by the verb—is unknown, not important, or when the subject of the passive sentence is the main topic of discussion.
동사의 행위를 하는 "행위자"가 누군지 모르거나, 중요하지 않거나, 수동문의 주어가 이야기의 주제일 때 수동태를 사용한다.

FOCUS

1 *In the active voice, the agent performs the action expressed by the main verb. In the* **passive voice***, the thing being acted upon—the object—moves to the subject position of the sentence. But though their positions in the sentence have changed, their relationship to each other remains the same.*

능동태에서는 행위자가 주요 동사의 행동을 하고, 수동태에서는 행동이 받는 목적어가 문장에서 주어의 위치로 이동한다. 문장에서의 위치는 달라지지만, 관계는 변하지 않는다.

Humans **have been domesticating** wild animals for thousands of years.[1] (active voice: agent-action-object)
Dogs **were domesticated** roughly 15,000 years ago in Central Asia.[2] (passive voice: object-action-[optional] agent)

2 *The* **passive voice** *is formed with a form of be and a past participle. (NOTE: Only transitive verbs—those that take objects—can be made passive.)*

수동태는 「be동사+과거분사」의 형태이다. (주의: 목적어를 취하는 타동사만 수동태를 만들 수 있다.)

An old stone wishing well **dominates** the temple courtyard.[1] (active)

→ The temple courtyard **is dominated** by an old stone wishing well. (passive)

The government **is building** a new sports complex in my hometown.[2]

→ A new sports complex **is being built** in my hometown by the government.

The school nurse **has given** each child a thorough physical.[3]

→ Each child **has been given** a thorough physical by the school nurse.

This book **will change** your life for the better.[4]

→ Your life **will be changed** for the better by this book.

3 *Intransitive verbs (e.g.: argue, bark, collapse, giggle) cannot be made passive. As well, a few transitive verbs (e.g.: have, lack, resemble, suit, fit) do not appear in the passive voice.*

목적어를 취하지 않는 자동사와 have, lack, resemble, suit, fit과 같은 몇몇 타동사는 수동태를 만들지 않는다.

My kids **argue** a lot, but deep down I know they love each other very much.[1]

The antique chair **collapsed** under the weight of the heavy encyclopedias.[2]

After the earthquake, the city **resembled** a war zone; it was ruined.[3]

(✗) After the earthquake, a war zone ~~was resembled~~ by the city; it was ruined.

My friend Jacob **had** the flu last week.④ (✗) The flu ~~was had~~ by Jacob.

That blue striped tie really **suits** you.⑤ (✗) You ~~are suited~~ by that blue striped tie.

4 *With two-object verbs, either the indirect object or the direct object can become the subject.*
목적어를 두 개 갖는 동사는 간접 목적어나 직접 목적어가 수동태의 주어가 될 수 있다.

> *Verbs with two-objects: give, send, lend, show, tell, offer, pay, promise ...*

Minji's parents promised <u>her</u> <u>a trip to England</u> if she passed her exams.
→ <u>Minji</u> **was promised** a trip to England if she passed her exams.
→ <u>A trip to England</u> **was promised** to Minji if she passed her exams.

5 *Stative passives are verb-like words that follow be and function as adjectives. They indicate states or conditions – not actions – and they frequently pattern with prepositions.*
상태 수동태는 be동사 뒤에 오고 형용사와 같은 기능을 한다. 행동이 아닌 상태나 조건을 나타내며 종종 전치사와 결합을 한다.

> *Stative passive + preposition: be interested in, be worried about, be terrified of, be limited to,*
> *be intimidated by, be crowded with, be exhausted from ...*

A: Your cat looks <u>hungry</u>. He keeps eying the food on my plate. (*hungry* = adjective)
B: His leg **is broken**, so he's looking for sympathy. Just pet him a little.① (*is broken* = stative passive)

Brad **is worried about** Jess, who is attending a conference in a strange city all by herself.②

Carol suffers from claustrophobia; in other words, she **is terrified of** small, cramped spaces.③

Jim **was caught up** in the excitement of the game, so he didn't notice his dinner burning in the kitchen.④

WRITING TIPS

The **passive voice** *is especially common in technical and scientific writing, legal documents, and lab reports, where the agent is the researcher and to say so would be inappropriate.*
수동태는 기술서나 과학적 내용의 글, 법문, 연구 보고 등 행위자를 언급하는 것이 부적절할 수 있는 장르의 글에서 주로 사용된다.

The heat **was increased** to 450°.①
Striking factory workers **will be held** responsible for lost productivity.②

The **passive voice** *is also used in descriptive writing, especially in descriptions of places.*
수동태는 특히 장소 묘사와 같은 설명문에 흔히 쓰인다.

The cottage **had been renovated** two years earlier, but it still smelled of old timber.③

---

1 ① 인류는 수천 년 동안 야생 동물을 가축화해 왔다. ② 개는 중앙아시아에서 대략 15,000년 전에 가축화되었다. 2 ① 소원을 비는 오래된 돌우물이 절의 안뜰을 차지하고 있다. ② 정부가 내 고향에 새 종합운동장을 짓고 있다. ③ 양호 선생님이 각각의 어린이를 꼼꼼하게 신체검사했다. ④ 이 책은 당신의 삶을 더 좋게 변화시켜 줄 것입니다. 3 ① 우리 아이들은 자주 언쟁을 하지만, 나는 그들이 마음속 깊이 서로 매우 사랑한다는 것을 안다. ② 골동품 의자가 무거운 백과사전의 무게에 눌려 주저앉았다. ③ 지진 후, 도시는 전쟁터를 방불케 망가졌다. ④ 내 친구 제이콥은 지난주에 독감에 걸렸다. ⑤ 그 파란색 줄무늬 넥타이는 너에게 정말 잘 어울린다. 4 민지의 부모님은 그녀가 시험에 합격하면 영국으로 여행을 보내준다고 약속했다. 5 ① A: 네 고양이는 배고파 보여. 그는 계속 내 접시의 음식을 주시하고 있어. B: 내 고양이는 다리가 부러져서 위로받고 싶어 해. 그를 약간 쓰다듬어 줘. ② 브레드는 제스를 걱정하고 있는데, 그녀는 낯선 도시에서 혼자 회의에 참가하고 있다. ③ 캐롤은 폐소 공포증이 있어. 다시 말하면 그녀는 작고, 비좁은 장소를 무서워해. ④ 짐은 게임의 재미에 푹 빠져서 부엌에서 저녁이 타는 것을 눈치채지 못했다. WT ① 온도가 450°로 증가했다. ② 파업한 공장 노동자들은 생산량 손실에 대한 책임을 지게 될 것이다. ③ 오두막집은 2년 전에 개조되었지만, 아직도 오래된 목재 냄새가 난다.

wheat 밀
harvest ~을 수확하다
disappear 사라지다
terrifically 굉장히, 엄청
globe 지구
threat 위협
phishing 피싱(전화 사기)
cyber bullying
사이버 불링(인터넷 상에서 특정한 사람을 괴롭히는 것)
expand 확대되다, 늘다

A ( ) 안에서 가장 알맞은 것을 고르시오.

1 Generally, wheat (harvested / is harvested) in the fall.

2 The flowers (will die / will be died) if you don't water them enough.

3 Suddenly, the strange man (disappeared / was disappeared) in front of my eyes.

4 More than 3,000 numbers (can store / can be stored) in this brand-new cell phone.

5 Some animals are terrifically intelligent and (can teach / can be taught) many amazing tricks.

6 All students who take this class (will expect / will be expected) to read several novels written in English.

7 Organizations like UNICEF and the World Health Organization (have helped / have been helped) millions of people around the globe.

8 Threats to ordinary citizens, which include virus attacks, phishing scams, and cyber bullying (are growing / are being grown) as the Internet expands.

Artic fox 북극 여우
trading company
무역회사
evolve 진화하다
frigid 매우 추운
explorer 탐험가
conduct ~을 수행하다
translate ~을 번역하다

B 주어진 동사를 각각 과거 시제나 과거완료 시제로 바꿔 문장을 완성하시오.

1 The Arctic fox _____ as the "snow fox" or "white fox." (know, 현재)

2 He _____ by a trading company to discover the Northwest Passage to Asia. (hire, 과거)

3 It _____ to survive in some of the most frigid temperatures on the planet. (evolve, 현재완료)

4 Henry Hudson, the great English explorer, _____ in London, England. (bear, 과거)

5 Of Glenn's three sons, Tom, the youngest, most closely _____ his father. (resemble, 현재)

6 The interview _____ by one of our faculty members at the end of the month. (conduct, 미래)

7 His latest novel _____ into ten languages since he published the first edition in 2017. (translate, 현재완료)

REVIEW

정답 및 해설 P. 11

A 다음 빈칸에 가장 알맞은 것을 고르시오.

semester 학기
English literature
영문학

1 A: Where would you like to go for dinner?

B: I _____ about having Chinese food. Does that sound good?

① will have thought   ② had been thinking

③ was thinking   ④ will think

2 A: Jerry, where did you spend your holiday last year?

B: Well, we _____ to go to Tahiti, but we decided against it at the last minute. So we went to Bali.

① plan   ② has planned

③ had planned   ④ are planning

3 A: Hyunjung, which courses _____ this semester?

B: I only have two courses: English literature and Korean history.

① are you taking   ② did you take

③ had you taken   ④ will you take

B 다음 대화를 읽고, 바르지 <u>않은</u> 문장을 고르시오.

pregnant 임신한
thrilled
몹시 흥분한, 신이 난
in-laws 인척, 친척
awful 끔찍한, 지독한
expressway 고속도로

1 ① A: Heather, what's your new roommate like?

② B: She's nice. She had moved in two days ago, and we're getting along fine.

③ A: That's good. Good roommates are hard to find.

④ B: Yes, that's true. And we are both interested in studying Korean, so we can help each other.

2 ① A: Michelle, I've got some great news. I went to the doctor last week, and I find out I'm pregnant.

② B: That's great news! Your husband must be thrilled.

③ A: Yes. Both he and my in-laws are very pleased. This will be their first grandchild.

④ B: That's wonderful! Congratulations! I wish you and your family all the best.

3 ① A: Traffic this evening was just awful. The expressway is still closed.

② B: I can't believe they haven't finished the repair work yet.

③ A: I know! They work on it for almost a month already.

④ B: It'll be finished by next week. Then things should get back to normal.

REVIEW PLUS

정답 및 해설 P. 12

A 다음을 읽고, 바르지 <u>않은</u> 문장을 고르시오.

1

dramatically 극적으로
worldwide
전 세계적으로
significant 중요한
enable A to+동사원형
A가 ~하는 것을 가능하게 하다
communicate
연락을 주고받다
along with
~와 더불어, 마찬가지로
function 기능
access ~에 접근하다

The Internet has dramatically changed the lives of people around the world. ① By using computers, we are able to contact people worldwide in a matter of seconds. ② The use of email is a significant part of the Internet. It enables us to communicate with each other quickly and cheaply. ③ Along with email, the World Wide Web is an important function of the Internet. ④ It is allowed us to easily access information on just about any topic. Using the World Wide Web is easy: all you need is a web browser and an Internet connection.

2

majority of 대부분의
operate ~을 운영하다
priest 성직자
monk 수도승
proper 적절한
merchant 상인
set up 세우다
enrollment 입학, 등록자

During the Middle Ages, there were many schools. ① However, the majority of schools were for boys only. ② The Church operated many of them, and classes taught in Latin because Christian prayers were spoken in Latin. ③ Boys who attended these schools were expected to become priests or monks when they reached the proper age. ④ In some towns, the merchants set up schools for boys who were planning to become merchants. These merchant schools, much like the Church schools, were not always open to female enrollment.

3

fossil fuel 화석연료
large amounts of
상당한 양의
emission 방출물, 배기
run out 떨어지다
viable 실행 가능한
alternative 대안
discover ~을 발견하다
method 방법
store
~을 저장하다, 비축하다
electricity 전기
replace ~을 대체하다

① Many people think that solar energy will be solving the energy problems of the future. ② Fossil fuels create large amounts of harmful emissions. In addition, supplies of most fossil fuels are quickly running out. ③ In order to make solar energy a viable alternative to fossil fuels, scientists need to discover a better method of storing the electricity for use at night and on cloudy days. ④ If we are able to improve battery technology, solar energy will soon replace highly polluting fuels like coal and oil.

B 다음 (A), (B), (C)에서 어법에 맞는 표현으로 가장 적절한 것을 고르시오. [기출 응용]

Taking photos on sunny, hot days is just as dangerous for you (A) _____ it is for your camera. While you can deal with a simple sunburn, your camera faces permanent damage from excessive sun exposure. Keeping the lens covered when you aren't using it (B) _____ . Photos of sunrises and sunsets are always fun to take and view later, but pointing your lens directly at the sun may damage it. The lens (C) _____ similar to the human eye; both are harmed by directly peering into sunlight.

sunburn
햇볕으로 입은 화상
face ~에 직면하다
permanent 영구적인
damage
손해, 피해, 해를 입히다
excessive 과도한
exposure
(햇빛 등에) 노출
be similar to
~와 유사하다
peer into 응시하다
recommend
~을 권장하다, 추천하다

	(A)		(B)		(C)
①	while	···	is recommended	···	are
②	while	···	is recommending	···	are
③	while	···	is recommending	···	is
④	as	···	is recommending	···	is
⑤	as	···	is recommended	···	is

C 다음 글의 밑줄 친 부분 중, 바르지 <u>않은</u> 것을 고르시오. [기출 응용]

There are no social conventions ① <u>regulating</u> our grief at the death of an animal. You can throw your cat's body in the garbage can or bury it with a gravestone. It is quite a different situation after the loss of a close family member when some mourning ② <u>is required</u>. In general, however, there is a notion that grief after the loss of an animal is suitable for children but not for adults. Mourning a dead pet ③ <u>provides</u> children with a useful "rehearsal" for the death of human family members, but ④ <u>it is not considering</u> appropriate for adults because there is a lack of social support for the mature person ⑤ <u>going through</u> such grief.

convention 관행
regulate ~을 규제하다
grief 슬픔
bury ~을 묻다, 매장하다
gravestone 묘비
mourn
~을 애도하다, 슬퍼하다
in general 일반적으로
notion 개념
be suitable for
~에 적당하다
provide ~을 제공하다
mature 성숙한
go through ~을 겪다

WRITING PRACTICE

정답 및 해설 P. 12

 Correct the errors and rewrite the sentences.

1 This time next year, we will <u>have been knowing</u> each other for ten years.

→ _____

2 This time next month, we <u>will backpack</u> around Europe. I'm so excited.

→ _____

3 New York City <u>will be repaired</u> lower Manhattan for several years to come.

→ _____

4 By the time Dr. Rogers retires, he <u>will be working</u> at this university for 30 years.

→ _____

5 Sean will have been dating Carrie for seven years when they <u>will get married</u>.

→ _____

 Rearrange the words. Follow the example.

> 「It is believed that S + V」 ~라고 믿어진다
>
> are / better than / it is believed that / those in others / the schools in this state
>
> → ___It is believed that the schools in this state are better than those in others.___

1 was formed / more than / it is believed that / four billion years ago / the earth

→ _____

2 a unified Korea / a global scientific powerhouse / it is believed that / would be

→ _____

3 by the human mind / many illnesses / it is believed that / are actually caused

→ _____

PART 4

Verbals

Overview

Unit 15

KEY CONCEPTS

English has three different kinds of **verbals**: **participles**, **gerunds**, and **infinitives**. Verbals look and feel like verbs because they are verbs in form and they express actions and states of being. But they do not function as verbs but rather as other parts of speech: adjectives, nouns, and adverbs.

영어에는 분사, 동명사, 부정사 세 가지 준동사가 있다. 준동사는 동사의 형태를 가지고 행동과 상태를 표현하기 때문에 동사처럼 보이지만, 동사의 기능을 하지 않고 형용사, 명사, 부사로서의 역할을 한다.

FOCUS

1 *A* **participle** *is a* **verb form** *that functions as an* **adjective**.

분사는 형용사의 기능을 하는 동사 형태이다.

The **sobbing** student was escorted to the nurse's office.① (*sobbing* modifies *student*)

Today's lecture on ancestry was a little **boring**.② (*boring* says something about *Today's lecture*)

The **enraged** bull charged the **frightened** matador.③ (*enraged* modifies *bull*, and *frightened* modifies *matador*)

2 *A* **gerund** *is a* **verb form** *that functions as a* **noun**. *And just like other nouns, gerunds can fill a number of different sentence slots.*

동명사는 명사의 기능을 하는 동사 형태로 주어 · 목적어 · 보어의 역할을 한다.

Since Julia was twelve years old, **collecting** rare stamps has been her passion.① (subject)

I love **meeting** new people and **visiting** exotic locals.② (object of transitive verb)

Are you looking forward to **graduating** next year?③ (object of preposition)

Jiho's favorite hobby is **playing** video game.④ (subject complement)

3 *An* **infinitive** *is a* **verb form** *that can function as a* **noun**, **adjective**, *or* **adverb**.

부정사는 명사, 형용사, 부사의 기능을 하는 동사 형태이다.

To question and **explore** is part of what it means to be human.① (subject)

Jim always refuses **to look** whenever I put in my contact lenses.② (object of transitive verb)

Wherever Melinda goes, she always brings a book **to read**.③ (adjective modifying book)

Richard went to the dentist **to have** his braces removed.④ (adverb explaining purpose)

---

1 ① 흐느껴 우는 학생이 양호실로 옮겨졌다. ② 조상에 관한 오늘의 강의는 약간 지루했다. ③ 성난 황소는 겁에 질린 투우사를 향해 달려왔다. 2 ① 줄리아는 열두 살 때부터, 희귀한 우표 수집을 매우 좋아했다. ② 나는 새로운 사람을 만나는 것과 이국적인 장소를 방문하는 것을 매우 좋아한다. ③ 너는 내년에 졸업하는 것이 기대되니? ④ 지호가 가장 좋아하는 취미는 비디오 게임을 하는 것이다. 3 ① 질문하고 탐구하는 것은 인간이라는 것을 의미하는 일부분이다. ② 짐은 내가 콘택트렌즈를 낄 때마다 쳐다보기를 항상 거부한다. ③ 멜린다는 가는 곳마다 항상 읽을 책을 가져간다. ④ 리처드는 교정기를 빼기 위해 치과에 갔다.

EXERCISES

정답 및 해설 P. 13

 A 밑줄 친 부분의 역할을 <보기>에서 골라 그 기호를 쓰시오.

보기	ⓐ subject	ⓑ subject complement
	ⓒ object of transitive verb	ⓓ object of preposition
	ⓔ adjective	ⓕ adverb

1 My first part-time job was <u>mopping</u> floors in a French restaurant. _____

2 The detective scrutinized the door knob <u>to discover</u> some fingerprints. _____

3 I totally forgot about <u>lending</u> you my portable disk. I thought I had lost it. _____

4 I'm not quite sure if we have enough time <u>to finish</u> all this work before I leave. _____

5 Jill continued <u>taking</u> taekwondo lessons even though she broke her wrist. _____

6 <u>Waiting</u> in the rain for his friends made Jake furious. _____

mop
~을 대걸레로 닦다, 청소하다
detective 탐정; 수사관
scrutinize
~을 세밀히 조사하다
knob (문) 손잡이
fingerprint 지문
portable
휴대용의, 가지고 다닐 수 있는
wrist 손목
furious 격노한, 격심한

B 주어진 단어를 알맞게 바꿔 문장을 완성하시오.

1 You refuse _____ (have) a serious conversation with me, don't you?

2 Chris had already left for the airport when I arrived. I was very _____ (disappoint).

3 The math teacher doesn't allow her students _____ (use) calculators during exams.

4 Mike's attempts _____ (find) accommodations in Vancouver were not very successful.

5 I have been reading your blog comments with _____ (grow) anger over the past few months.

6 Once I changed the wall _____ (cover) in my room, the atmosphere totally brightened up. It was a great idea!

7 I always listen to music on my smartphone, but today I'm listening to an English lecture _____ (improve) my listening.

disappoint
~을 실망시키다
allow
~을 허락하다, 허용하다
calculator 계산기
attempt 시도
accommodation
숙박 시설
atmosphere 분위기
brighten 밝아지다

Participles

Participle is the name of the *-ing* or *-ed* verb form that functions as an adjective. In sentences, participles are used to modify nouns. However, participles do not form or establish the tense of the sentence; they cannot be main verbs.

분사는 형용사와 같은 기능을 하는 −ing 또는 −ed의 동사 형태를 말한다. 분사는 명사를 수식하고, 시제에 영향을 주지 않는다.

FOCUS

1 *Like main verbs,* **participles** *express time and have* **present** *and* **past forms**.

분사는 본동사처럼 시간을 표현할 수 있고 현재형과 과거형으로 나타낼 수 있다.

Working part-time, Jeff gained valuable on-the-job training.[1] (present participle)

Prepared by experience, the coach knew not to expect too much.[2] (past participle)

Having been a lifeguard, Sam was able to save the drowning man.[3] (present perfect participle)

2 *Both the* **present** *and* **past participle** *can be used as an adjective to* **modify** *a noun. Participles can come before the nouns they modify or follow linking verbs like be, become, and seem.*

현재분사와 과거분사 모두 명사를 수식하는 형용사로 쓸 수 있다. 분사는 수식하는 명사 앞에 오거나 be, become, seem과 같은 연결 동사 다음에 올 수 있다.

a **Present participles** *have an* **active meaning**. *The nouns they modify "perform" the action, which affects the person or thing being described.*

현재분사: 능동의 의미, 현재분사가 수식하는 (대)명사는 행위자의 역할을 한다.

Don't get too close to that **barking** dog.[1] (The dog is performing "the action of barking.")

Steven ran into the **burning** house.[2] (The house was performing "the action of burning.")

This is my first garage sale. It's really **interesting**![3]

b **Past participles** *have a* **passive meaning**. *The nouns they modify "receive" the action; in other words, they are acted upon.*

과거분사: 수동의 의미, 과거분사가 수식하는 명사는 행동을 받는다.

John's **sprained** ankle will heal in about a month.[1] (Something sprained John's ankle.)

The **terrified** children sat huddled together.[2] (Something terrified the children.)

You seem **confused**. Can I clarify the instructions for you?[3]

3

*A **participle phrase** includes the participle plus its modifier(s), object(s), and/or complement(s).*

분사구는 분사와 수식어(들), 목적어(들), 보어(들)로 구성된다.

<u>Removing</u> her shoes, Lily entered the tiny house and greeted her host with a bow.[①]

("Removing" = participle; "her shoes" = direct object of the action expressed by the participle)

Tasha, <u>**embarrassed** by the sudden attention</u>, stopped talking and sat back down.[②]

("embarrassed" = participle; "by the sudden attention" answers the question "why?")

Our swimsuits, <u>**lying** in a pile on the bathroom floor</u>, were still too wet to pack.[③]

("lying" = participle; "in a pile" answers the question "how?", and "on the bathroom floor" answers the question "where?")

After we arrived at school, we saw the teachers <u>**talking** quietly to each other.</u>[④]

("talking" = participle; "quietly to each other" answers the question "how?")

---

1 ① 제프는 시간제로 일하면서, 소중한 직업 훈련을 받았다. ② 코치는 경험을 바탕으로, 너무 많은 것을 기대하지 말아야 한다는 것을 알았다. ③ 샘은 인명 구조원이어서 물에 빠진 남자를 구할 수 있었다. 2 a ① 저 짖고 있는 개에게 너무 가까이 가지 마라. ② 스티븐은 불타는 집 안으로 뛰어들어갔다. ③ 이것은 나의 첫 번째 중고품 세일이야. 정말 재미있어! b ① 존의 삔 발목은 한 달 정도면 나을 것이다. ② 겁에 질린 어린이들은 함께 웅크려 앉아 있었다. ③ 너 혼란스러워 보여. 지시사항을 명확하게 말해 줄까? 3 ① 릴리는 신발을 벗으면서, 작은 집 안으로 들어가 주인에게 허리를 숙여 인사하였다. ② 갑작스러운 관심에 부끄러워진 타샤는 말하는 것을 멈추고 다시 앉았다. ③ 화장실 바닥에 쌓여 있는 우리의 수영복은 짐을 싸기엔 여전히 너무 젖어 있었다. ④ 우리는 학교에 도착한 후, 선생님들이 서로 조용하게 이야기하는 것을 보았다.

EXERCISES

정답 및 해설 P. 13

face ~을 직면하다
exhaust
~으로 몹시 지치다
murmur ~을 중얼거리다
washing-up 설거지
ridiculous
웃기는, 터무니없는
sparsely
드문드문, 띄엄띄엄
breathless 숨을 죽인
carve ~을 새기다
clan 씨족
represent ~을 대표하다
status 지위
occupation 직업
profession 전문직
physician 의사
clergy 성직자

A 밑줄 친 분사구문의 행위자(*agents*)를 찾아 쓰시오.

1 Many senior high school students are having a tough time <u>deciding on a career</u>.

2 <u>Facing serious illness</u>, most people learn that there is much to hope and wish for in their lives.

3 <u>Exhausted</u>, Eugene murmured that starting the washing-up at such a late hour would be ridiculous.

4 The audience, <u>sitting sparsely in the auditorium</u>, watched the basketball game with breathless interest.

5 At the front of the house, there were carved images of clan symbols <u>representing the families living there</u>.

6 The top-status occupations are the professions: physicians, lawyers, professors, and clergy, <u>requiring many years of education and training</u>.

transplant
(기관·조직 등을) 이식하다
organ 기관
stimulate ~을 자극하다
strategy 전략
debt 빚
apparently
명백히, 분명히
extremely 극도로
tedious 지루한, 따분한

B ( ) 안에서 가장 알맞은 것을 고르시오.

1 Kidneys have become the most commonly (transplanting / transplanted) organ.

2 The newly (releasing / released) movie playing was the best one I have ever seen.

3 We need a really (stimulating / stimulated) marketing strategy to attract public attention.

4 If Lawrence's family can't pay their debt by the (fixing / fixed) date, they will lose their house.

5 The entrance exam was a complete success, and Mackey was apparently extremely (pleasing / pleased).

6 The work was (tiring / tired) and tedious. All I had to do was sit on a bench and watch people swim all day long.

7 My brother asked me to babysit for him that evening. I spent time folding (coloring / colored) paper into airplanes with his son.

C 주어진 단어를 알맞게 바꿔 문장을 완성하시오.

1 Sophia was _____ (disturb) to hear of her father's illness.

2 It is _____ (disconcert) to watch Isaac make one mistake after another on the stage.

3 This TV program shows that the current situation is not only _____ (confuse) but also dangerous.

4 The teacher found the new student's attitude _____ (bewilder). She decided to call the student's parents.

5 Unlike my boyfriend, I'm not _____ (satisfy) to spend my days doing nothing. That's why I often argue with him.

6 Jane is easily _____ (embarrass) when she can't express herself well in English to her Australian friends.

disturb
~을 불안하게 하다
disconcert
~을 당황하게 하다
attitude 태도
bewilder
~을 당황하게 하다
satisfy ~을 만족시키다
argue with
~와 논쟁하다
embarrass
~을 당황케 하다
express oneself 의견을 말하다, 자신을 표현하다

D 주어진 단어를 알맞게 바꿔 문장을 완성하시오.

1 (conflict) ① There were _____ reports on whether he had been sentenced to death.
② Ann often feels _____ about who to choose because of her feelings for both boys.

2 (admire) ① Bradley received many _____ letters from women who found him attractive.
② She was widely _____ for her elegance and warmth as the First Lady of America.

3 (captivate) ① Harry was so _____ by the band's musical sound that he watched their concert twice.
② Loran has had wide success as a singer due to her _____ voice.

4 (astound) ① David whined from hunger, but soon he began to work again with his usual _____ speed.
② I was _____ when my best friend told my secret to everyone within earshot.

conflict (의견·생각 등이)
충돌하다, 대립하다
sentence to death
사형을 선고하다
admire
~을 찬양하다, 높이 평가하다
attractive 매력적인
elegance 우아함, 기품
captivate ~을 사로잡다
astound
~을 놀라게 하다
whine 투덜거리다
hunger 굶주림
within earshot
불러서 들리는 곳에

Gerunds

Unit 17

KEY CONCEPTS

Gerund is the name of the *-ing* verb form that functions as a noun. In sentences, gerunds are used as subjects, complements, and objects. However, gerunds — like participles — do not form or establish the tense of the sentence; they cannot be main verbs.

동명사는 명사의 기능을 하는 –ing 형의 동사 형태를 말한다. 문장 안에서 동명사는 주어, 보어, 목적어로 쓰인다. 하지만 분사와 마찬가지로 동명사도 본동사가 아니기 때문에 문장에서 시제에 영향을 주지 않는다.

FOCUS

1   *Like main verbs,* **gerunds** *can express time and have* **present**, **perfect** *and* **passive forms**.

동명사는 본동사처럼 시간을 표현할 수 있고 현재형, 완료형, 수동태를 가진다.

Now that my father has retired, his favorite pastime is **gardening**.① (present gerund)

A witness reported **having seen** a strange man milling about.② (perfect gerund)

Everyone hates **being ignored**.③ (simple gerund passive)

I appreciated **having been corrected** on my English grammar.④ (perfect gerund passive)

2   *Gerunds commonly function as* **subjects** *and describe* **general activities** *and* **abstract ideas**.

동명사는 주로 주어의 기능을 하며 일반적인 활동과 추상적인 생각을 설명한다.

Jogging and **swimming** are fantastic forms of cardiovascular exercise.①

Making a friend is easy, but **maintaining a friendship** requires a lifetime of effort.②

Talking on a cell phone can be dangerous when you're behind the wheel of a car.③

NOTICE

When the subject of the sentence is a gerund, the subject is **singular**.

동명사가 문장의 주어일 때 단수 취급한다.

The boy's **painting** on the walls is a serious offense.④

3   *Gerunds also function as* **objects**. *They follow certain verbs and verb + preposition combinations, for example adore, avoid, consider, deny, dislike, delay, enjoy, finish, imagine, involve, mind, miss, postpone, practice, suggest, give up, keep on, plan on and put off.*

동명사는 또한 목적어 역할을 하며 위에 제시된 특정 동사나 동사와 전치사가 결합된 동사구 뒤에 온다.

Your son <u>denies</u> **writing** the email, but we are fairly certain that it was him.①

I've <u>given up</u> **eating junk food** because it's making me feel a little unhealthy.②

We <u>postponed</u> **going** overseas this year because of the high cost of air travel.③

4   *A gerund is made* **negative** *by adding* **not** *or* **never**.

동명사의 부정형은 「not/never+동명사」이다.

I really hate **never seeing** you anymore. I wish you lived closer to me.①

Not drinking enough fresh water would be unhealthy for anyone.②

5   *A gerund can have its own* **subject** *and* **object**.

동명사는 주어와 목적어를 가질 수 있다.

She can't understand <u>his</u> **behaving** in such a rude way. ①

I love **buying** small, inexpensive <u>gifts</u> for my friends, especially when they're feeling down.②

The subject of the gerund usually appears in the possessive case.

동명사의 주어는 주로 소유격으로 나타낸다.

I can understand **your** not **telling** him the truth.③

Sue was shocked at **Jim's refusing** to help.④

---

1 ① 이제 우리 아버지는 은퇴하셨고, 가장 즐기시는 취미는 정원 가꾸기이다. ② 한 목격자가 이상한 남자가 돌아다니는 것을 보았다고 신고했다. ③ 모든 사람은 무시당하는 것을 싫어한다. ④ 나는 내 영문법을 교정해 주는 것에 감사했다.   2 ① 조깅과 수영은 심장혈관 운동의 훌륭한 예이다. ② 친구를 만드는 것은 쉽지만, 우정을 유지하는 것은 평생의 노력을 요구한다. ③ 운전할 때 휴대 전화를 사용하는 것은 위험할 수 있다. ④ 그 소년이 벽에 그림을 그린 것은 중범죄에 해당한다.   3 ① 당신의 아들은 그 이메일을 쓴 것을 부정하지만, 우리는 그가 했다고 거의 확신합니다. ② 나는 정크푸드가 건강에 좋지 않다는 기분이 들어 먹는 것을 그만두었다. ③ 비싼 항공 여행 비용 때문에 우리는 올해 해외에 가는 것을 연기했다.   4 ① 나는 더는 너를 볼 수 없다는 것이 정말 싫어. 네가 근처에 살았으면 좋겠어. ② 누구든지 신선한 물을 충분히 마시지 않는 것은 건강에 해로울 것이다.   5 ① 그녀는 그가 그렇게 무례하게 행동하는 것을 이해할 수 없다. ② 나는 친구들에게, 특히 그들이 기분이 좋지 않을 때 작고 값싼 선물을 하는 것을 매우 좋아한다. ③ 나는 네가 그에게 진실을 말하지 않는 것을 이해할 수 있다. ④ 수는 짐이 도와주기를 거절해서 매우 놀랐다.

EXERCISES

adore ~을 아주 좋아하다
hold ~을 열다, 개최하다
favor 호의
involve ~을 포함하다
surround ~을 둘러싸다
concentrate on
~에 집중하다
run into 우연히 마주치다
appreciate
~에 감사하다
application 지원서
candidate 지원자

A 주어진 단어를 알맞게 바꿔 문장을 완성하시오.

1 John and I both adore _____ (visit) art museums.

2 _____ (hold) the conference on this island would be very expensive.

3 I can do any favor for you as long as it doesn't involve _____ (ask) me for money.

4 Avoid being _____ (disturb) by people surrounding you and concentrate on your own job.

5 Corley mentioned having memories of _____ (lose) her younger brother whenever I ran into her.

6 While we all appreciate _____ (receive) your applications, only the chosen candidates will be contacted.

imply ~을 나타내다
squint 실눈으로 보다
crow's feet
눈꼬리의 주름살
environment 환경
well-designed
잘 설계된
fingerprint 지문
banister 난간
conclusive 결정적인
proof 증거
guilt 범죄; 죄책감
apologize
~에 대해 사과하다

B 〈보기〉에서 단어를 골라 알맞게 바꿔 문장을 완성하시오.

보기	offer	imply	squint	leave

1 _____ in bright sunlight causes wrinkles and crow's feet around the eyes.

2 This park is appreciated for _____ guests a quiet environment. It has several well-designed gardens.

3 John wore gloves to avoid _____ fingerprints, but his fingerprints on the banister were conclusive proof of his guilt.

4 _____ otherwise was an awful mistake. I expect you to apologize for having made those comments.

Infinitives

Infinitive is the name of the to + *verb* form that functions as a noun, adjective, or adverb. In sentences, infinitives are used as subjects and objects. However, infinitives — like participles and gerunds — do not form or establish the tense of the sentence; they cannot be main verbs.

부정사는 명사, 형용사, 부사의 역할을 하는 「to+동사원형」 형태를 말한다. 문장 안에서 부정사는 주어와 목적어로 사용된다. 하지만 분사와 동명사처럼 부정사 역시 본동사가 아니므로 문장에서 시제에 영향을 주지 않는다.

FOCUS

1 *Like main verbs,* **infinitives** *can express time and have* **present, perfect** *and* **passive forms**. *An infinitive is made* **negative** *by adding* **not**.

부정사는 시간을 표현할 수 있고 현재형, 완료형, 수동태를 가지며, 부정형은 「not+to부정사」이다.

Our recruiter has agreed **to review** your application.[①] (present infinitive)

These materials are not **to be removed** from the library.[②] (present infinitive passive)

The weather appears **to be getting** better.[③] (present progressive infinitive)

He pretended **to have been studying**.[④] (perfect progressive infinitive)

Bigfoot is said **to have roamed** this forest many years ago.[⑤] (perfect infinitive)

Jerry is lucky **to have been elected**.[⑥] (perfect infinitive passive)

Try **not to bump** the sofa against the wall. We've just had it painted.[⑦]

2 *Infinitives can function as* **subjects**. *However, the word* it *will often replace the infinitive as the subject. (NOTE: Gerunds are more commonly used as subjects.)*

부정사는 주어 기능을 할 수 있지만, it이 종종 주어로서 부정사를 대신한다. (주의: 주어로 동명사가 더 보편적으로 사용된다.)

To find a reliable study partner who has a flexible schedule can be a real challenge.

→ **It** can be a real challenge **to find** a reliable study partner who has a flexible schedule.

→ **Finding** a reliable study partner who has a flexible schedule can be a real challenge.[①]

To ride a motorcycle without wearing any protective gear, especially a helmet, is insane.

→ **It** is insane **to ride** a motorcycle without wearing any protective gear, especially a helmet.

→ **Riding** a motorcycle without wearing any protective gear, especially a helmet, is insane.[②]

NOTICE

When the subject of the sentence is an infinitive, the subject is **singular**. 부정사가 문장의 주어일 때 단수 취급한다.

To find a reliable rock climbing partner is a real challenge.[③]

3 Infinitives also function as **objects**.

부정사는 문장에서 목적어 역할을 한다.

a *Verbs that take infinitives as objects include agree, ask, decide, hope, learn, need, pretend, promise, try, and want.* 부정사를 목적어로 받는 동사

Dr. Richard reluctantly <u>agreed</u> **to resign** as managing director of the company.①

My baby brother <u>needs</u> **to go** to the toilet. Could you show us where it is, please?②

A: Are you sad that Seth has gone back to the UK?

B: I am, but he <u>promised</u> **to call** me often.③

b *Other verbs take infinitives as objects, but usually only following a noun or pronoun: allow, encourage, force, invite, order, permit, remind, tell, and warn.* 명사나 대명사 뒤에서 부정사를 목적어로 받는 동사

I'm surprised that you <u>allowed</u> <u>Jake</u> **to borrow** your car.①

Principal Park <u>encourages</u> <u>all students</u> **to learn** a foreign language.②

The new security system will not <u>permit</u> <u>anyone</u> **to enter** without the correct password.③

c *Some verbs can be followed by either gerunds or infinitives without changing the meaning of the sentence: begin, continue, intend, like, and start.* 문장의 의미를 바꾸지 않으면서 동명사 또는 부정사 앞에 오는 동사

Lisa <u>starts</u> **preparing** breakfast for her family at 7:30 a.m.

→ Lisa <u>starts</u> **to prepare** breakfast for her family at 7:30 a.m.①

 NOTICE

The following verbs cannot be used interchangeably without changing the meaning of the sentence: forget, regret, remember, stop, and try.

목적어로서 부정사 혹은 동명사가 올 때 의미가 달라지는 동사

Grandma Kim's grandchildren <u>stopped</u> **to visit** her.② (Her grandchildren visited her.)

Grandma Kim's grandchildren <u>stopped</u> **visiting** her.③ (Her grandchildren don't visit her anymore.)

4 We use **bare infinitives** *(an infinitive without to).*

원형부정사(to가 없는 부정사)를 사용하는 경우

a *after modal auxiliary verbs* 조동사 다음에 올 때

I <u>can't</u> **wait** for summer vacation this year.①

You <u>must</u> **have** been having a bad dream.②

b *after let, help, make, have, I'd rather, and I'd better* let, help, make, have, I'd rather, I'd better 다음에 올 때

My father sometimes <u>lets</u> me **drive** his car on the weekends.①

My mother <u>made</u> me **clean** the whole apartment yesterday.②

I'd rather **play** basketball this afternoon than **watch** a movie.③

c *with verbs of perception (e.g.: feel, hear, notice, see, observe)* 지각 동사와 함께 쓰일 때

At eight o'clock Lisa <u>heard</u> Jeff **go** out.①

A teacher <u>observed</u> her **climb** over the fence.②

5
When an infinitive follows an **adjective***, it usually comments on how a person feels about something.*
감정을 나타내는 형용사 다음에 부정사가 올 때는 그 감정의 원인이나 이유를 보충 설명한다.

> *Adjectives of feelings: anxious, eager, happy, pleased, shocked, relieved, surprised, disappointed ...*

On the phone, Michelle sounded very <u>eager</u> **to meet** you.①

We're all so <u>pleased</u> **to hear** you're feeling better.②

6
Infinitives also help define **abstract nouns***.*
부정사는 추상명사를 보충 설명한다.

> *Abstract nouns: advice, decision, desire, opportunity, permission, proposal, refusal, reminder, suggestion ...*

I spoke to Mom about my <u>decision</u> **to attend** college in the UK.①

This exhibition is a unique <u>opportunity</u> **to see** Picasso's early work.②

The phone company insists on texting me <u>reminders</u> **to pay** my bill.③

---

1 ① 신입 모집 담당자가 너의 지원서를 재검토하는 것에 대해 동의했다. ② 도서관의 이 자료들은 폐기되어서는 안 된다. ③ 날씨가 점점 좋아지고 있는 듯하다. ④ 그는 공부하는 척했다. ⑤ 오래전에 새스콰치가 이 숲을 돌아다녔다고 한다. ⑥ 제리가 운 좋게도 당선이 되었다. ⑦ 벽에 소파를 부딪치지 않도록 해. 우리가 방금 페인트칠했어. 2 ① 변경 가능한 스케줄을 가진 믿을 수 있는 스터디 파트너를 구하는 것은 정말 힘든 일이다. ② 보호 장비, 특히 헬멧 없이 오토바이를 타는 것은 미친 짓이다. ③ 믿을 만한 암벽 등반 파트너를 찾는 것은 정말 힘든 일이다. 3 a ① 리처드 박사는 회사의 전무 이사직을 그만두는 것에 대해 마지못해 동의했다. ② 내 남동생은 화장실에 가야 해요. 화장실이 어디에 있는지 알려 주실래요? ③ A: 너는 세스가 다시 영국으로 돌아가서 슬프니? B: 응, 하지만 나에게 자주 전화하기로 약속했어. b ① 나는 네가 제이크에게 차를 빌려 줘서 놀랐다. ② 박 교장 선생님은 모든 학생들에게 외국어를 배우도록 권하신다. ③ 새로운 보안 시스템은 정확한 비밀번호 없이는 누구도 들어오는 것을 허락하지 않을 것이다. c ① 리사는 오전 일곱 시 삼십 분에 가족들을 위해 아침 식사 준비를 시작한다. ② 김 씨 할머니의 손주들은 그녀를 방문하기 위해 멈추었다. ③ 김 씨 할머니의 손주들은 그녀를 방문하는 것을 그만두었다. 4 a ① 나는 올해 여름 방학이 너무나 기다려진다. ② 너는 나쁜 꿈을 꾸고 있었던 것이 틀림없다. b ① 우리 아버지는 주말에 가끔 내게 자신의 차를 운전할 수 있도록 해준다. ② 우리 어머니는 어제 내게 아파트 청소를 시켰다. ③ 나는 오늘 오후에 영화를 보느니 차라리 농구를 하겠다. c ① 8시에 리사는 제프가 나가는 소리를 들었다. ② 한 선생님이 그녀가 담을 넘는 것을 지켜보았다. 5 ① 전화상으로, 미셸이 너를 매우 만나고 싶어하는 것처럼 들렸다. ② 네 건강이 회복되고 있다니 우리는 매우 기뻐. 6 ① 나는 영국에 있는 대학에 가겠다는 내 결심을 엄마에게 말했다. ② 이 전시회는 피카소의 초기 작품들을 볼 수 있는 좀처럼 없는 기회이다. ③ 전화 회사에서 계속 나에게 요금을 내라는 독촉장을 문자로 보내온다.

PART 4 * UNIT 18_ **81**

EXERCISES

정답 및 해설 P. 14

overjoy
~을 크게 기쁘게 하다

astonish
~을 놀라게 하다

flame 불길, 불꽃

unreasonable
불합리한

as of today
오늘로서, 현재로서는

yellow dust 황사

affect ~에 영향을 미치다

appreciate
~의 가치를 인정하다

vocalist 가수

console
(컴퓨터 등의) 조작 테이블

mention
~을 언급하다, 말하다

in process 진행 중인

pretend ~인 체하다

fatally 치명적으로

evidence 증거

indicate ~을 나타내다

tragically 비극적으로

pass away
돌아가시다, 사망하다

passage 통과, 허가

private bill 개인 법안

permit ~을 허가하다

immigrate 이주하다

A ( ) 안에서 알맞은 것을 모두 고르시오.

1 When Jamie invited Tim (have / to have) dinner, he was overjoyed.

2 It was astonishing to watch the band (perform / to perform) at the concert.

3 The strong winds and dry conditions helped (keep / to keep) the flames going.

4 It is unreasonable that he should ask you (quit / to quit) within two weeks.

5 As of today, we may not (be / to be) able to deliver your order as quickly as in the past.

6 Kelly broke her promise (giving / to give) the electronic dictionary back to me within a week.

7 Strong yellow dust clouds will continue (affecting / to affect) the nation this weekend.

8 The show made me (appreciate / to appreciate) what a great vocalist Martina McBride is.

9 I'm almost ready to buy a computer game console, but I fear I may regret (buying / to buy) it soon after.

10 I think we'd better not (mention / to mention) the issue anymore because it is already in process.

11 The tornado struck the south end of the city. High winds also forced a highway bridge (close / to close).

12 I provide my students with all the information they need and let them (decide / to decide) for themselves.

13 The main actress in the story pretended (being / to be) fatally ill, despite medical evidence indicating she could live another twenty years.

14 Tragically, Lora passed away on May 14, 1983, the very day of the passage of a private bill permitting her (immigrate / to immigrate) to the United States.

B 주어진 단어를 알맞게 바꿔 문장을 완성하시오.

1 ① Remember _____ (include) a small blanket for the journey.

② Do you remember _____ (switch) the lights off before we left?
I remember _____ (lock) the door.

2 ① I forgot _____ (mention) where we should meet. I've got to get back to her.

② It was a wonderful day. I shall never forget _____ (hear) the president's address.

3 ① If I try _____ (locate) my biological parents, I'm afraid it might hurt their feelings.

② Try _____ (do) something active that makes you feel motivated, such as dancing to your favorite music or going out with your friends.

4 ① I don't want to look back and regret _____ (have) started something that ended in disaster.

② I regret _____ (say) that we're here to discuss solutions and strategies, not problems.

include ~을 포함하다
journey 여행
switch A off A를 끄다
address 연설
locate ~의 소재를 파악하다. 위치를 알아내다
biological 생물학(상)의
active 활동적인
motivate ~의 동기를 부여하다
look back 뒤돌아보다
disaster 실패; 재앙
discuss ~에 대해 논의하다
solution 해결책
strategy 전략

C 문장을 읽고, 밑줄 친 부분을 바르게 고쳐 문장을 다시 쓰시오.

1 The website would not allow me copying and pasting the text.

→ _____

2 Both my brothers tend to dread and postpone to clean the house.

→ _____

3 After you have finished to read the magazine, put it back where it was.

→ _____

4 Eric was relieved discovering that at least one person enjoyed the food he made.

→ _____

5 I'd better to stop asking you questions. Let's just get started with the easiest part of the process.

→ _____

6 Remember that as dogs enjoy human company, they will not appreciate be left alone for long periods.

→ _____

_____

allow ~을 허용하다
paste ~을 붙이다
dread ~을 몹시 꺼리다, 두려워하다
postpone ~을 연기하다, 늦추다
relieve ~을 안심시키다

REVIEW

정답 및 해설 P. 15

retire from
~에서 은퇴하다

take up ~을 시작하다

expect ~을 기대하다

relate to ~와 관계가 있다

reception 피로연

be familiar with
~에 익숙하다

A 다음 빈칸에 가장 알맞은 것을 고르시오.

1 A: I think you sound like an engineer. What did you do before getting a job
as a teacher?

B: _____ retired from engineering, I took up teaching.

① Have   ② Had   ③ Having   ④ To have

2 A: I was expecting you to come to my house party last weekend. What
happened?

B: I'm so sorry not _____ come. I had to babysit my nephews that
evening.

① have   ② had   ③ having   ④ to have

3 A: I can't see anyone related to Vicky here. Who do you think these people
are?

B: Most of the people _____ to the reception are her old friends.
That's why we are not familiar with anyone.

① invite   ② invited   ③ inviting   ④ to invite

keep one's fingers
crossed 행운을 빌다

exception 예외

disciplinarian
규율이 엄한 사람

childhood 유년기

solitary 외로운

influence
~에 영향을 주다

B 다음 대화를 읽고, 바르지 않은 문장을 고르시오.

1 ① A: I'd like to be in front of the Opera House in Sydney.

② B: Why don't you go to Australia this summer vacation?

③ A: I can't. Because of a medical exam, I must postpone travel to Sydney
until the end of the year.

④ B: I'll keep my fingers crossed for you.

2 ① A: It's already eleven o'clock. I forgot calling my father and tell him I
would be late.

② B: It will be all right. He may understand we are having fun at the
graduation party.

③ A: There are no exceptions with him. If I don't get home by ten without
calling, I'll get locked out.

④ B: Wow, he is a real disciplinarian.

3 ① A: I would like to ask you about your childhood. How was it?

② B: My childhood was very solitary. My parents were busy working as
doctors.

③ A: How did your childhood influence the father you have become?

④ B: To have been a father for many years, I'm now aware of how precious
time with my children is.

REVIEW PLUS

정답 및 해설 P. 15

 A 다음을 읽고, 바르지 <u>않은</u> 문장을 고르시오.

1

> ① No wonder Americans are gaining weight. ② A new study shows that cookies, candy, and bacon have gotten two percent cheaper, whereas the costs of vegetables and fresh fruit have increased 20 percent. ③ One encouraged finding from the University of Maryland is that prices have stayed steady for many canned and frozen vegetables and fruits, which retain almost all their nutritional value. ④ It is helpful to buy produce in season and scout out deals at a farmers' market.

encourage ~을 격려하다
finding 발견
steady 끊임없는; 한결같은
can ~을 통조림하다
frozen 언, 얼어붙은
retain ~을 유지하다
nutritional
영양의, 영양상의
value 가치
scout out
~을 찾다, 찾아내다

2

> ① Dreams are a way for the subconscious mind to communicate with the conscious. ② Dreaming of something you're worried about are the way that the brain helps you get ready for a disaster in case it arises. ③ Dreaming of a challenge such as a swimming competition or giving a presentation at school may improve your performance. ④ Cognitive neuroscientists have also discovered that dreams and the rapid eye movement that happens while you're sleeping are related to our ability to learn and remember.

subconscious
무의식의, 잠재의식의
conscious 의식
arise 발생하다
competition 경쟁, 대회
cognitive 인식의
neuroscientist
신경과학자

3

> ① While accompanying polar bear biologists during late-winter field research at a Canadian national park, Daniel had a very unusual opportunity taking a snapshot of a pair of three-month-old cubs squeezing tight inside their den. ② He tried to avoid frightening them by moving extremely slowly. ③ The texture in the walls of the den was made by the mother bear's claws during excavation. ④ Although he wound up getting frostbite, he believed it was absolutely worth it.

accompany
~와 동행하다
biologist 생물학자
cub 새끼
squeeze ~을 꼭 껴안다
den 동굴
texture 결, 감촉
claw 발톱
excavation 땅파기, 발굴
wind up
(~ 상황에) 처하게 되다
frostbite 동상

B 다음 (A), (B), (C)에서 어법에 맞는 표현으로 가장 적절한 것을 고르시오. [기출 응용]

What is a "webinar," and what benefits can it generate for a company? As more businesses look for creative ways to reach new customers as well as cut costs of (A) _____, the subject of webinars often comes up. The word webinar is (B) _____ from two root words: web and seminar. A webinar is a seminar (C) _____ the web and conferencing software. One of the most immediate benefits of a webinar is that it can eliminate a large portion of your company's travel budget. While there will always be those occasions where a face-to-face meeting is necessary, many business exchanges can be handled with the use of web conferences.

	(A)		(B)		(C)
①	communicating	⋯	derived	⋯	used
②	communicating	⋯	deriving	⋯	used
③	communication	⋯	derived	⋯	used
④	communication	⋯	deriving	⋯	using
⑤	communicating	⋯	derived	⋯	using

C 다음 글의 밑줄 친 부분 중, 바르지 않은 것을 고르시오. [기출 응용]

Legend has it that, during the Chinese Tang dynasty, a poor public official was so honest that he refused ① to take bribes. He could not buy meat ② to feed his family, so he invented tofu. To this day, some Chinese call honest government officials "tofu officials." ③ Knowing as "the cow of China," tofu's protein is similar in quality to that of meat. But tofu is really more like cheese in the way it is ④ made. Soy milk is thickened with a mineral salt, ⑤ forming curds—that's why tofu's other popular name is "bean curd."

86

WRITING PRACTICE

A Rewrite sentences using the given words with *to-infinitives* or *gerunds*.

1 To please our parents is sometimes a difficult task. (It)

→ _____ our parents.

2 To study all day at the library is not good for your health. (It)

→ _____ at the library.

3 My friend Jackie is interested in an on-line company. (work for)

→ My friend Jackie _____ an on-line company.

4 Cathy has lived in Spain for a year, but she's still poor at Spanish. (speak)

→ Cathy has lived in Spain for a year, but _____ .

B Correct the errors and rewrite the sentences.

1 Go down these stairs and keep on to walk across until you reach the other side.

→ _____

2 We already own many of the things that we need cleaning a house and mending a household items.

→ _____

3 I consider Tanya's ideas not as establishing facts, but rather as provocative ideas that stimulate others.

→ _____

4 I have been hoping becoming a member of the Korean national team. I will put a great deal of effort into doing so.

→ _____

5 Listened to the tremendous ovation, I was ushered into Seoul Stadium along with the other members of my team.

→ _____

C Rearrange the words. Follow the examples.

> 「S + cannot help -ing」 ~하지 않을 수 없다
>
> couldn't / slipped / when / laughing / her brother / help / on the ice
>
> → She _____ couldn't help laughing when her brother slipped on the ice _____.

1 with our school administration / cannot / serious concerns / raising / help

→ Such a fact _____.

2 wondering / was conversing with / whom / my sister / couldn't / on the Internet / help

→ I _____.

3 help / me / of the surrounding mountains / in Germany / couldn't / impressing

→ The magnificent view _____.

D Rearrange the words. Follow the examples.

> 「To tell the truth,」 사실대로 말하자면
>
> haven't paid back / you / to tell the truth, / lent you / the money I
>
> → _____ To tell the truth, you haven't paid back the money I lent you. _____

1 my professor's lectures / have / to tell the truth, / interest in / I / little

→ _____

2 several workers including you / rumor has it that / to tell the truth, / be laid off / will

→ _____

3 have put / for a month / the kidnappers / him / in solitary confinement / to tell the truth,

→ _____

PART 5

Adverbials

Adverbs

Adverbs are words that modify verbs, adjectives, and other adverbs. The term **adverbial** refers to the structures that perform the same function as adverbs do in sentences. Adverbial structures include prepositional phrases and adverb clauses.

부사는 동사, 형용사, 그리고 다른 부사를 수식한다. 부사적 어구(adverbial)는 부사와 같은 기능을 하는 구문을 말하며, 부사 구문에는 전치사구와 부사절이 있다.

FOCUS

1 **Adverbs** *modify verbs, adjectives, and other adverbs. They answer the questions when, why, where, how, or to what extent. Adverbs that modify adjectives or other adverbs usually come before the words they modify.*

부사는 동사, 형용사, 다른 부사를 수식한다. "언제, 어디서, 왜, 어떻게, 어느 정도인가"라는 질문에 대한 답이 되며 주로 수식하는 형용사나 다른 부사의 앞에 위치한다.

Fish **often** return to the place where they were born to mate.[①]

The package the courier left for you is **extremely** heavy. Can you come pick it up yourself?[②]

Our buses are departing **quite** regularly despite the city-wide transit strike.[③]

> ! NOTICE
>
> *The adverbs ago and enough are exceptional: they usually follow the adjectives or adverbs they modify.*
>
> 부사 ago와 enough는 예외적으로 수식하는 형용사나 부사 뒤에 위치한다.
>
> That happened long **ago**. I'd almost forgotten about it.[④] (ago long)
>
> Peter is old **enough** to make his own decisions.[⑤] (enough old)
>
> The dog ran fast **enough** to catch the squirrel.[⑥] (enough fast)

2 *Adverbs that modify adjectives and other adverbs, but which are not usually used to modify verbs, are called* **intensifiers**.

일반적으로 동사를 수식하는 데 사용되지 않고 형용사와 부사를 수식하는 부사를 강조어(intensifier)라고 한다.

Intensifiers: fairly, quite, rather, so, too, very ...

He's quite attractive, but not in the classic sense.[①]

I know I've been demanding. Thank you for being **so** patient with me.[②]

Your father answered the telephone **rather** angrily. Is everything all right?[③]

3 *Six different types of adverbs are used to modify verbs: adverbs of* **frequency**, **manner**, **location**, **time**, **conjunctive adverbs**, *and* **negative adverbs**.

빈도, 태도(방법), 위치(장소), 시간, 접속부사, 부정부사는 동사를 수식한다.

White marble is **frequently** streaked with gray, black, or green.[①] (frequency)

The large crowd had been waiting **patiently** for the play to begin.[②] (manner)

Margaret leaned **forward** to whisper something in Perry's ear during dinner.[③] (location)

I've got a ton of work to get through before **tomorrow**. I'll have to take a rain check.[④] (time)

We try to be as careful as we can; **nevertheless**, accidents do happen.[⑤] (conjunctive adverb)

You **hardly** ate anything at all. Please, have some more. I insist![⑥] (negative adverb)

4 *Adverbs that follow certain groups of verbs do so in a predictable order.*

특정 그룹의 동사 다음에 나오는 부사는 정해진 어순에 따른다.

a *With verbs of motion: place → means → time → purpose*

이동을 나타내는 동사와 함께: 장소 → 방법(수단) → 시간 → 목적

Verbs of motion: arrive, come, fly, go, leave, run, walk ...

We **arrived** here on foot last night to conduct a survey.[①]

b *With all other verbs: manner → place → time → purpose*

기타 동사와 함께: 태도 → 장소 → 시간 → 목적

Beth **swims** enthusiastically in the pool every morning to keep in shape.[①]

---

1 ① 물고기는 흔히 번식을 하려고 태어난 곳으로 돌아온다. ② 택배 기사가 두고 간 짐은 상당히 무거워. 직접 와서 가져갈 수 있겠니? ③ 도시 전역에서 발생한 도시 교통 기관의 파업에도 저희 버스는 상당히 정기적으로 출발하고 있습니다. ④ 그것은 오래전에 일어난 일이었다. 나는 그것에 대해 거의 잊고 있었다. ⑤ 피터는 자기 스스로 결정을 내릴 만큼 나이가 들었다. ⑥ 그 개는 다람쥐를 잡을 만큼 빨리 달렸다. 2 ① 그는 꽤 매력적이지만, 전형적인 미남형은 아니다. ② 내가 너무 많이 요구해왔다는 것을 나도 알아. 나를 잘 참아줘서 고마워. ③ 네 아버지가 전화를 좀 화난 듯이 받으셨어. 별일 없니? 3 ① 하얀색 대리석은 흔히 회색, 검은색, 녹색의 줄무늬가 있다. ② 많은 관중이 연극이 시작되기를 침착하게 기다렸다. ③ 마거릿은 저녁 식사 중에 페리의 귀에 뭔가를 속삭이려고 앞으로 몸을 숙였다. ④ 내일이 되기 전에 끝내야 할 일이 너무 많아. 약속을 미뤄야 할 것 같아. ⑤ 최대한 조심하겠지만, 사고가 일어날 수도 있어. ⑥ 너는 거의 아무것도 먹지 않았어. 좀 더 먹으렴. 부탁할게! 4 a ① 우리는 어젯밤에 여론 조사를 하려고 걸어서 여기에 왔다. b ① 베스는 몸매를 유지하려고 아침마다 수영장에서 열심히 수영을 한다.

EXERCISES

predictable
예측할 수 있는, 뻔한
take on ~을 떠맡다
handle ~을 다루다
spice 양념
value
~을 소중히 하다, 평가하다
commodity 상품
valuable 값비싼, 귀중한

 A ( ) 안에서 가장 알맞은 것을 고르시오.

1 The curry at the new Indian restaurant down the road is (quite / too) tasty.

2 In recent years, horror movies have become so (predictable / predictably).

3 Do you think you are (enough old / old enough) to take on adult responsibilities?

4 The suitcase you bought today is (surprising / surprisingly) light and easy to handle.

5 Spices and tobacco were (high / highly) valued in the past and used as commodities for trade.

6 Sangmi was robbed on the subway, and luckily she didn't lose anything (extreme / extremely) valuable.

tone 몸을 탄탄하게 만들다
prevent ~을 예방하다
choir 합창단

B 우리말과 같은 뜻이 되도록 주어진 단어를 알맞게 배열하시오.

1 오늘 아침 기차가 기차역에 거의 2시간 늦게 도착했다.

(almost two hours / this morning / late / at the station)

→ The train arrived _____ .

2 마이클은 몸을 탄탄하게 만들려고 매일 저녁 체육관에서 정기적으로 운동을 한다.

(at the gym / to tone his body / every evening / regularly)

→ Michael exercises _____ .

3 우리 아버지는 사고를 예방하기 위해 겨울에 빙판 도로에서는 조심스럽게 운전하신다.

(to prevent accidents / on icy roads / carefully / in winter)

→ My father drives _____ .

4 우리 학교 합창단은 지난주 호주의 건국 기념일을 기념하기 위해 홀에서 크게 노래를 불렀다. (last week / in the hall / to celebrate Foundation Day / loudly)

→ Our school choir sang _____ .

5 농구 선수들은 어젯밤 샤워를 하기 위해 서둘러 운동장을 떠났다.

(to have a shower / in a hurry / last night / the playground)

→ The basketball players left _____ .

6 철새들은 겨울이 다가오면 추위를 피하려고 재빨리 남쪽으로 날아간다.

(quickly / to escape the cold / when the winter approaches / south)

→ Migratory birds fly _____ .

Unit 20

Prepositional Phrases

 **KEY CONCEPTS**

A **prepositional phrase** consists of a preposition (e.g: at, in, from, by, about) and its object (a noun or pronoun). Prepositional phrases can be used—like adverbs—to modify verbs, adjectives, or other adverbs. When used **adverbially**, a prepositional phrase will answer one of the following questions: *when, why, where, how,* or *to what extent.*

전치사구는 전치사와 전치사의 목적어로 이루어져 있다. 전치사구는 부사와 마찬가지로, 동사, 형용사, 또는 다른 부사들을 수식한다. 부사적으로 사용되는 전치사구는 "언제, 왜, 어디(에)서, 어떻게, 어느 정도인가"하는 질문에 대한 답이 된다.

FOCUS ···

1 *Prepositional phrases modify verbs, adjectives, or other adverbs.*

전치사구는 동사, 형용사, 다른 부사를 수식한다.

The exhausted trekkers arrived <u>late</u> **at night.**① (*At night* modifies the adverb *late.*)

The unfortunate tourist <u>lost</u> her way **in the dense jungle.**② (*In the dense jungle* modifies the verb *lost.*)

Mr. Park was not <u>happy</u> **about his new student's attitude.**③

(*About his new student's attitude* modifies the adjective *happy.*)

2 *Prepositional phrases often follow one another. (NOTE: "Place" normally comes before "time")*

종종 전치사구 다음에 또 다른 전치사구가 나오기도 한다. (주의: 일반적으로 장소 전치사구가 시간 전치사구 앞에 위치한다.)

I found this rare old coin <u>at the beach under a rock.</u>①

Let's meet <u>at the cafe across from the library at three o'clock.</u>②

3 *Sometimes, you can move the prepositional phrase to the beginning of the sentence. In opening position, the prepositional phrase modifies the verb.*

때때로 전치사구를 문장 맨 앞에 올 수 있으며, 문장의 맨 앞에 위치한 전치사구는 동사를 수식한다.

We <u>decided</u> to stay indoors and play a game of cards **because of the weather.**

→ **Because of the weather,** we <u>decided</u> to stay indoors and play a game of cards.①

The carpenter <u>pounded</u> the nails into the weakened floor **with tremendous force.**

→ **With tremendous force,** the carpenter <u>pounded</u> the nails into the weakened floor.②

In English, the new and important information normally comes at the end of the sentence—that's where the listener or reader expects it to be. So avoid stringing together a long series of prepositional phrases at the end of a sentence, especially if they add no new information.

영어에서는 일반적으로 새롭고 중요한 정보가 문장의 맨 뒤에 온다. 글을 읽는 사람이나 듣는 사람 또한 문장의 마지막에 정보가 있을 것이라고 예상한다. 따라서 문장 맨 마지막에 전치사구들을 계속 나열하는 것을 조심해야 하며, 특히 그 내용이 앞서 언급된 정보일 경우에는 더 주의해야 한다.

My brother saved up for almost three years to buy himself a beautiful new German sports car. Finally, last week, he became the proud owner of a new G-Motors ~~because of his savings from last three years.~~[①]

The prepositional phrases "because of his savings" and "from last three years" add no new information, so they don't belong at the end of the sentence. Worse, they obscure the important new information the writer wants to focus on, which is the kind of car his brother bought: a G-Motors.

전치사구 because of his savings와 from last three years는 새로운 정보를 제공하지 않으므로 문장 맨 마지막에 오는 것이 적절하지 않다. 게다가 화자가 강조하고자 하는 것은 그의 남동생이 산 차의 종류인 G-Motors인데, 잇달아 붙는 전치사구가 이러한 중요한 정보를 알아보기 어렵게 만든다.

---

1 ① 지친 도보 여행자들이 밤늦게 도착했다. ② 운이 없는 관광객이 빽빽한 정글 안에서 길을 잃었다. ③ 박 선생님은 새로 온 학생의 태도가 마음에 들지 않았다. 2 ① 나는 이 낡고 희귀한 동전을 바닷가 바위 밑에서 발견하였다. ② 세 시에 도서관 맞은편에 있는 카페에서 만나자. 3 ① 우리는 날씨 때문에 집 안에서 카드 게임을 하기로 결정했다. ② 목수는 약해진 바닥에 못을 엄청난 힘으로 내리쳤다. WT ① 내 남동생은 아름다운 독일산 신형 스포츠 자동차를 사려고 거의 3년간 돈을 모았다. 드디어, 지난주에 그는 새 G-Motors의 자랑스러운 주인이 되었다.

EXERCISES

A 밑줄 친 구가 수식하는 단어를 찾아 쓰시오.

1 The playful kitten always jumps <u>over the table</u> and hides <u>behind the chair</u>.

2 All the kindergarten children were happy <u>about going to the amusement park</u>.

3 Hamsters make great pets, but if left unattended, they may quickly run <u>into small spaces</u>.

4 Even though the plane's departure was delayed <u>by an hour</u>, they arrived early <u>in the morning</u>.

> playful 쾌활한
> kindergarten 유치원
> unattended
> 보살핌을 받지 못하는, 방치된
> departure 출발
> be delayed 연착하다

B 문장을 읽고, 밑줄 친 부분을 바르게 고쳐 쓰시오.

1 Only experienced fishermen in Busan go <u>at five in the morning out to sea</u>.
  → Only experienced fishermen in Busan go _____ .

2 David and Victoria first met each other <u>ten years ago at a fashion event</u>.
  → David and Victoria first met each other _____ .

3 Billy usually plays soccer <u>on Wednesdays and Thursdays in the playground</u>.
  → Billy usually plays soccer _____ .

4 The security guard saw the robbers <u>before they went into the bank across the street</u>.
  → The security guard saw the robbers _____ .

> experienced
> 경험이 있는
> security guard 경비원
> robber 강도

C 글을 읽고, 불필요한 부분을 삭제하시오.

1 Hojun, who is the editor of our school newspaper, wrote a good review about the new school play. On the opening night of the play, many students and teachers attended because of his good review.

2 My sister attended many institutes and did a lot of independent study to go to university abroad. Last week, she was accepted into a prestigious French university because of her hard work and studying.

> review 평론
> attend ~에 참석하다
> institute 학원
> independent
> 독립된; 자립적인
> accept
> ~을 입학시키다, 받아들이다
> prestigious
> 명성이 있는, 훌륭한

Unit 21 Adverb Clauses

 **KEY** CONCEPTS

Adverb clauses—also called subordinate clauses—provide information about verbs. They answer the questions: *when, why, where, how,* or *to what extent.* **A subordinate clause** is a kind of dependent clause, so it must be linked to a complete sentence(the main clause); it cannot stand alone.

종속절이라고도 불리는 부사절은 본동사에 대한 정보를 제공한다. 부사절은 언제, 왜, 어디서, 어떻게, 어느 정도인가 하는 질문에 대한 답이 된다. 종속절은 주절인 완전한 문장에 연결되어야 하며, 단독으로 문장을 만들지 못한다.

 FOCUS ··

1 *Adverb clauses begin with* **subordinating conjunctions**. *These conjunctions show the relationship between the adverb clause and the main clause.*

부사절은 종속접속사로 시작하며, 이때 접속사는 부사절과 주절과의 관계를 나타낸다.

 Subordinating conjunctions: when, as, because, although, whereas, if, unless ...

When Jim saw the tornado approaching, he quickly ran downstairs into the basement.①

Alex wasn't able to play in the championship game **because** he had a broken wrist.②

If I save up enough money this year, I'll visit you in London next summer.③

> ! **NOTICE**
>
> **Commas** *always set off an adverb clause that opens the sentence.*
>
> 문두에 부사절이 위치할 때는 항상 콤마로 주절과 구분시켜 주어야 한다.

2 *Adverb clauses that show* "**time relationships**" *begin with when, before, after, while/as, by the time, since, until/till, and as ~ as.*

when. before, after, while/as, by the time, since, until/till, as ~ as로 시작하는 절은 시간을 나타내는 부사절이다.

Make sure your hands are clean **before** you wash those vegetables, please.①

After Rebecca graduates from law school, she will work for her father in Singapore.②

3 *The verb tense in the adverb clause will affect the verb tense choice in the main clause.*

부사절에서 동사의 시제는 주절의 동사 시제에 영향을 준다.

When Sherry got home, her husband, Steve, was preparing dinner.①

While I was riding home, my brand-new hat blew off in the wind.②

I haven't seen Greg **since** he moved back home last summer.③

Jeff stayed with his dog **until** the vet finished bandaging his leg.④

4 *Adverb clauses that show "**cause** and **effect**" relationships begin with because, since, now that, and as long as. (NOTE: Because introduces an expected result, and since is also used in time clauses.)*

because, since, now that, as long as로 시작하는 절은 원인과 결과를 나타내는 부사절이다. (주의: because는 예상된 결과를 알려주며, since는 시간절에도 사용된다.)

The bridge was temporarily closed **because** <u>it was in a state of disrepair</u>.①

<u>**Since** the world's supply of oil is limited</u>, we should enact laws to regulate its use.②

I'm looking forward to a bit of a break **now that** <u>all of my work is done</u>.③

5 *Adverb clauses that show "**concession** and **contrast**" begin with even though, although, and though. Adverb clauses that show "**direct contrast**" begin with while and whereas. (NOTE: Even though introduces an unexpected result, and while is also used in time clauses.)*

양보와 대조를 나타내는 부사절은 even though, although, though로 시작하고, 직접적인 대조를 나타내는 부사절은 while, whereas로 시작한다. (주의: even though는 예상하지 못한 결과를 알려줄 때 사용하고, while은 시간절에도 사용된다.)

<u>**Even though** Bill Gates left college before graduating</u>, he still managed to become a success.①

Frighteningly, the living room lights came on, **although** <u>no one was near the switch</u>.②

Mario is interested in ice hockey, **whereas** <u>Abigail is more interested in figure skating</u>.③

6 *Adverb clauses that show "**condition**" begin with if, in case, as long as, unless, only if, provided (that), and in the event (that).*

if, in case, as long as, unless, only if, provided (that), in the event (that)으로 시작하는 절은 조건을 나타내는 부사절이다.

Let's stop at the next gas station. <u>**If** we run out of gas</u>, we'll be in big trouble.①

I'll help you with your homework **only if** <u>you promise to help me clean the kitchen</u>.②

<u>**In the event that** I'm late</u>, please don't leave. Just wait for me until I arrive.③

Future forms are not used in adverb clauses of condition with if.

조건을 나타내는 부사절에서 if는 미래 시제와 쓰이지 않는다.

(×) If ~~we'll run out of~~ gas, we'll be in big trouble.

 WRITING TIPS

*Adverb clauses can be used to **combine** two short sentences. Doing so will add **variety** to your writing and give it a "tighter" feel.*

부사절은 두 개의 짧은 문장을 결합할 때 사용할 수 있다. 부사절을 효과적으로 사용하면 글의 의미가 풍부해지고 짜임새 있어진다.

Linda looked unfazed. Her brother jumped out of the closet wearing a *Scream* mask.[①]

These two ideas can be joined for greater effect.

위의 두 문장을 부사절을 사용해 합치면 글의 짜임새가 보다 튼튼해짐을 알 수 있다.

Linda looked unfazed **when** her brother jumped out of the closet wearing a *Scream* mask.[②]

If the two sentences have unequal importance, save the most important one for the end so that your reader will remember it.

두 개의 문장이 서로 다른 비중의 중요도를 가진다면 가장 중요한 것을 맨 마지막에 써야 독자들에게 쉽게 각인됨을 알아두자.

Leslie shrieked out loud **because** she heard her name called at the raffle.[③]

(We are more interested in *why* Leslie shrieked than the noise she made.)

---

1 ① 짐은 폭풍이 오는 것을 보고, 재빨리 아래층 지하실로 달려갔다. ② 알렉스는 팔목이 부러져서 결승전에 참가할 수 없었다. ③ 올해 돈을 충분히 모으면 내년 여름에 내가 너를 보러 런던에 갈게. 2 ① 저 채소를 씻기 전에 당신의 손을 깨끗하게 하는 것을 명심하세요. ② 레베카는 법대를 졸업하고, 싱가포르에서 그녀의 아버지를 위해 일할 것이다. 3 ① 셰리가 집에 왔을 때 그녀의 남편인 스티브는 저녁 식사를 준비하고 있었다. ② 집에 차를 타고 오는 중에 새로 산 모자가 바람에 날아갔다. ③ 나는 그레그가 지난여름에 고향으로 이사 간 뒤로 그를 본 적이 없어. ④ 제프는 수의사가 그의 개의 다리에 붕대를 다 감을 때까지 개와 같이 있었다. ⑤ 네가 한 일에 대해 사과하면 용서해 줄게. ⑥ 영화가 시작할 때쯤에는 네가 팝콘을 다 먹어 치우고 없겠어. 4 ① 그 다리는 파손이 된 상태였기 때문에 임시로 폐쇄되었다. ② 세계의 석유 공급량은 한계가 있으므로 사용을 규제하는 법 조항을 만들어야 한다. ③ 내 일이 모두 끝나서 나는 약간의 휴식을 기대하고 있다. 5 ① 빌 게이츠는 대학을 중퇴했지만, 그는 성공했다. ② 무섭게도, 스위치 근처에 아무도 없었음에도 거실의 불이 켜졌다. ③ 마리오는 아이스하키에 관심이 있지만, 애비게일은 피겨 스케이팅에 더 관심이 있다. 6 ① 다음 주유소에 들르자. (차에) 기름이 다 떨어지면 우리는 큰 곤란을 겪게 될 거야. ② 부엌 치우는 것을 도와준다고 약속하면 네 숙제를 도와줄게. ③ 내가 만약 늦더라도, 떠나지 말아 주세요. 내가 도착할 때까지 기다려 줘요. WT ① 린다는 전혀 동요되지 않아 보였다. 그녀의 남동생은 스크림 가면을 쓰고 벽장에서 튀어나왔다. ② 린다는 그녀의 남동생이 스크림 가면을 쓰고 벽장에서 튀어나왔을 때 전혀 동요되지 않아 보였다. ③ 레슬리는 복권 추첨에서 자신의 이름이 불렸기 때문에 크게 비명을 질렀다.

EXERCISES

 A ( ) 안에서 가장 알맞은 것을 고르시오.

1 Some of the students fell asleep (while / if) the principal was addressing them.

2 (Even though / If) we leave early and are lucky tonight, we'll get front row seats at the concert.

3 (When / Although) Switzerland is famous for manufacturing watches, I didn't find one that I liked.

4 Dean was absent for two weeks (because / although) he broke his leg and had to stay in the hospital.

5 An article published in a magazine last week said that it was unhealthy to eat meat just (before / after) going to bed.

6 You should take off your shoes when you enter a house in Korea, (whereas / because) in South Africa you don't need to.

> fall asleep 잠들다
> address ~에 연설하다
> manufacture
> ~을 제작하다
> article 기사

B 문장을 읽고, 밑줄 친 부사절이 어디에 속하는지 〈보기〉에서 골라 쓰시오.

> 보기
> ⓐ cause and effect   ⓑ concession
> ⓒ condition   ⓓ contrast
> ⓔ time

1 Although Kevin is not very talkative, he is really fluent in English. _____

2 The courier company delivered the package while I was walking the dog.

_____

3 John's already traveled to seventeen countries while Jessica has only traveled to ten. _____

4 I'm going to accept the job offer from the company if the working conditions are suitable. _____

5 All the students seem to be relaxed and enthusiastic now that their final projects have been completed. _____

6 Mr. Park's new method of teaching pronunciation is interesting and fun, whereas his previous method was boring. _____

> talkative
> 말이 많은; 말하기를 좋아하는
> courier company
> 운송회사
> working condition
> 근로조건
> suitable 적절한, 알맞은
> enthusiastic 열정적인
> complete ~을 끝내다
> previous 이전의

C 두 문장의 뜻이 통하도록 주어진 접속사를 이용하여 문장을 완성하시오.

1 Jack realized his spelling mistakes, but he had already sent the email.
(by the time)

→ _____, he had already sent the email.

2 The dress that she wore was made of silk, but the sleeves were made of satin. (while)

→ The dress that she wore was made of silk _____.

3 You can play computer games, but you must complete your homework.
(as long as)

→ You can play computer games _____.

4 We want to go to Thailand this summer, but we have to find cheap plane tickets. (if)

→ _____, we'll go to Thailand this summer.

5 The girls in our class are good at math, but the boys are good at geography.
(whereas)

→ The girls in our class are good at math, _____.

D 〈보기〉에서 알맞은 접속사를 골라 문장의 뜻이 통하도록 문장을 완성하시오.

| 보기 | if | although | whereas | because |

1 Many guests complained about the food. They had a good time at the party.

→ _____, they had a good time at the party.

2 Summer is really hot this year. I'll spend most of my time in the swimming pool.

→ _____, I'll spend most of my time in the swimming pool.

3 The comedian felt lousy and disappointed. Nobody laughed at his jokes that night.

→ The comedian felt lousy and disappointed _____

_____.

4 Adam preferred to take a test for the evaluation. His classmates wanted to make a presentation.

→ Adam preferred to take a test for the evaluation, _____

_____.

Participle Phrases

 **KEY CONCEPTS**

Adverb clauses can sometimes be reduced, or shortened, to phrases. Three different types of participle phrases can be used to reduce an adverb clause to a phrase: the present participle, the perfect participle, and the passive perfect participle.

부사절은 구로 축약되기도 한다. 부사절은 현재분사구, 완료분사구, 그리고 수동형 완료분사구로 줄일 수 있다.

FOCUS

1 *The* **present participle** *(-ing) can be used to shorten an adverb clause to a phrase when the two clauses have the same subject. (NOTE: The action in the participle phrase may come before, after, or at the same time as the action in the clause.)*

현재분사구는 두 개의 절이 같은 주어를 가질 때 부사절을 구로 줄이는 데 쓰인다. (주의: 분사구는 동시에 일어난 행동을 의미한다.)

While I was frying eggs this morning, I burned my hand badly on the stove.
→ **Frying** eggs this morning, I burned my hand badly on the stove.[1]

Because I was surprised at her sudden question, I was not able to answer.
→ **(Being) Surprised** at her sudden question, I was not able to answer.[2]

After Suki made the last fold, she proudly admired her paper crane.
→ **Making** the last fold, Suki proudly admired her paper crane.[3]

2 *The* **perfect participle** *(having + p.p.) is used to shorten, or combine clauses that have the same subject. (NOTE: The action in the participle phrase comes before the action in the clause.)*

완료분사구는 주어가 같은 두 절을 줄이거나 결합시킬 때 쓰인다. (주의: 분사구에서의 행동은 주절에서의 행동보다 먼저 일어난다.)

Ally applied plenty of moisturizer to her sunburned face before she went to bed.
→ **Having applied** plenty of moisturizer to her sunburned face, Ally went to bed.[1]

Because Steven grew up poor, he was highly motivated to succeed.
→ **Having grown up** poor, Steven was highly motivated to succeed.[2]

I wasn't able to concentrate in class because I had not slept well for days.
→ I wasn't able to concentrate in class, **not having slept** well for days.[3]

3 *The* **passive perfect participle** *(having + been + p.p.) is used to shorten passive clauses that have the same subject. (NOTE: The action in the participle phrase comes before the action in the clause.)*

수동형 완료분사구는 주절과 주어가 같은 수동태절을 줄이는데 쓰인다. (주의: 분사구에서의 행동은 주절에서의 행동보다 먼저 일어난다.)

After <u>Mr. Obama</u> **was elected**, <u>he</u> quickly moved to implement his election pledges.

→ **(Having been) Elected**, <u>Mr. Obama</u> quickly moved to implement his election pledges.①

After <u>Jenny</u> **was stung** by the wasp, <u>she</u> burst out crying and ran toward home.

→ **(Having been) Stung** by the wasp, <u>Jenny</u> burst out crying and ran toward home.②

! NOTICE

The understood subject of the participle clause is always the subject of the clause; otherwise, the sentence "dangles." This is not only ungrammatical but also illogical.

분사절의 생략된 주어는 주절의 주어와 동일하다는 것이 전제되어 있다. 분사절의 주어가 주절의 주어와 동일하지 않으면 비문(非文)이 될 뿐 아니라 의미가 통하지 않을 수도 있다.

Mrs. Choi was driving to the supermarket today when her baby spoke his first word.③

(×) ~~Driving to the supermarket today, Mrs. Choi's baby spoke his first word.~~

Who was driving the car? The second sentence incorrectly reports that Mrs. Choi's baby was driving the car. 두 번째 문장은 최 여사의 아기가 운전을 하고 있다는 내용이 된다.

Negative participle clauses are also possible. We use "not" before the -ing form or past participle

분사구문의 부정은 분사 앞에 not을 쓴다.

Not knowing what to say to her, he just smiled.④

EXERCISES

 A ( ) 안에서 가장 알맞은 것을 고르시오.

1 While (having looked / looking) for a shoe store, I saw many clothing stores having sales.

2 Before (watching / having watched) television, Byron finished his homework and fed the pets.

3 (Raising / Having raised) a cat for ten years, Jennifer decided to become an animal psychologist.

4 While (reading / having read) the article, William looked up the unfamiliar words in the dictionary.

5 (Having seen / Having been seen) him at the gym regularly, people assume that he is fit and healthy.

6 Before (going / having gone) to university to major in Spanish, Dennis spent two years in South America.

7 After (having seen / having been seen) the accident, someone in the crowd immediately called the police.

> feed ~에게 먹이를 주다
> psychologist 심리학자
> look up ~을 찾다
> assume ~을 가정하다
> fit (몸이) 탄탄한
> immediately 즉시, 즉각

 **B** 두 문장의 의미가 통하도록 분사구문을 이용하여 문장을 완성하시오.

1 Before Woojin sang, he cleared his throat and did voice exercise backstage.
→ Before _____, Woojin cleared his throat and did voice exercises backstage.

2 I had broken my new glasses by mistake; I went to the optometrist yesterday.
→ _____ my new glasses by mistake, I went to the optometrist yesterday.

3 Because Emilio has good taste in clothes, he was asked to choose a dress for the bride.
→ _____ good taste in clothes, Emilio was asked to choose a dress for the bride.

4 While Joseph was talking on the phone, he saw the cat break the expensive Chinese vase.
→ _____ on the phone, Joseph saw the cat break the expensive Chinese vase.

> throat 목구멍, 목
> by mistake 실수로
> optometrist 검안사
> have good taste in ~
> ~에 안목이 있다

confidence 자신감
volunteer
자진해서 ~ 하다

C 두 문장의 의미가 통하도록 분사구문을 이용하여 문장을 완성하시오.

1 As Ben had no confidence, he never volunteered to speak in class.

→ _____, Ben never volunteered to speak in class.

2 After you have completed the form, send it with all the necessary documents to this address.

→ _____, send it with all the necessary documents to this address.

3 Because Jamie didn't have a lot of money, she decided to buy the cheapest pen in the shop.

→ _____, Jamie decided to buy the cheapest pen in the shop.

4 Before Betty went out, she turned off all the lights and made sure the windows were closed.

→ _____, Betty turned off all the lights and made sure the windows were closed.

collapse on
~에 드러눕다, 주저앉다
disturb ~을 방해하다
immediately 즉시, 즉각

D 두 문장의 의미가 통하도록 부사절을 이용하여 문장을 완성하시오.

1 After having finished work on the weekend, I collapsed on my bed because I was so tired.

→ _____,

I collapsed on my bed because I was so tired.

2 Being disturbed by his noisy neighbors, Franklin decided to ask them to turn down the music.

→ _____,

he decided to ask them to turn down the music.

3 As soon as having heard that he passed the entrance exam, Sangjun immediately called his mother.

→ _____,

he immediately called his mother.

4 After having met in Rome, they got married. They return there every year to celebrate their wedding anniversary.

→ _____

They return there every year to celebrate their wedding anniversary.

REVIEW

정답 및 해설 P. 19

A 다음 빈칸에 가장 알맞은 것을 고르시오.

be on strike 파업 중이다
strike 파업을 하다
salary 급여, 봉급

1 A: We're going to Jejudo for the summer. What are you doing during the vacation?

B: Oh, my grandmother usually visits _____.

① our house every summer for three weeks

② for three weeks every summer our house

③ every summer our house for three weeks

④ for our house three weeks every summer

2 A: Did you see the news? The automobile workers are on strike again.

B: Yes. They are striking _____.

① because of poor conditions and low salaries

② since poor working conditions and low salaries

③ as long as poor working conditions and low salaries

④ now that poor working conditions and low salaries

B 다음 대화를 읽고, 바르지 <u>않은</u> 문장을 고르시오.

take place
일어나다, 개최되다
various 다양한
diverse 다양한
admire ~을 존경하다
determination
결단, 결심
strength 힘, 용기
go through
~을 겪다, 경험하다

1 ① A: Have you heard about the restaurant festival that will take place this week?

② B: No, but it sounds interesting. What is it about?

③ A: Well, various restaurants are taking part, so you can try diverse foods from all over the world.

④ B: OK. So I guess we have to make reservations after we go to these restaurants.

2 ① A: Wow, I really admire people who can survive the toughest test in life.

② B: Yeah, me too. It's amazing to see their determination and strength.

③ A: Because they go through terrible situations, they still manage to succeed.

④ B: I hope I can develop the same qualities.

3 ① A: I'm so excited about our trip to Europe. I think it's going to be really interesting.

② B: Definitely! Europe is charming, especially in the summer. Which countries will you be visiting?

③ A: First we're going to France for a week, then Italy, Switzerland, and Germany.

④ B: I think Switzerland is great for its nature, even though the others are great for their food.

PART 5 ＊ REVIEW_ **105**

REVIEW PLUS

정답 및 해설 P. 19

정답 및 해설 P. 19

A 다음을 읽고, 바르지 <u>않은</u> 문장을 고르시오.

1

suffer from
~으로 고통받다

acupuncture
treatment 침술 요법

suggest ~을 제안하다

willingly 기꺼이

① Having suffering from backache for many weeks, I decided to see the doctor in my neighborhood. ② He gave me some acupuncture treatment and suggested that I do yoga because it will stretch the muscles in my back. ③ I willingly took his advice and found a yoga class at the gym near my office. ④ I now attend yoga class in the morning from seven to eight-thirty every day and I feel much better.

2

considerable 상당한

popularity 유행, 인기

feathered
깃털 장식이 있는

rapidly 빨리, 신속하게

① Badminton, an exciting racket sport, has enjoyed considerable popularity because of its Olympic status. ② Badminton uses a shuttlecock, which flies very differently from balls used in most other racket sports. ③ This makes badminton unique since a shuttlecock is a cone-shaped feathered device. ④ Having hit, the feathers in the shuttlecock create a higher pull which causes it to lose speed much more rapidly than a ball.

3

groom (털을) 다듬다

essential 중요한

enhance
~을 높이다, 향상시키다

appearance 외모

decrease 감소하다

establish a close
relationship
친밀한 관계를 맺다

① Horse grooming is an essential part of keeping horses because it enhances a horse's appearance for competitions. ② Since not always necessary, it is recommended that a horse be groomed daily as it provides many benefits for the horse. ③ Having been groomed regularly, a horse's skin becomes healthier and the risk of health problems decreases. ④ Horse grooming also helps in quickly establishing a close relationship between the horse and the groomer, who is often the owner.

B 다음 (A), (B), (C)에서 어법에 맞는 표현으로 가장 적절한 것을 고르시오. [기출 응용]

One evening I arrived at campus after work and found the parking lot full. (A) _____ for a parking space, I found Margaret, my eldest daughter, who was a student at the same school. She was walking to her car to go home after her last class of the day. A few drivers eager to get the spot she would be leaving were following her. Desperate to get (B) _____, I stopped my car, jumped out, and ran over to my daughter. I traded keys with her and told her to drive my car home (C) _____ that I would bring her car home after my class. As I dashed past the other drivers on the way to class, she gave me a look of open-mouthed astonishment.

	(A)		(B)		(C)
①	Searched	⋯	to class on time	⋯	during explaining
②	Searching	⋯	to class on time	⋯	while explaining
③	Searched	⋯	on time to class	⋯	while explaining
④	Searching	⋯	on time to class	⋯	during explaining
⑤	Searched	⋯	to class on time	⋯	while explaining

C 다음 글의 밑줄 친 부분 중, 바르지 <u>않은</u> 것을 고르시오. [기출 응용]

The teddy bear is a ① <u>stuffed</u> toy bear. Strangely enough, the Teddy Bear Effect refers to the phenomenon where a passive listener appears to give wisdom to a speaker ② <u>without doing</u> anything other than listening. ③ <u>Suppose</u> you ask someone a question ④ <u>expected</u> to learn something from the answer. You often discover the answer for yourself simply through the act of expressing the question verbally. In this situation, the listener is ⑤ <u>compared to</u> a teddy bear because toy bears would serve the same purpose.

WRITING PRACTICE

정답 및 해설 P. 20

A Change the adverb clauses, into participle phrases.

1 Before James joined the gym, he was terribly overweight and got tired easily.

→ _____

2 After the suit was sent to the dry cleaners, it looked good as new and it smelled great.

→ _____

3 Because Janet felt really ill, she quickly decided to postpone her birthday picnic at the riverside.

→ _____

4 While the archeologists were excavating the site, they discovered the ruins of an unknown civilization.

→ _____

5 As Kay had not received any news about her university application, she was very worried about next year.

→ _____

B Correct the errors and rewrite the sentences.

1 The teacher makes an announcement <u>every morning in class</u>.

→ _____

2 My mother likes Italian food <u>because</u> my father prefers Chinese food.

→ _____

3 <u>When</u> it rains tomorrow, I'll wear my black coat and take an umbrella.

→ _____

4 <u>Having been mixed</u> the chemicals, they observed the chemical reaction.

→ _____

5 The children were happy <u>because of</u> their father bought them gifts overseas.

→ _____

C Fill in the blanks to make the two sentences have the same meaning.

> 「because+S+V」 → 「because of+Noun (phrase)」 ~때문에, 왜냐하면
> We couldn't go out because the weather was really bad.
> → We couldn't go out _____because of the bad weather_____ .

1 The school band and choir couldn't practice yesterday because the hall was locked.

→ The school band and choir couldn't practice yesterday _____ .

2 The amusement park was really crowded on Saturday because the weather was gorgeous.

→ The amusement park was really crowded on Saturday _____ .

3 Jennifer couldn't access her email account today because her computer froze.

→ Jennifer couldn't access her email account today _____ .

D Fill in the blanks to make the two sentences have the same meaning.

> 「while+S+V」 → 「during +Noun (phrase)」 ~동안에
> The sports fans were chanting and singing while their team was playing soccer.
> → The sports fans were chanting and singing _____during the soccer match_____ .

1 My family stayed in Hawaii while we were on summer vacation.

→ My family stayed in Hawaii _____ .

2 The waiters and chefs were preparing the food while the director was making a speech.

→ The waiters and chefs were preparing the food _____ .

3 My mother and father cooked dinner while we were watching a game show on television.

→ My mother and father cooked dinner _____ .

Correct the errors and rewrite the sentences.

1 A: Did you read the news about the new government policy on taxes?

B: Yes, before <u>reached</u> a decision, the politicians mulled it over for a week.

→ Yes, _____ .

2 A: I always thought you were a vegetarian <u>although</u> you never ate red meat.

B: Really? Although I don't eat red meat, I do eat chicken and fish, but mostly vegetables.

→ I always thought you were a vegetarian _____ .

3 A: Even though he's really good at telling stories animatedly, he isn't very confident.

B: Oh, that's why he sits quietly <u>every day at the back of the class</u>.

→ Oh, _____ .

4 A: Wow! Tina is really good at her job and is always praised by her boss.

B: Yes. <u>Worked</u> as an intern, she learned the skills she needed for her job very quickly.

→ _____ she needed for her job very quickly.

5 A: How was <u>the last night concert</u>? I heard the singer was one hour late.

B: Although the singer arrived late, the crowd was waiting patiently for her to start.

→ _____

PART 6

//

Adjectivals

//

Unit 23 · Adjectives

 **KEY CONCEPTS**

The term adjectival refers to a function. Any structure or form that modifies a noun is performing the role of an adjectival. Nouns can be modified in a number of ways.

형용사 상당어구는 명사를 수식하는 모든 구조나 형태가 형용사 역할을 하는 것을 말한다. 명사는 아래와 같이 다양한 방법으로 수식될 수 있다.

determiner 한정사	adjective 형용사	noun 명사	NOUN 명사	prepositional phrase 전치사구	participle phrase 분사구	adjective clause 형용사절
a	tasty		pizza			
her	leather	baseball	glove			
my	old		friend	from Canada		
the			dog		barking loudly	
another			person			who likes

Adjectives are words that modify nouns. Adjectives typically answer one of these three questions about the noun: What kind? How many[much]? Which one?

명사를 수식하는 형용사는 명사에 대한 세 가지 종류의 질문에 대한 대답이 될 수 있다. 어떠한 종류인가? 양[수]이 얼마나 되는가? 어느 것인가?

FOCUS

1 *Adjectives used before nouns are called* **attributive adjectives**.

한정 형용사는 명사 앞에 오는 형용사이다.

We fed the **cute** deer at the zoo.[1]

Strong winds toppled the **old** tree.[2]

This **portable** computer is just the right size.[3]

2 *Adjectives that follow linking verbs are called* **predicate adjectives**. *Predicate adjectives tell us something about the subject of the sentence.*

서술 형용사는 연결 동사 다음에 나오는 형용사로 주어에 대한 정보를 제공한다.

Linking verbs: be, become, look, seem, appear, sound, smell, and taste ...

My grandmother's house smells **funny**.[1]

The streets here are **narrow** and **windy**.[2]

This backpack is too **large**, **heavy**, and **ugly**.[3]

3 *The following adjectives can only be used as predicate adjectives, not as attributive adjectives: afloat, afraid, aglow, alive, alone, and asleep.* 접두사 a가 붙은 형용사는 서술 형용사로만 쓰인다.

Justin is **afraid** of the water.① (~~Afraid Justin~~)

The kids were **aglow** with excitement.② (~~The aglow kids~~)

Susan's son fell **asleep** straight away this afternoon.③ (~~Susan's asleep son~~)

Some predicate adjectives have "partner"—or related—attributive adjectives.

한정 형용사와 관련이 있거나 짝이 되는 서술 형용사이다.

Is Michael all right? He looks **ill**.④ (predicate adjective)

My son Michael is an **unhealthy** boy.⑤ (attributive adjective)

The monkeys are fast **asleep** in their cages.⑥ (predicate adjective)

The **sleeping** monkeys are cuddled up together.⑦ (attributive adjective)

4 *Attributive adjectives tend to follow a predictable order:* 한정 형용사의 어순은 다음과 같다.

a *determiners (e.g.: both, the, his, this, another)* 한정사

b *cardinal numbers (e.g.: one, two, three)* 기수

c *general adjectives describing opinions and qualities such as size, weight, shape, age*
의견이나 크기, 무게, 형태, 나이 등의 성질을 설명하는 일반 형용사

d *and adjectives describing color, origin, material, and purpose* 색, 근원, 재료, 목적을 설명하는 형용사

I bought my brother **a small wooden Japanese** mask.①

Justin says he really loves **traditional Korean** food.② (~~Korean traditional food~~)

Will you buy me **this cute pink one piece** dress?③

> **!NOTICE**
>
> *General adjectives from different classes are not normally separated by commas; however, adjectives from the same class generally are.*
>
> 다른 종류의 일반 형용사들은 콤마로 구분하지 않는다. 하지만 같은 종류의 형용사들은 콤마로 구분한다.
>
> My brother bought himself <u>a beautiful new German sports car.</u>④
>
> The treasure hunters uncovered <u>an **ancient, antique** treasure chest.</u>⑤
>
> *In some cases, adjectives describing origin, shape, color, and materials may require commas. Use commas if the adjectives help identify the thing being described.*
>
> 경우에 따라, 기원, 모양, 색과 재료를 설명하는 형용사도 콤마를 필요로 할 수 있다. 형용사가 무엇을 한정하는지를 분명히 해야 할 때 콤마를 사용한다.
>
> a beautiful Korean painting⑥ (=a beautiful, Korean painting)
>
> a brown leather handbag⑦ (=a brown, leather handbag)
>
> a tiny oval mirror⑧ (=a tiny, oval mirror)

5

Normally we need to include a noun with an adjective. But if the adjective is describing a well-known, general group of people, we can omit the noun.

일반적으로 형용사는 명사와 같이 쓰이지만, 잘 알려진 사람이나 집단을 수식할 경우 명사를 생략하기도 한다.

Susan's brother trains guide-dogs for **the blind.**[1] (the blind = blind people)

The council has pledged to build more shelters for **the homeless.**[2] (the homeless = people without homes)

The government ought to spend more money taking care of **the poor.**[3] (the poor = poor people)

6

Use a hyphen (-) between two (or more) words—nouns, adjectives, adverbs—that modify a noun.

하이픈(-)은 두 개 이상의 단어(명사, 형용사, 부사)가 명사를 수식할 때 사용한다.

<u>This</u> is a **well-developed** essay.

→ This <u>essay</u> is well developed.[1]

My boyfriend loves **chocolate-covered** <u>peanuts</u>.[2]

But if the first word is an -ly adverb, no hyphen is used.

첫 단어가 -ly로 끝나는 부사의 경우에는 하이픈(-)을 사용하지 않는다.

This is a **highly unusual** request.[3] (highly-unusual)

That was a **completely surprising** result.[4] (completely-surprising)

---

1 ① 우리는 동물원에서 귀여운 사슴에게 먹이를 주었다. ② 강한 바람이 오래된 나무를 쓰러뜨렸다. ③ 이 휴대용 컴퓨터는 딱 알맞은 크기다.   2 ① 우리 할머니 댁에서 희한한 냄새가 난다. ② 이 곳의 거리들은 좁고 바람이 세다. ③ 이 책가방은 너무 크고, 무겁고, 볼품이 없다.   3 ① 저스틴은 물을 무서워한다. ② 어린이들은 신이 나서 얼굴이 붉게 달아올랐다. ③ 수잔의 아들은 오늘 오후에 바로 잠이 들었다. ④ 마이클은 괜찮니? 그는 아파 보여. ⑤ 내 아들 마이클은 건강하지 못한 소년이야. ⑥ 원숭이들은 우리 안에서 곤히 잠을 자고 있다. ⑦ 잠자고 있는 원숭이들은 서로 부둥켜 안고 있다.   4 d ① 나는 우리 형에게 나무로 된 작은 일본 가면을 사 주었다. ② 저스틴은 한국의 전통 음식을 정말 좋아한다고 말한다. ③ 나에게 이 귀여운 분홍색 원피스를 사 줄래요? ④ 우리 형은 멋진 새 독일 스포츠카를 샀다. ⑤ 보물 사냥꾼들은 고대의 골동품 보물 상자를 발견했다. ⑥ 아름다운 한국 그림 ⑦ 갈색 가죽 핸드백 ⑧ 작은 타원형 거울   5 ① 수잔의 오빠는 맹인들을 위한 맹도 견을 훈련한다. ② 의회는 집이 없는 사람들에게 더 많은 보호소를 지을 것이라고 서약했다. ③ 정부는 가난한 사람들을 돌보는 데 더 많은 돈을 사용해야 한다.   6 ① 이것은 잘 다듬어진 에세이이다. ② 내 남자 친구는 초콜릿으로 덮인 땅콩을 매우 좋아한다. ③ 이것은 매우 이례적인 요청이다. ④ 그것은 완전히 놀라운 결과였다.

114

A ( ) 안에서 가장 알맞은 것을 고르시오.

aglow 벌겋게 단
reboot 재시동하다
certain 특정한
avian 새의
species (동식물 분류상의) 종(種)
professionalism 전문성
perseverance 인내
afloat (물에) 뜬
alight 불타는, 불붙은
cause 원인
accidental 우연한, 돌발적인

1 The child was (aglow / glow) with excitement that his father was coming home after being away for so long.

2 To restart your computer system after the screen comes (alive / live), push the F8 key repeatedly until the system reboots.

3 Certain types of birds are (like / alike) only in that they are all members of the avian species. Penguins and eagles are prime examples.

4 Only through the crew's professionalism and perseverance were they able to keep the damaged boat (afloat / float) during the storm.

5 Last Saturday firefighters were called to a fire. Upon arrival, they found the building well (alight / light). The cause of the fire was believed to be accidental.

B 〈보기〉알맞은 단어를 골라 문장을 완성하시오.

portable 가지고 다닐 수 있는
palm 손바닥
prepare ~을 준비하다
costume 의상
originally 원래는
tribe 부족, 종족

보기	portable	wooden	tiny	beautiful	traditional

1 When we go camping in the mountains, Dad always brings our _____ stove so we can prepare our own meals.

2 I think that traditional Korean hanboks are very _____. They are much more colorful than most Western clothing.

3 When I brought my new puppy home, I could not believe how _____ he was. I could hold him in the palm of my hand.

4 Mom is preparing many different kinds of food for Chusuk, and the children are all dressed up in their _____ costumes.

5 My brother has a huge _____ mask hanging on the wall of his room. Originally, it belonged to a member of a West African tribe.

electrical storm
(= thunderstorm)
뇌우

celadon 청록색

priceless 대단히 귀중한

precise 명확한, 정확한

mathematical 수학의

waft 떠돌다, 흐르다

vivid 생생한

fresco 프레스코화(새로 석회를 바른 벽이 마르기 전에 그린 그림)

applicant 지원자

participate in
~에 참가하다

strenuous
힘든, 큰 노력을 필요로 하는

agility test
민첩성 테스트

exhausting 기진맥진한

utilize ~을 이용하다

tundra 툰드라(북쪽 북극해 연안에 분포하는 넓은 벌판)

C 주어진 단어를 이용하여 문장을 완성하시오. [필요하면 하이픈(−)과 콤마(,)를 사용할 것]

1 My (jacket / black / leather/ old) is the warmest coat I own.

→ My _____ is the warmest coat I own.

2 (electrical storm / of the year / the most dangerous) took place last night.

→ _____ took place last night.

3 (celadon / two / those / vases) are priceless antiques from the Goryeo Dynasty.

→ _____ are priceless antiques from the Goryeo Dynasty.

4 My engineering examination asked (precise / many / questions / mathematical).

→ My engineering examination asked _____ _____.

5 What are (watering / smells / those / mouth / wafting up) from the street?

→ What are _____ from the street?

6 I saw (brightly / colored / vivid / the walls / covering / frescos) of the church.

→ I saw _____ of the church.

7 Before becoming a firefighter, all applicants must participate in a very strenuous (agility test / exhausting / physical).

→ Before becoming a firefighter, all applicants must participate in a very strenuous _____.

8 The Space shuttle is a (designed / well / precision / very) aircraft utilized for space travel.

→ The Space shuttle is a _____ aircraft utilized for space travel.

9 During our trip to northern Canada we experienced (bone / the extreme / cold / chilling) of the tundra.

→ During our trip to northern Canada, we experienced _____ of the tundra.

Unit 24
Prepositional Phrases

 **KEY** CONCEPTS

A **prepositional phrase** is a kind of adjectival. A prepositional phrase consists of a preposition and its object (a noun or pronoun). Prepositional phrases function adjectivally when they modify nouns.
전치사구는 형용사 상당 어구의 한 종류로 전치사와 전치사의 목적어(명사나 대명사)로 이루어져 있다. 전치사구는 명사를 수식하는 형용사 기능을 한다.

FOCUS

1

As adjectives, **prepositional phrases** *identify "which one." They follow the nouns they modify.*
형용사 역할을 하는 전치사구는 수식할 명사 뒤에 나온다.

The black **sneakers** <u>on the shelf</u> belong to me.[①]

This **note** <u>from the nurse</u> excuses John from gym class.[②]

The **sweet potatoes** <u>in the crisper</u> have gone off; they smell terrible![③]

2

Within the prepositional phrase itself, the object of the preposition too can be modified.
전치사구 내에서 전치사의 목적어도 수식을 받을 수 있다.

Hand me the atlas <u>on the second shelf</u>.[①]
("On the second shelf" modifies *atlas* while "second" modifies *shelf*.)

Bring me all of the dirty towels <u>from the second-floor bathroom</u>.[②]
("From the second-floor bathroom" modifies *towels* while "second-floor" modifies *bathroom*.)

The fence <u>around the old wooden barn near the lake</u> needs to be repainted.[③]
("Around the old wooden barn" modifies *fence* while "old wooden" and "near the lake" modify *barn*.)

3

A prepositional phrase will never contain the subject of a sentence.
전치사구는 문장의 주어를 포함하지 않는다.

Every **one** <u>of the volunteers</u> **was** ready on time.[①] (*One* is singular.)

Neither <u>of these coursebooks</u> **is** very well written.[②] (*Neither* is singular.)

The **printers** <u>in the computer lab</u> **are** not working.[③] (*Printers* is plural.)

Kerry, <u>along with his friends</u>, still **believes** in the Tooth Fairy.[④] (*Kerry* is singular.)

All <u>of the students</u> <u>in the class</u> **collect** money for the needy.[⑤] (*All* is plural.)

---

1 ① 선반 위의 검은색 운동화는 내 것이다. ② 간호사로부터 받은 이 메모는 존이 체육 수업 출석하지 않게 해준다. ③ 채소 칸의 고구마가 상했어. 그것들은 냄새가 지독해! 2 ① 두 번째 선반에 있는 지도책을 나에게 건네줘. ② 2층 화장실에서 더러운 수건들을 모두 나에게 가져다주세요. ③ 호수 근처에 있는 낡은 목제 헛간 주위의 울타리는 다시 페인트칠해야 한다. 3 ① 자원 봉사자들 각각 제시간에 준비되어 있었다. ② 이 교과서 두 권 모두 매우 잘 쓰여진 것은 아니다. ③ 컴퓨터실의 프린터는 작동되지 않는다. ④ 그의 친구들과 마찬가지로 케리는 여전히 이(tooth)의 요정을 믿고 있다. ⑤ 학급의 모든 학생들은 경제적으로 어려운 사람들을 위해 돈을 모은다.

EXERCISES

stall 귀빈석
in search of ~을 찾아서
remarkable 주목할 만한
royal azalea 철쭉
on the other side of
~의 반대쪽에
in the meantime
그 사이에

A 문장을 읽고, 밑줄 친 부분의 역할을 〈보기〉에서 찾아 쓰시오.

| 보기 | ⓐ adjectival | ⓑ adverbial |

1 Mary is jumping rope <u>in the backyard</u>.

2 Do you want me to bring you the blanket <u>in the closet</u>?

3 Steven Jobs gave a presentation <u>about the new product</u>.

4 The seats <u>in the circle</u> are cheaper than those <u>in the stalls</u>.

5 Matthew went into the mountains <u>in search of</u> lost treasure.

6 There was a remarkable growth <u>in sales</u> <u>before Christmas</u>.

7 There are some royal azaleas <u>on the other side of the Mountain</u>.

8 I haven't been home <u>in six years</u>. <u>In the meantime</u>, my family has moved.

9 Go down this street <u>for three blocks</u> and turn left <u>at the corner</u>, you can't miss it.

background 배경
botanical 식물의
employ ~을 고용하다
occupy (공간·시간을)
차지하다, 거주하다
supplementary
추가의, 보충의
check-in counter
체크인 카운터 (공항의 탑승
수속 장소)
prior to ~전에

B (   ) 안에서 가장 알맞은 것을 고르시오.

1 Each of the four members (has / have) a different background.

2 The flowers at the botanical garden (is / are) beautiful.

3 Both Kate and I (am / are) employed at the automobile factory.

4 Half of the homes in this neighborhood (is not / are not) occupied.

5 The perfume in Duty Free shops (is / are) cheaper than anywhere else.

6 An ever increasing number of Ph.D. holders (is / are) having difficulty finding jobs.

7 All of the supplementary material for the students (was / were) supplied by the school.

8 The carpet on the floor (was cleaned / were cleaned) by the housekeeping staff yesterday.

9 The check-in counter at Goldsky Airlines (insist / insists) that travelers check in at least two hours prior to departure.

Unit 25 Adjective Clauses

 **KEY CONCEPTS**

In addition to adjectives and prepositional phrases, **adjective clauses**—also called relative clauses—can be used to modify nouns. An adjective clause is a kind of dependent clause, so it must be linked to a complete sentence; it cannot stand alone.

형용사절은 관계사절이라고도 하는데 형용사와 전치사구처럼 명사를 수식한다. 형용사절은 일종의 종속절로 완전한 문장과 연결되어야 하며 홀로 쓰일 수 없다.

FOCUS ···

1   **Adjective clauses** *begin with* **relative pronouns** *and* **relative adverbs.** *They follow the nouns (or pronouns) they modify.*

형용사절은 관계대명사나 관계부사로 시작하며 수식하는 명사나 대명사 뒤에 쓰인다.

> *Relative pronouns: who, that, which, whom, whose*

> *Relative adverbs: when, where, why, how*

Stacey found the **money** <u>that she had lost</u> in her jeans pocket.①
Michael Gray is the **boy** <u>who just transferred here from Ellis High School.</u>②
The **neighborhood** <u>where I grew up</u> looks totally different now.③

2   **Subject** *relative pronouns are required; object relative pronouns may be omitted.*

주격 관계대명사는 생략할 수 없지만, 목적격 관계대명사는 생략할 수 있다.

The clerk **who** sold you these shoes quit last **week.**① (*Who* is the subject of the clause.)
The car **that** crashed into the building was badly damaged.② (*That* is the subject of the clause.)
The mysterious Venus flytrap is a plant **which** eats insects.③ (*which* is the subject of the clause.)
The manager **(who[m])** I spoke to last week was really helpful.④ (*Who[m]* is the object of the clause.)
The movie **(that)** we saw last Saturday was really great!⑤ (*That* is the object of the clause.)

3   *The relative pronoun* whose *is used to show possession. It cannot be omitted.*

관계대명사 whose는 소유를 나타내며 생략할 수 없다.

The girl **whose** dictionary I borrowed isn't here today.① (whose dictionary=*her dictionary*)
Passengers **whose** bags have been checked in may not leave the security area.②
(whose bags=*passengers' bags*)

4 *To punctuate (with commas) an adjective clause, first decide if the clause contains* **essential** *or* **non-essential** *information.*

형용사절이 중요한 정보를 가지고 있는지 아닌지에 따라 콤마 표시 유무가 달라진다.

a *Clauses that contain* **essential information** *do not require commas. Information is essential if it helps the reader identify which noun the writer is referring to.*

형용사절이 말하고자 하는 명사의 중요한 필수 정보를 포함하고 있을 때 콤마 표시를 하지 않는다.

The <u>children</u> who scored highest on the test will be rewarded.[1] (which children?)

The <u>hotel</u> where I met your mother is being torn down.[2] (which hotel?)

Now compare the following. In each case the nonspecific noun has been made specific, so we use commas.

선행사를 명확하게 해 주어야 할 경우에는 콤마를 사용할 수 있다.

<u>Martin and Sarah</u>, who scored highest on the test, will be rewarded.[1]

<u>The Lexington Hotel</u>, where I met your mother, is being torn down.[2]

 NOTICE

Clauses with that are never set off with commas, even if the noun is specific.

명사가 구체적이어도 that절에는 콤마를 사용하지 않는다.

Jim's dog, which was tied up to the pole, barked loudly.[3]

(✗) ~~Jim's dog, that~~ was tied up to the pole, barked loudly.

The dog that was tied up to the pole barked loudly.[4]

(✗) ~~The dog, that~~ was tied up to the pole, barked loudly.

 NOTICE

If the clause is essential, any relative pronoun can be used. Object relative pronouns can be omitted.

형용사절이 필수적인 경우, 모든 관계대명사 사용이 가능하며 이때 목적격 관계대명사는 생략 가능하다

b **Non-essential clauses** *do require commas. A relative clause is non-essential when we know specifically who or what is being referred to.*

who나 what이 구체적으로 무엇인지 알 수 있는 경우, 관계사절은 중요하지 않으며 이처럼 필수적이지 않은 절은 콤마를 필요로 한다.

c **Proper nouns** 고유 명사

Ottawa, **which** is the capital of Canada, is a charming city.[1] (There is only one Ottawa.)

Mr. Kim, **who** teaches at Brown College, is popular.[2] (There is only one Mr. Kim at Brown College.)

d **Common nouns** *(When the referent is known, or if there is only one possible referent.)*

보통 명사(지시 대상이 잘 알려져 있거나, 유일무이할 경우)

My mother, **who** quit college to raise me, has returned to school.[1] (You have only one mother.)

Mrs. Wilson's husband, **who** retired last year, has offered to help.[2] (Mrs. Wilson has only one husband.)

The highest mountain in the world, **which** was not summitted until 1953, has been climbed many times since.③ (There can be only one "highest mountain in the world.")

If the clause is non-essential, any relative pronoun can be used **except** *that. Object relative pronouns* **cannot** *be omitted.*

형용사절이 필수적이지 않을 경우 that을 제외한 관계대명사가 모두 사용 가능하다. 이때 목적격 관계대명사는 생략할 수 없다.

5 *Sometimes which is used to modify a whole sentence.*

which는 전체 문장을 수식하는 데 쓰이기도 한다.

I woke up this morning with a pimple on my nose, **which** really embarrassed me.①

My brother gave up playing computer games, **which** really surprised me.②

My friends threw me a surprise birthday party, **which** made me happy.③

Instead of referring to a specific noun, which refers to the idea expressed in the main clause. Though common in speaking, this kind of **broad reference** *should be avoided in writing–especially on a writing test.*

which는 특정 선행사가 아닌 주절 전체를 표현할 때 사용한다. 이것은 말할 때는 많이 쓰이지만, 문장이 모호해지므로 쓰기 시험에서 사용하지 않도록 한다.

To fix this kind of sentence in your writing, find a <u>noun</u> *that sums up the idea expressed in the main clause and put it before the relative pronoun that.*

쓰기에서 이러한 문장을 고치기 위해서는 주절에서 개요를 나타내는 명사를 찾아 관계대명사 that 앞에 쓰면 모호해진 문장을 고칠 수 있다.

I woke up this morning with a pimple on my nose, a <u>problem</u> **that** really embarrassed me.①

My brother gave up playing computer games, a <u>decision</u> **that** really surprised me.②

My friends threw me a surprise birthday party, an <u>event</u> **that** made me happy.③

---

1 ① 스테이시는 청바지 주머니에서 잃어버린 돈을 찾았다. ② 마이클 그레이는 엘리스 고등학교에서 전학 온 소년이다. ③ 내가 자란 동네는 이제 완전히 달라졌다. 2 ① 너에게 신발을 판 그 점원은 지난주에 그만두었다. ② 건물을 들이받은 차는 심하게 망가졌다. ③ 신비로운 파리지옥은 곤충을 먹는 식물이다. ④ 지난주에 내가 이야기했던 매니저가 매우 도움이 되었다. ⑤ 우리가 지난 토요일에 본 영화는 정말 흥룡했다! 3 ① 내가 사전을 빌린 소녀는 오늘 여기에 없다. ② 가방을 체크인한 승객들은 안전 구역을 떠나지 마십시오. 4 a ① 시험에서 가장 높은 점수를 받은 어린이에게 상을 줄 것이다. ② 내가 네 엄마를 만났던 호텔이 철거되고 있다. ③ 시험에서 가장 높은 점수를 받은 마틴과 사라가 상을 받게 될 것이다. ④ 내가 네 엄마를 만났던 렉싱턴 호텔은 철거되고 있다. ⑤ 기둥에 묶여 있었던 짐의 개가 크게 짖었다. ⑥ 기둥에 묶여 있었던 개가 크게 짖었다. c ① 캐나다의 수도인 오타와는 매력적인 도시이다. ② 브라운 대학에서 가르치시는 김 선생님은 인기가 많다. d ① 나를 키우기 위해 대학을 그만두신 엄마는 다시 학교로 가셨다. ② 작년에 은퇴한 윌슨 부인의 남편이 도와주겠다고 제안했다. ③ 세계에서 가장 높은 그 산은 1953년에서야 비로소 정복되었고 그 이후로 많은 사람들이 등정을 하고 있다. 5 ① 나는 오늘 아침에 일어나보니 코에 여드름이 나 있었고, 이것은 정말로 나를 당황하게 했다. ② 내 남동생이 컴퓨터 게임하는 것을 그만두었는데, 이것은 정말로 나를 놀라게 했다. ③ 내 친구들이 나에게 깜짝 생일 파티를 열어 주었는데, 이것은 나를 행복하게 했다. WT ① 아침에 일어나보니 코에 여드름이 나 있었는데, 이 문제는 나를 정말로 당황하게 했다. ② 내 남동생은 컴퓨터 게임하는 것을 그만두었는데, 이 결정은 나를 정말로 놀라게 했다. ③ 내 친구들은 나에게 깜짝 생일 파티를 열어 주었는데, 이 이벤트는 나를 행복하게 했다.

EXERCISES

정답 및 해설 P. 21

babysit
남의 아이를 돌보다
playwright 극작가
a great deal 많은 양
quarterback
쿼터백(미식축구에서 공격을
지휘하는 선수)
take off 이륙하다
turbulence 난기류
distract 집중이 안 되게
하다, 산만하게 하다
odd 이상한
ringtone 신호음
no-frills
기본적인, 군더더기 없는
get into shape
건강해지다

A ( ) 안에서 알맞은 것을 모두 고르시오.

1 We moved into a new house (which / that) had recently been built.

2 Justin King, (whose / whom) I babysat as a child, has become a famous playwright.

3 My neighbor told me something (which / that) I'm sure will shock you a great deal.

4 The quarterback is the player (who / whose) responsibility is to lead the football team.

5 Flight 5340, (which / that) took off smoothly, quickly began to shake violently due to turbulence.

6 The taxi driver, (who / whose) was distracted by his passengers' odd sounding cell phone ringtone, clearly caused the accident.

7 The new "no-frills" exercise program (which / that) was prescribed by Carrie's personal trainer failed to help her get into shape.

bud (가지, 잎의) 싹, 눈
blossom 꽃이 피다
patio 테라스
story (건물의) 층; 이야기
cuisine 요리
assist ~을 돕다
respected
높이 평가되는 훌륭한
admired 존경받는
chemistry 화학
ambition 야망

B 관계대명사 who, whose, which, whom 중 알맞은 것을 골라 문장을 완성하시오.

1 The boy _____ fell down the stairs broke his arm.

2 Don't buy roses _____ buds have already blossomed.

3 The house, _____ has two large patios in the front and the rear, is two stories tall.

4 The Italian restaurant _____ Jane recommended to us served real Toscana cuisine.

5 The Korean flight attendant _____ assisted us was fluent in both Spanish and English.

6 Mr. Wilcox, _____ all of the students respected and admired, was a chemistry teacher.

7 Sehyun, _____ ambition is to work at the UN, spends most of her time learning foreign languages.

C 문장을 읽고, 밑줄 친 부분을 바르게 고쳐 문장을 다시 쓰시오.

1 Venus is one <u>whose</u> we would call a natural beauty.

→ _____

2 My brother turned out his light, which <u>mean</u> he is ready to sleep.

→ _____

3 Donald Trump was the candidate <u>whose</u> won the presidential election.

→ _____

4 An architect, who designs and draws buildings, <u>are</u> often confused with an "archeologist".

→ _____

turn out ~을 끄다
presidential election 대통령 선거
architect 건축가
be confused with ~와 혼동하다
archeologist 고고학자

D 두 문장의 뜻이 통하도록 〈보기〉와 같이 that을 이용하여 문장을 완성하시오.

> 보기 We watched the new Broadway musical *Wicked*, which is based on a best-selling novel. (story)
> → We watched the new Broadway musical *Wicked*, ___a story that___ is based on a best-selling novel.

1 Every spring, the annual River Run event comes to Laughlin, Nevada, which increases the population by approximately 20,000. (influx)

→ Every spring, the annual River Run event comes to Laughlin, Nevada, _____ increases the population by approximately 20,000.

2 Recently, computers have become smaller and more portable than they were in the past, which has really helped increase sales. (improvement)

→ Recently, computers have become smaller and more portable than they were in the past, _____ has really helped increase sales.

3 Every year thousands of dolphins are inadvertently trapped in fishermen's nets, which is endangering the species. (occurrence)

→ Every year thousands of dolphins are inadvertently trapped in fishermen's nets, _____ is endangering the species.

annual 1년의
approximately 대략적으로
improvement 개선, 향상
inadvertently 부주의로, 우연히
be trapped in ~에 갇히다
endanger ~을 위험에 빠뜨리다
occurrence 발생, 일어남

Unit 26

Adjective Phrases

KEY CONCEPTS

Adjective phrases are reduced adjective clauses. And like adjective clauses, they follow the nouns and pronouns they modify.

형용사구는 형용사절의 축약이다. 형용사절과 마찬가지로 수식하는 명사나 대명사 다음에 나온다.

The boy <u>taking attendance</u> is the class leader.①

Cars <u>traveling over the speed limit</u> will be ticketed automatically.②

The little fern, <u>moved in front of the window</u>, grew quickly.③

OCUS ···

1
To reduce an adjective clause containing a subject relative pronoun (e.g.: who, which, that) to an adjective phrase, do one of the following.

주격 관계대명사를 포함하고 있는 형용사절을 다음과 같이 형용사구로 줄일 수 있다.

Omit the relative pronoun and the form of be. 관계대명사와 be 동사를 생략한다.

The boy (who is) taking attendance is the class leader.

→ The boy **taking attendance** is the class leader.①

The towels (that are) in this cupboard are for you to use.

→ The towels **in this cupboard** are for you to use.②

NOTICE

Only adjective clauses with subject relative pronouns can be reduced.

주격 관계대명사가 있는 형용사절만 줄일 수 있다.

Omit the relative pronoun and change the non-be verb to its -ing form.

관계대명사를 생략하고, be동사가 아닌 동사는 ing형으로 고친다.

Cars <u>that travel over the speed limit</u> will be ticketed automatically.

→ Cars **traveling over the speed limit** will be ticketed automatically.③

The fence <u>that surrounds the army barracks</u> is lined with barbed wire.

→ The fence **surrounding the army barracks** is lined with barbed wire.④

2

Sometimes the reduction of an adjective clause to a phrase leaves only a single adjective. If so, move the adjective before the noun.

형용사절을 형용사구로 줄일 때 형용사 하나만 남는 경우, 형용사를 명사 앞으로 이동시킨다.

Shoes (that are) old should not be donated to charity.

→ **Old shoes** should not be donated to charity.[①]

Milk (that is) cold tastes better than milk at room temperature.

→ **Cold milk** tastes better than milk at room temperature.[②]

3

If both the adjective clause and participle phrase are nonessential, the use of commas is required.

형용사절과 분사구 모두 필수적이지 않다면, 콤마로 표시해야 한다.

Toronto, (which is) the largest city in Canada, is my hometown.

→ Toronto, **the largest city in Canada**, is my hometown.[①]

The little fern, (which was) moved in front of the window, grew quickly.

→ The little fern, **moved in front of the window**, grew quickly.[②]

EXERCISES

hang 걸리다
encircle ~을 둘러싸다
embassy 대사관
security 안전, 보안
border 국경
require ~을 필요로 하다

A 형용사절을 형용사구로 바꿔 문장을 다시 쓰시오. (생략 가능한 부분을 생략하거나 -ing형을 이용할 것)

1 Paris, which is the City of Lights, is my hometown.

→ _____

2 The suit that is hanging in the closet belonged to my uncle.

→ _____

3 The wall that encircles the embassy is for the security of the workers inside.

→ _____

4 Canadians that travel across the border to the U.S. are now required to show their passports.

→ _____

reserved
남겨둔, 따로 떼어둔
depart 출발하다
pier 부두
en route 도중에
Tahiti
타히티 섬(남태평양의 섬)
ecological
생태학의, 환경의
damage 피해, 파괴
pollution 오염
poisonous
유해한, 독을 함유한
substance 물질
reach ~을 잡다, 도달하다

B 〈보기〉와 같은 형용사절을 관계대명사(*who*, *which*)를 이용하여 절로 바꿔 문장을 다시 쓰시오.

보기	Do you know the man looking for his wallet?
	→ _____Do you know the man who is looking for his wallet?_____

1 The woman holding the sign is waiting for my mother to arrive.

→ _____

2 Young people should not sit in seats reserved for the elderly.

→ _____

3 The cruise ship departing from pier 11 is en route to the island of Tahiti.

→ _____

4 This documentary is about the ecological damage being caused by pollution.

→ _____

5 Poisonous substances should not be left out where children can reach them.

→ _____

126

REVIEW

정답 및 해설 P. 22

A 다음 빈칸에 가장 알맞은 것을 고르시오.

install ~을 설치하다
worn-out 낡은
antiquated 구식의, 낡은
secondhand 중고의

1 A: Did you get tickets for the figure skating competition?

B: Unfortunately not. All of the seats _____.

① is sold   ② was sold   ③ are sold   ④ were sold

2 A: Is there anyone _____ name hasn't been called yet?

B: Excuse me, Mr. Sanderson. Mine hasn't been called.

① that   ② who   ③ whose   ④ whom

3 A: I had some difficulty installing Photoshop on this _____ computer.

B: Why don't you buy a new one? They're not as expensive as they used to be.

① worn-out, antiquated secondhand

② secondhand worn-out antiquated

③ antiquated secondhand worn-out

④ worn-out secondhand antiquated

B 다음 대화를 읽고, 바르지 <u>않은</u> 문장을 고르시오.

career 직업
demanding
힘든, 까다로운
reward 보상
consider
~을 생각하다, 고려하다
household chore
집안일
elegantly
우아하게, 고상하게
romantically
낭만적으로
long-distance
장거리의

1 ① A: Many people believe that being a pilot is a good career choice.

② B: How so? It sounds like quite a difficult job.

③ A: It is a highly demanding and stress job, but it has its rewards too: free travel and high salary.

④ B: I see. Maybe I should consider that as a career option.

2 ① A: Hello, Julia. I haven't seen you for a while. What have you been up to?

② B: Hi, Eric. Yeah, it's been a while. I am keeping busy by volunteering with the elderly.

③ A: That's great. What do you do for them?

④ B: I help older people whom live alone. I take them food or magazines. I help them with their household chores too.

3 ① A: Where are you going for your honeymoon?

② B: My fiancee wants to go to Santorini, which is elegantly and romantically, but I want to go to somewhere in Asia.

③ A: Oh, no! It's your honeymoon! It has to be somewhere special!

④ B: I know, but I don't want to go too far away. I really hate long-distance flying.

REVIEW PLUS

정답 및 해설 P. 23

A 다음을 읽고, 바르지 <u>않은</u> 문장을 고르시오.

1

state ~을 말하다
harmless 무해한
improve
~을 개선하다, 향상시키다
relieve ~을 풀다
anxiety 걱정, 근심, 불안
unify ~을 하나로 만들다
establish ~을 확립하다
individual identity
개인의 정체성

① A well-known professor once stated that joking is a harmless way to improve relationships with others. Many people joke to relieve stress and anxiety. ② Furthermore, members of groups often joke about people whose are not members of their group. ③ These types of jokes help to unify the group as well as establish individual identities. ④ Whatever the reasons are that people continue to joke, many still feel that laughter is the best medicine.

2

artificial 인공의
method 방법
discovery 발견
replace
~을 대신하다, 대체하다
revolutionize
~에 대변혁을 일으키다
complicated 복잡한
rubbery 탄성이 있는
cool ~을 식히다, 식다
replacement
대체, 교환
tissue 조직(생물)

① Researchers who have been working on a way to create artificial muscles have recently discovered a method using a type of artificial silk. ② The discovery of this product what purpose is to replace or repair damaged muscles has revolutionized the medical field. ③ The method that is used to create this material is somewhat complicated. ④ The researchers experimented with Orlon, which is an artificial silk, by boiling it until it turned into a rubbery substance. Once the Orlon cooled, it is ready to be used as an artificial replacement for human muscle tissue.

3

coastal 해안을 따라 있는
shortage 부족
abundance of
풍부한, 많은
evaporate 증발하다
triangular 삼각형의
weave ~을 짜다
net 그물
suspend
~을 매달다, 걸다
droplet 방울

① Many of Chile's northern coastal villages have been suffering from a water shortage, even though they have an abundance of fog and clouds. ② However, the sun is so hot that the clouds and fog evaporate before they can develop into rain. One village is experimenting with a solution. ③ Using a triangular woven polypropylene net which is suspended between two wooden poles, the villagers capture water droplets from the clouds and fog. ④ The villagers whose are using this method are able to collect about 40 gallons of water per net each day. The village has been able to create up to 2,500 gallons of water per day, enough for everyone to drink, cook, clean, and even water small gardens.

polypropylene 폴리프로필렌(보온병 등에 쓰이는 원료)

B 다음 (A), (B), (C)에서 어법에 맞는 표현으로 가장 적절한 것을 고르시오. [기출 응용]

The summer Olympic Games contain many events with (A) _____ names. For instance, the triple jump is a track and field event. The name implies that the event includes three jumps, but it is made up of a hop, a skip, and a jump. The athletes who (B) _____ in this event look as if they are dancing as they bounce down the runway. Another event is the hammer throw. This event's name is misleading because the hammer does not look like a carpenter's tool at all. The hammer in the Olympic event is a metal ball (C) _____ hangs from a wire handle. The athlete holds the handle with both of his or her hands, spins around to build power, and then releases the hammer into the air.

	(A)		(B)		(C)
①	misled	⋯	compete	⋯	what
②	misleading	⋯	competes	⋯	what
③	misled	⋯	compete	⋯	that
④	misled	⋯	competes	⋯	that
⑤	misleading	⋯	compete	⋯	that

triple jump 3단뛰기
track and field
육상 경기
hop 짧은 도약
skip 가볍게 뛰기
athlete 운동선수
bounce 뛰어오르다
hammer throw
해머던지기
mislead 오해하게 하다
release
(잡고 있던 것을) 날려 보내다

C 다음 글의 밑줄 친 부분 중, 바르지 <u>않은</u> 것을 고르시오. [기출 응용]

Gila monsters are one of the only two kinds of venomous lizards in the world. Their venom is about as ① <u>poisonous</u> as a diamondback rattlesnake's venom. They have thick tails that grow thicker after meals because that's ② <u>why</u> they store fat. These lizards have been known to eat up to one-third of their body weight in one meal! That is ③ <u>like</u> a 60-pound kid eating 80 quarter-pound hamburgers. They eat ④ <u>mostly</u> small birds, eggs, and insects. Gila monsters track their prey by picking up a scent. Gila monsters also sometimes eat carrion, ⑤ <u>which</u> is an animal that is already dead.

venomous 독이 있는
lizard 도마뱀
venom (독사 따위의) 독액
diamondback
등에 다이아몬드 모양의 무늬
가 있는
rattlesnake 방울뱀
store
~을 비축하다, 저장하다
track ~을 추적하다
scent 향기, 냄새
carrion
죽은 동물의 고기, 썩은 고기

WRITING PRACTICE

정답 및 해설 P. 23

 A   Correct the errors and rewrite the sentences.

1   I'm looking for the book <u>what</u> you gave me.

→ _____

2   The orchard where Jimmy grows oranges <u>are</u> very large.

→ _____

3   The child <u>whom</u> is playing over there is my neighbor's son.

→ _____

4   The dinner includes a special dance performance and a feast of <u>Maori traditional food</u>.

→ _____

5   I want to speak to the woman <u>that</u> job is to make reservations.

→ _____

B   Correct the errors and rewrite the sentences.

1   The cars we saw at the auto show <u>was</u> really nice.

→ _____

2   The woman wearing the baseball cap <u>look</u> very kind.

→ _____

3   The manuscripts written by the author <u>was</u> sent to the publisher.

→ _____

4   Four hours and thirty minutes <u>are</u> an extremely long time to be talking on the phone.

→ _____

5   In ancient Rome, gladiators, <u>whose are</u> highly trained, fought to the death.

→ _____

C Rearrange the words in the correct order.

1 who / the baby / is / Amber / my niece, / is crying

→ _____

2 whom / today / I / a woman / had never met before / I met

→ _____

3 these couches / of / very attractive nor comfortable / neither / is

→ _____

4 enormous / two / the tsunami victims / helped / those / gray elephants

→ _____

5 was / where / to return to the town / the old man's dream / he was born

→ _____

D Translate Korean into English using the given words. Use commas if necessary.

1 그녀는 리노로 이사했고, 거기서 그녀는 사회 선생님이 되었다.
(she / where / Reno, / a social studies teacher / moved to / she became)

→ _____

2 그 식당은 주방 직원을 잘 다룰 수 있는 주방장이 필요하다.
(who / is capable of / managing the kitchen staff / needs / a chef / the restaurant)

→ _____

3 아프리카의 많은 사람들이 극심한 빈곤 속에 사는데, 이 상황이 나를 슬프게 한다.
(a situation / many people / that / abject poverty, / live in / saddens me / in Africa)

→ _____

4 그 젊은 남자는 법대에서 1등으로 졸업했는데 국선 변호사로 일하고 있다.
(is working / his law class, / who / as a public defender / at the top of / graduated / the young man,)

→ _____

E Complete the dialogs using the words in parentheses.

1 A: One quarter of the house _____ (have) been renovated.

B: When do you think the rest of the house will be finished?

2 A: The number of tigers in the wild _____ (have) decreased.

B: Yes, I know. It is really sad.

3 A: The elderly woman down the street found a wallet that _____ (be) on the road.

B: I wonder if it's the one I lost.

4 A: The man wearing black pants and sunglasses _____ (be) a famous author.

B: Really? I didn't know that. What books has he written?

5 A: What scared him _____ (be) the big brown Recluse spider. It crept up his arm.

B: It crept up his arm? I would have been scared too. I hate spiders.

PART 7

Nominals

Overview

Unit 27

Nouns name people, things, and concepts, and they fill a number of different sentence slots: subject, direct/indirect object, subject complement, object complement, and object of prepositions. However, several other structures (e.g.: gerunds, infinitives, noun clauses) also fit where nouns do in sentences. Collectively, these forms are referred to as **nominals**.

명사는 문장 안에서 주어, 직접/간접 목적어, 주격 보어, 목적격 보어, 전치사의 목적어 역할을 한다. 동명사, 부정사, 명사절이 명사 역할을 하기도 하는데, 이를 총체적으로 '명사 상당어구(nominals)'라고 한다.

Noun phrases as

Subject:	The Taj Mahal is one of India's best-known landmarks.① 주어
Subject Complement:	The highlight of my trip to Europe was definitely Paris.② 주격 보어
Object Complement:	My best friend Stacey dyed her hair blonde yesterday.③ 목적격 보어
Direct Object:	The security guard approached the car cautiously.④ 직접 목적어
Indirect Object:	You didn't allow us enough time to finish the test.⑤ 간접 목적어
Object of Preposition:	Louis has just returned from the Maldives.⑥ 전치사의 목적어

OCUS ···

1 *Gerunds, infinitives, and **noun clauses** can also fill many of the sentence slots that nouns do: subjects, direct/indirect objects, subject complements, object complements, and objects of prepositions. In the following examples, the nominal structures are underlined.*

동명사, 부정사, 명사절은 문장 내에서 주어, 직접/간접 목적어, 주격 보어, 목적격 보어, 전치사의 목적어로서 명사 역할을 한다.

a Subject:

Learning begins in infancy.① (gerund)

Decorating the Christmas tree is the best part of Christmas.② (gerund phrase)

To fix a modern car engine requires a lot of training.③ (infinitive phrase)

What you said the other day really upsets me.④ (noun clause)

b Subject Complement:

My kid brother's hobby is model airplane building.① (gerund)

The highlight of the trip was watching the sunset.② (gerund phrase)

Carol's ambition is to fly before the age of twenty.③ (infinitive phrase)

My mistake was that I refused to take lessons.④ (noun clause)

c Direct object:

The people next door don't appreciate my <u>singing</u>.[1] (gerund)

Sam loves <u>seeing good movies with his friends</u>.[2] (gerund phrase)

Peter wants <u>to finish his homework by ten</u>.[3] (infinitive phrase)

I just knew <u>that it was going to be a disaster!</u>[4] (noun clause)

d Indirect object:

Nowadays, Marcel gives <u>golfing</u> all of his energy and time.[1] (gerund)

Some people give <u>gossiping</u> too much time.[2] (gerund)

My mother gave <u>my cooking</u> two thumbs-up.[3] (gerund phrase)

e Object of preposition:

I'm a little nervous *about* <u>driving</u> tomorrow.[1] (gerund)

You'll get in trouble *for* <u>faking an illness</u>.[2] (gerund phrase)

The school had no choice *except* <u>to elect Alice chairperson</u>.[3] (infinitive phrase)

You are not responsible *for* <u>what your brother did</u>.[4] (noun clause)

KC ① 타지마할은 인도에서 가장 유명한 유적지 중 하나이다. ② 내 유럽 여행 중 하이라이트는 당연히 파리였다. ③ 나의 가장 친한 친구 스테이시는 어제 금발로 염색했다. ④ 경비원은 조심스럽게 차에 접근하였다. ⑤ 당신은 우리에게 시험을 끝낼 만큼 시간을 충분히 주지 않으셨어요. ⑥ 루이스는 방금 몰디브에서 돌아왔다. 1 a ① 유아기 때 배움이 시작된다. ② 크리스마스트리를 꾸미는 것은 크리스마스의 백미이다. ③ 최신식 자동차 엔진을 고치는 것은 많은 훈련을 요구한다. ④ 며칠 전에 네가 한 말은 나를 정말로 화나게 했다. b ① 내 남동생의 취미는 모형 비행기를 만드는 것이다. ② 그 여행 중 하이라이트는 일몰을 보는 것이었다. ③ 캐롤의 야망은 20세가 되기 전에 비행하는 것이다. ④ 수업을 받지 않은 것이 나의 실수였다. c ① 옆집 사람들이 내가 노래 부르는 것을 싫어한다. ② 샘은 그의 친구들과 좋은 영화를 보는 것을 매우 좋아한다. ③ 피터는 열 시까지 숙제를 끝내고 싶다. ④ 나는 그 일이 이렇게 엉망이 될 줄 알았어! d ① 요즘 마르셀은 그의 모든 에너지와 시간을 골프에 쏟고 있다. ② 어떤 사람들은 남의 얘기를 하며 너무 많은 시간을 보낸다. ③ 우리 어머니는 내 요리에 극찬을 해주었다. e ① 나는 내일 운전하는 것이 약간 긴장이 된다. ② 아프다고 거짓말해서 너는 혼이 날 것이다. ③ 학교는 앨리스를 학과장으로 선임하는 것 말고는 더 이상의 선택권이 없다. ④ 네 형이 한 일에 너는 책임이 없다.

PART 7 ＊ UNIT 27_ **135**

EXERCISES

정답 및 해설 P. 24

A 문장을 읽고, 밑줄 친 부분에 해당하는 것을 〈보기〉에서 고르시오.

> **보기** ⓐ subject ⓑ subject complement
> ⓒ object ⓓ object of preposition

spend money like a drunken sailor
돈을 물 쓰듯 쓰다

detective 형사, 탐정

robbery 강도 (행위)

inside job 내부 범행

get in one's way
~에게 방해가 되다

bribery 뇌물 수수

embezzlement 횡령

contribute to
~하는 데 원인이 되다

1 You should stop underline{spending money like a drunken sailor}. _____

2 The detective seems to believe underline{that the robbery was an inside job}. _____

3 The problem is underline{that the cost of housing is high in this neighborhood}. _____

4 Walter keeps underline{getting in our way}. Someone is going to have to ask him to leave. _____

5 underline{Spreading false rumors on the Internet} is a crime, and it will be treated as such. _____

6 I don't read tabloid newspapers. I simply don't believe in much of underline{what they say}. _____

7 Bribery and embezzlement rumors contributed to underline{damaging the company's image}. _____

B 문장을 읽고, 밑줄 친 부분을 바르게 고치시오.

encourage
~을 촉진하다, 조성하다

be fascinated by
~에 매료되다

natural selection
자연 선택

horrible 끔찍한

goblin 작은 도깨비,

typical 전형적인

just around the corner
바로 앞으로 다가온

1 As time goes by, I dislike underline{live} in the big city.

2 Field trips will encourage the students underline{be} more interested in what the teacher talks about in class.

3 Alex was fascinated by underline{that} he heard from his teacher about Darwin's theory of natural selection.

4 Since their horrible argument two weeks ago, Yunhee has been thinking about underline{end} her relationship with Hoon.

5 underline{Decorate} a house with pictures of ghosts and goblins is a typical Halloween tradition in many parts of North America.

6 As spring is just around the corner, the community will hold an event to celebrate the underline{planted} of wild flowers throughout the city.

Unit 28 Apposition

An **appositive** is a noun or noun phrase that follows another noun and renames it. Appositives, like adjective clauses, can carry nonessential or essential information.

동격어는 명사 뒤에 위치하며 앞에 나온 명사에 새로운 이름을 붙이는 명사(구)이다. 형용사절과 같이 동격어는 필수적인 정보일 수도, 필수적이지 않은 정보일 수도 있다.

FOCUS

1 *An* **appositive** *is a* **noun** *or* **noun phrase** *that* **renames** *another noun right before it. Appositives can be short or long, nonessential or essential.*

동격어는 바로 앞에 나온 명사를 재정의하는 명사(구)이다. 동격어는 짧거나 길 수 있고, 필수적 또는 필수적이지 않을 수도 있다.

a *Appositives are set off by* **commas** *when they add nonessential or extra information.*

동격어가 필수적이지 않거나, 추가 정보일 때는 콤마로 구분된다.

<u>Sarah's husband</u>, **Louis King**, works as a talent scout for an NBA team in Miami.[1]
(Sarah has only one husband, so Louis King adds nonessential or extra information.)

<u>Mexico City</u>, **the most populous city in North America**, has many interesting archaeological sites.[2]
(There can be only one most populous city in North America, so this is extra information.)

On <u>Mercury</u>, **the eighth largest planet**, the temperature varies from 90 K to 700 K![3]
(There is only one Mercury, so the eighth largest planet is extra information.)

b *Appositives are* **not** *set off by* **commas** *when they add* **essential** *information telling us "which one."*

동격어가 "어느 것"인지 알려 주는 필수적인 정보일 경우 콤마로 구분하지 않는다.

<u>Evan's friend</u> **John** cheated on the test.[1] (Evan has more than one friend, so John tells us which friend.)

<u>We</u> **Canadians** are just as patriotic as Americans are. (Canadians defines we.)[2]

! NOTICE

Appositives normally follow nouns, but they can come at the beginning of sentences too.

동격어는 보통 명사 뒤에 위치하지만, 문장 맨 앞에 오기도 한다.

The most populous city in North America, <u>Mexico City</u> has many interesting archaeological sites.[3]

2

We use a colon (:) to signal an appositive (or list of appositives) at the end of a sentence.

동격어(특히 복수의 동격어)를 표시하기 위해 문장 맨 끝에 콜론(:)을 사용하기도 한다.

In this course, students will practice using <u>all four language skills</u>: speaking, listening, reading, and writing.[1]

 WRITING TIPS

Student writers often overuse the verb be. The result is a number of short, choppy sentences when one would be better. To fix this problem, use an appositive to combine two sentences into one.

학생들은 종종 be동사를 남용한다. 그 결과로 짧고 고르지 못한 문장들이 여러 개 생긴다. 이러한 문제를 해결하기 위해서는 두 문장을 하나로 만들어 주는 동격어를 사용해야 한다.

Hanbok is a traditional Korean dress. It is both colorful and very beautiful.

→ *Hanbok*, a traditional Korean dress, is both colorful and very beautiful.[1]

Kim Yuna is a world-champion figure skater from Korea. She is the first person in history to score more than 200 points in an international skating event.

→ Kim Yuna — <u>a world-champion figure skater from Korea</u> — is the first person in history to score more than 200 points in an international skating event.[2]

---

1 a ① 사라의 남편인 루이스 킹은 마이애미 NBA팀에서 인재 발굴 담당자로 일한다. ② 북미에서 가장 인구가 많은 멕시코시티는 흥미로운 고고학적 유적지를 많이 가지고 있다. ③ 여덟 번째로 큰 행성인 수성의 온도는 90K에서 700K까지 변한다! b ① 에반의 친구 존은 시험에서 부정행위를 했다. ② 우리 캐나다인들은 미국인들만큼 애국적이다. ③ 북미에서 가장 인구가 많은, 멕시코시티는 흥미로운 고고학적 유적지를 많이 가지고 있다. 2 ① 이 과목에서 학생들은 언어의 네 가지 영역, 말하기, 듣기, 읽기, 쓰기를 연습할 것이다. WT ① 전통적인 한국 옷, 한복은 색채가 풍부하고 매우 아름답다. ② 한국의 세계 챔피언 피겨 스케이트 선수 김연아는 국제 스케이트 대회에서 최초로 200점 이상을 받은 사람이다.

EXERCISES

 A 〈보기〉와 같이 구두점을 추가하여 문장을 다시 쓰시오.

> **보기** To come up with an accurate diagnosis a psychologist uses two basic tools a personal interview and a genealogy report.
> → To come up with an accurate diagnosis, a psychologist uses two basic tools: a personal interview and a genealogy report.

come up with ~을 찾아내다, 내놓다, 발견하다
accurate 정확한
diagnosis 진단
psychologist 심리학자
genealogy 혈통, 가계
pharmacist 약사
multi-legged 다리가 많은
scurry 빨리 움직이다, 황급히 달리다

1 Here comes Mr. Campbell our school's new math teacher and athletic coach.

→ _____

2 John Styth Pemberton an Atlanta-based pharmacist created the original recipe for Coca-Cola in 1886.

→ _____

_____

3 When I saw the insect a large, multi-legged creature scurrying toward me across the kitchen floor, I screamed.

→ _____

_____

B 〈보기〉와 같이 두 문장을 한 문장으로 만드시오.

> **보기** Mitch Albom is the author of *Tuesdays with Morrie*. He works as a newspaper columnist and broadcaster.
> → Mitch Albom, _the author of Tuesdays with Morrie_, works as a newspaper columnist and broadcaster.

broadcaster 방송인
tourist attraction 관광 명소
organic compost 유기농 비료
require ~을 필요로 하다
element 요소, 성분
carbon 탄소
nitrogen 질소
outbreak 발병, 발생
swine flu 돼지 독감
disrupt ~을 방해하다, 지장을 주다
descendant 유래한 것, 후손, 자손
infamous 악명 높은

1 Graceland is the former home of Elvis Presley. It is one of the most popular tourist attractions in the United States.

→ Graceland, _____, is one of the most popular tourist attractions in the United States.

2 Organic compost requires four basic elements. The four basic elements are carbon, nitrogen, air, and water.

→ Organic compost requires four basic elements: _____.

3 An outbreak of swine flu has disrupted air travel to and from Mexico. It is a descendant of the infamous Spanish flu virus.

→ An outbreak of swine flu, _____, has disrupted air travel to and from Mexico.

Noun Clauses

Unit 29

Noun clauses perform the same roles in sentences that nouns do: subjects, direct/indirect objects, subject complements, object complements, and objects of prepositions. A noun clause is a kind of **dependent clause,** so it must be linked to a complete sentence(the main clause); it cannot stand alone.

명사절은 문장 내에서 주어, 직접/간접 목적어, 주격 보어, 목적격 보어, 전치사의 목적어로서 명사와 같은 역할을 한다. 명사절은 종속절로 단독으로 쓰이지 못하고 주절과 연결되어야 한다.

FOCUS

1 **Noun clauses** *formed from statements are introduced by the word **that**. They are commonly used as* **direct objects***, especially with the verbs agree, answer, believe, claim, decide, explain, forget, hear, know, learn, mean, realize, say, and think.*

that은 명사절을 이끌며, 특히 위에 열거된 동사의 직접 목적어로 쓰인다.

I believe <u>(that) scientists will one day discover a cure for cancer.</u>①

The president announced <u>(that) more financial assistance would be provided.</u>②

Jenny suddenly realized <u>(that) she had made an appointment with Jackie later today.</u>③

When a noun clause is used as the subject of a sentence, **that** *cannot be omitted. Commonly, however, we use* **it** *as the subject and move the noun clause to the end of the sentence.*

명사절이 문장의 주어로 사용될 때 that은 생략될 수 없으며 일반적으로 it을 가주어로 사용하고 명사절이 문장 맨 끝으로 이동한다.

<u>That</u> Susan refused to ride the roller coaster didn't surprise anyone.

→ It didn't surprise anyone <u>that Susan refused to ride the roller coaster.</u>④

(×) ~~Susan refused to ride the roller coaster didn't surprise anyone.~~

2 **Yes/no question** *can be turned into noun clauses using* **if***, or the more formal* **whether***.*

Yes/no 의문문의 대답은 if나 whether를 사용하여 명사절로 전환할 수 있다. whether는 좀 더 격식 있는 상황에서 쓰인다.

A: Is there a bathroom in the building?

B: I'm sorry, but I don't know <u>if there's one in the building.</u>①

A: Did Jennifer contact Dr. Lee?

B: I wonder <u>whether (or not) Jennifer contacted Dr. Lee.</u>②

A: Does she need help?

B: I don't know <u>if/whether she needs help (or not).</u>③

Question words and whether are sometimes followed by infinitives, which express the meaning "should" or "can[could]."

부정사 앞에 오는 의문사와 whether는 때때로 "should" 또는 "can[could]"의 의미를 나타낸다.

Question words: what, which, where, when, who, whom, whose, why, how

Did you tell Greg **how to get** to the party?④ (= how he can[should] get)

I'm wondering **whether to have** the fish or the beef.⑤ (= whether I should have)

3 ***Wh-questions*** *can also be turned into noun clauses using question words.*

wh-의문(문) 역시 의문사를 사용해서 명사절로 바뀔 수 있다.

A: When does the movie start?	B: I'm not sure when the movie starts.①
A: Where is the new student from?	B: I'm not sure where the new student is from.②
A: What do you want for dinner?	B: I can't decide what I want for dinner.③
A: Who was knocking at the door?	B: I didn't see who was knocking at the door.④
A: How old is this church?	B: I don't know how old this church is.⑤

Statement word order (subject + verb) is always used in noun clauses. The auxiliary verbs do, does, and did are omitted.

간접 의문문의 명사절에서는 주어+동사의 어순을 따르며 조동사 do, does, did는 생략된다.

4 *Noun clauses are used as subject complements, objects of prepositions, and adjective complements.*

명사절은 주격 보어, 전치사의 목적어, 형용사 보어로 사용된다.

a *As subject complements*

The truth is that Billy was not very well behaved in class today.①

The question is whether we will be able to deliver the products on time.②

The winner of the English speech contest **will be** whoever speaks most fluently.③

b *As objects of prepositions*

You obviously didn't listen **to** what I said earlier.①

The top prize will go **to** whoever wins the race.②

c *As adjective complements*

My brother seems **happy** that he is learning English.①

We are all **afraid** that the final exam will be difficult this year.②

5 *Subjunctive noun clauses use the simple form of the root verb to advise and suggest, or to stress importance or urgency.*

충고나 제안, 중요성 또는 긴급함을 나타내는 동사의 목적어로 that절이 사용되며, 이때 명사절에는 동사원형을 쓴다.

The Ministry of Health recommends <u>that people **eat** five servings of fresh vegetables every day</u>.①

Tina's teacher recommended <u>that she **study** math and science at summer school</u>.②

Our neighbors downstairs asked <u>that you not **play** your music so loud</u>.③

It is essential <u>that pets **be** given love and attention, just like people</u>.④

 WRITING TIPS

Sentences containing a noun clause are commonly found in persuasive essay writing.

명사절이 들어있는 문장은 일반적으로 논설문에서 많이 쓴다.

a *In the **introductory paragraph**, we can use a noun clause to state our position.*

서론에서 명사절은 본인의 주장을 나타낼 때 쓴다.

Topic: Do the advantages of studying abroad outweigh the disadvantages?

In this essay, I will argue <u>that the advantages of studying abroad outweigh the disadvantages</u>.①

Topic: Some people believe that cell phones are harmful to society and should be banned. Others, however, believe that cell phones are harmless. Discuss both these views and give your own opinion.②

People have begun to question <u>whether cell phones are harmful to society</u>. In my opinion, I believe <u>that cell phones do more harm than good</u>.④

b *In the **conclusion**, we can use a **noun clause** to recommend a course of action.*

결론에서는 상대방에게 어떤 행동을 제안할 때 명사절을 쓴다.

I recommend <u>that parents be encouraged to send their children abroad for one year</u>.①

For these reasons, I believe <u>that children under the age of 16 should not be allowed to own a cell phone</u>.②

EXERCISES

정답 및 해설 P. 25

A 문장을 읽고, 밑줄 부분의 역할을 〈보기〉에서 찾아 쓰시오.

> 보기   ⓐ Subject Complement   ⓑ Objects of Preposition
>   ⓒ Adjective Complement

1 The thief seemed relieved <u>that the judge let him off with a warning</u>.

_____

2 The bottom line is <u>that we still don't know exactly what caused the fire</u>.

_____

3 A reward of $50,000 will go to <u>whoever apprehends the fugitives first</u>.

_____

4 We will send the money, clothing, and other donations to <u>whichever aid agency requests them</u>.

_____

5 Another interesting fact is <u>that Kamloops, B.C., was called "Cumcloups" by the original inhabitants of the area, the Shuswap Indians</u>.

_____

> relieved 안심한, 안도한
> bottom line
> 핵심, 중요한 것, 요점
> reward 보상
> apprehend
> ~을 체포하다
> fugitive 탈주자
> donation 기증(품), 기부
> inhabitant 주민

B 주어진 단어를 어법에 맞게 바꿔 문장을 완성하시오.

1 (stay)   You should decide where _____ in Tokyo before leaving home.

2 (drink)   I don't recommend that you _____ more than one can of soda pop per day.

3 (make)   The students continued to discuss how _____ the most of this rare opportunity.

4 (be)   It is important that all the students _____ required to learn English and Math.

5 (deal with)   When faced with a barrage of questions from the journalists, the rookie district attorney didn't know how _____ the situation.

> rare 드문
> be faced with
> ~에 직면하다
> a barrage of
> questions 질문 공세
> rookie 신예, 신참
> district attorney
> 지방 검사

real estate agent
공인중개사

intermediary 중재자

make fun of ~을 놀리다

put a person on
~을 장난으로 속이다

regular customer
단골

C 〈보기〉에서 알맞은 것을 골라 빈칸에 쓰시오.

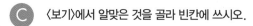

| 보기 | that | whether | if |

1 The question is _____ her apology would make any difference now.

2 Robert soon became aware _____ the application deadline had already passed.

3 Richard hoped _____ his real estate agent would serve as an intermediary.

4 A: Charlie makes fun of me all the time. It's hard to know _____ or not to take it personally.

    B: Don't take it too seriously. He just enjoys putting you on.

5 A: Do you know a lady named Carrie? I think she comes in here to this beauty salon from time to time.

    B: I'm not sure _____ or not she is a regular customer. The name doesn't sound familiar, but I'm new here.

clarify ~을 명백히 하다

capitalize
투자하다, 자본을 제공하다

merger 합병

pop tab
알루미늄캔 따개 고리(캔을 딸
수 있도록 붙어 있는 고리)

offender 범죄자

equipped 장비를 갖춘

correctional facility.
교정시설, 교도소

move forward
전진하다, 성장하다

D 문장을 읽고, 밑줄 친 부분을 어법에 맞게 고치시오.

1 I have forgotten how much <u>did it cost</u> to travel to England and back.

2 It should be clarified <u>who to capitalize</u> most on the merger last month.

3 I recommend that Esther <u>discusses</u> the situation with her parents first.

4 The Hahn family has been considering <u>whether change</u> the name of their shop.

5 I don't remember when <u>did my children became</u> interested in collecting pop tabs.

6 We need to ask Ken <u>if or not</u> he is leaving the school next year. It must be a rumor!

7 The criminal psychologist proposed that offenders <u>are</u> placed in specially equipped correctional facilities.

8 You might wonder how <u>would the banks</u> be able to lend out enough money to keep the economy moving forward.

E 문장을 읽고, "It ~ that" 구문을 이용하여 문장을 완성하시오.

behave 행동하다
amnesia
건망증, 기억 상실증
exposure 노출
hearing loss
청력 상실, 난청
disadvantage 단점
wind power 풍력
blade 날개, 칼날
promote
~을 촉진하다, 장려하다
consumerism
소비자 중심주의

1 That both of you behave like you own the world upsets me.

→ _____ both of you behave like you own the world.

2 That I should get this weird haircut was my mother's idea, not mine.

→ _____ I should get this weird haircut, not mine.

3 That Julian's boyfriend suffered from amnesia after the car accident shocked me.

→ _____ Julian's boyfriend suffered from amnesia after the car accident.

4 That long-term exposure to noise can lead to hearing loss doesn't surprise me.

→ _____ long-term exposure to noise can lead to hearing loss.

5 That one of the disadvantages of wind power is that many birds are killed by the blades amazed us.

→ _____ one of the disadvantages of wind power is that many birds are killed by the blades.

6 That the television industry is controlled by people who are more interested in promoting consumerism than culture is no big surprise.

→ _____ the television industry is controlled by people who are more interested in promoting consumerism than culture.

Indirect Speech

KEY CONCEPTS

Indirect speech—also called reported speech—is used to tell others what we have **heard** or **read**.
간접 화법은 우리가 듣거나 읽은 것을 상대방에게 이야기할 때 쓴다.

OCUS ···

1   *We commonly use noun clauses to report what others have said or written. (NOTE: The tense of the main verb affects the tense of the verb in the noun clause.)*

다른 사람들의 말이나 글을 보고할 때 명사절을 사용한다. (주의: 본동사의 시제는 명사절에 쓰인 동사의 시제에 영향을 미친다.)

  a *Present forms change to past forms.* 현재형은 과거형으로 바꾼다.

    Claire: "Hi everyone! I'm happy to be your new English instructor."

    → Claire **announced** to the class **(that) she was** happy to be **their** new English instructor.①

  b *The simple past changes to the past perfect.* 단순과거는 과거완료로 바꾼다.

    Sebastian: "Mom, I finished doing my homework an hour ago."

    → Sebastian **told** his mother **(that) he had finished** doing **his** homework an hour **before.**①

    ! NOTICE

    Pronouns and time or place expressions must change too.
    대명사와 시간 또는 장소 표현도 바꿔야 한다.

    your → their, my → his/her, ago → before, now → then, today → that day ...

    Rob: "I met Julia by chance at the mall two weeks ago."

    → Rob **said (that) he had met** Julia by chance at the mall two weeks **before.**②

  c *Will, can, and may change to would, could, and might. When must means have to, it changes to had to.*

    will, can, may는 would, could, might로 바꾸고, must가 have to의 의미일 때는 had to로 바꾼다.

    Jen: "I promise, Mrs. Kim. I'll work hard to earn a spot on the English debate team."

    → Jen promised Mrs. Kim **(that) she would work** hard to earn a spot on the English debate team.①

    Chris: "I must take Bowser out for a walk; otherwise, he'll never settle down."

    → Chris said **(that) he had** to take Bowser out for a walk; otherwise, he **would** never settle down.②

d *When the reporting happens soon after speaking, or when reporting facts, the noun clause verb may stay in the simple present:*

말한 다음 바로 알려주거나, 사실을 보고할 때는 명사절의 동사가 단순현재로 남을 수 있다.

A: "What did the waiter just say?"

B: "He <u>said</u> he **wants** to take our order. Hurry up and decide what you're going to have."[1]

A: "The Chrysler Building is one of New York City's finest examples of Art Deco architecture."

→ The guide <u>told</u> us that the Chrysler Building **is** one of New York City's finest examples of Art Deco architecture.[2]

2

The verb say is followed directly by a noun clause, whereas tell is followed first by a noun or pronoun and then the noun clause.

say 다음에는 바로 명사절을 쓰는 반면에, tell 다음에는 명사나 대명사를 먼저 쓰고 명사절을 쓴다.

The weather forecaster **said** <u>**(that)** it would rain today, but I guess he was wrong.</u>[1]

Jessica **told me** <u>that she would meet me here after class.</u> I wonder where she is.[2]

3

The verb ask is used with if and whether. 동사 ask는 if와 whether와 같이 쓰인다.

Mom <u>asked</u> **if/whether** we wanted something to eat.[1] (Mom asked that)

He <u>asked</u> **if/whether** she could translate English play scripts into Korean.[2]

---

1 a ① 클레어: "안녕, 여러분! 여러분의 새로운 영어 강사가 되어서 기뻐요." → 클레어는 학생들에게 그녀가 그들의 새로운 영어 강사가 되어 기쁘다고 말했다. b ① 세바스찬: "엄마, 한 시간 전에 숙제를 끝마쳤어요." → 세바스찬은 엄마에게 그가 한 시간 전에 숙제를 끝냈다고 말했다. ② 롭: "나는 2주 전에 쇼핑몰에서 우연히 줄리아를 만났어." → 롭은 그가 2주 전에 쇼핑몰에서 우연히 줄리아를 만났다고 말했다. c ① 젠: "김 선생님, 약속할게요. 영어 토론 팀에 들어가기 위해 열심히 할게요." → 젠은 김 선생님에게 그녀가 영어 토론 팀에 들어가기 위해 열심히 하겠다고 약속했다. ② 크리스: "바우저를 산책 시키러 나가야 해. 그렇게 하지 않으면 그는 절대로 진정하지 않을 거야." → 크리스는 자신이 바우저를 산책 시키지 않으면 진정하지 않을 것이라서 그를 산책 시키러 가야만 한다고 말했다. ③ 빅토리아: "나 호준이와 곧 결혼할지도 몰라." → 빅토리아는 곧 호준이와 결혼할지도 모른다고 했다. d ① A: "웨이터가 방금 뭐라고 말했니?" B: "그는 주문을 받고 싶다고 했어. 무엇을 먹을 건지 서둘러서 결정해." ② A: "크라이슬러 건물은 뉴욕의 아르 데코 건축 양식의 대표적인 건물이야." → 그 가이드가 크라이슬러 건물이 뉴욕의 아르 데코 건축 양식의 대표적인 건물이라고 말해 주었다. 2 ① 일기 예보관은 오늘 비가 올 것이라고 했지만, 그가 틀린 것 같다. ② 제시카는 여기서 방과 후에 나를 만나자고 했어. 나는 그녀가 어디에 있는지 궁금해. 3 ① 엄마는 우리에게 뭔가를 먹고 싶은지 물어보셨다. ② 그는 그녀에게 영어 연극 대본을 한국어로 번역할 수 있는지 물어보았다.

EXERCISES

weather forecaster
일기 예보관
announce ~을 알리다
steamship 증기선
oboe 오보에
request ~을 요청하다
investigation
수사, 조사
prior to ~전에
incident 사건, 사고

A ( ) 안에서 가장 알맞은 것을 고르시오.

1 His father whispered to me that he (is preparing / was preparing) a surprise party for his son.

2 The weather forecaster had announced that (there is / there was) a 50% chance of rain.

3 The famous photographer (said / told) us that the building looked like the front end of a huge steamship.

4 The guide said we (need / had needed) to catch that bus right away! It makes only one round trip per day.

5 Stephanie said that she (will be studying / would be studying) the oboe with Professor Lee that summer.

6 Philip told me that he was going to the career workshop to talk to a counselor who (will / would) be speaking there.

7 My uncle told me that he (requested / had requested) a closer investigation of the National Police Agency two weeks prior to the incident.

cut down ~을 줄이다
stand a person up
~을 바람맞히다
admit ~을 인정하다
be away 부재중이다
television
commercial
텔레비전 광고

B 문장을 읽고, 밑줄 친 부분을 바르게 고쳐 문장을 다시 쓰시오.

1 While Chris was in Korea, he was often asked where <u>did he come</u> from.
 → _____

2 Garry had promised his wife that he <u>will</u> cut down eating burgers and fries.
 → _____

3 When Ryan told me that Wendy <u>stands</u> him up twice, I knew that something was wrong.
 → _____

4 My neighbor admitted that she had forgotten to feed my dogs while I <u>am</u> away on vacation.
 → _____

5 Todd asked me <u>that</u> whether I was the famous child actor in the Kellogg's television commercials.
 → _____

148

C 주어진 직접 화법 문장을 간접 화법 문장으로 바꿔 문장을 완성하시오.

conduct ~을 행하다
be divided into
~로 나뉘다
thorax 흉부
abdomen 복부
black sheep 골칫거리
get into trouble
곤경에 빠지다
landlord (집) 주인
get rid of ~을 없애다
allow ~을 허락하다
cope with ~에 대처하다
security threat
안보 위협
face 직면하다
cannot afford
~하면 안 된다

1 Shelly said, "I will conduct interviews with people from all parts of the country."

→ Shelly said that _____.

_____

2 Ms. Kim said, "The body of the bee is divided into three parts: the head, thorax, and abdomen."

→ Ms. Kim said that _____

_____.

3 My parents said to my brother, "You are the black sheep of the family, always getting into trouble."

→ My parents told my brother that _____

_____.

4 My landlord said to me, "You must get rid of your dog because pets aren't allowed in the building."

→ My landlord told me that _____

_____.

5 The soldiers said, "We are prepared to cope with any kind of security threat our country faces."

→ The soldiers said that _____

_____.

6 John said, "My knee hurts, but I can't afford to miss any more practices. I've missed too many already."

→ John said that _____

_____.

D 문장을 읽고, 밑줄 친 부분을 바르게 고쳐 문장을 다시 쓰시오.

1 The cashier said she <u>was</u> closing her register now. Let's use the self-service checkout machine over there.

→ _____

_____

2 Ms. Choi, the athletic coach, saw Stephen sitting on the grass. He complained that <u>I</u> had been having leg cramps.

→ _____

_____

3 After Jeff confessed to me that he started going out with Mary three month <u>ago</u>, I spent a sleepless night wondering what to do.

→ _____

_____

4 Mrs. Smith asked Mark <u>that</u> he had seen her reading glasses around anywhere. She said she needed them to read the morning paper.

→ _____

_____

E 주어진 간접 화법 문장을 직접 화법 문장으로 바꿔 문장을 완성하시오.

1 Silvia asked me what topics we were going to discuss today.

→ Silvia said to me, _____

2 All of a sudden, the leader asked me if I had anything to share with them.

→ All of a sudden, the leader said to me, _____

3 One day, my son asked me how babies quickly develop such a large vocabulary.

→ One day, my son said to me, _____

4 Professor Morgan told Jennifer that she'd got the scholarship for the winter program at Berkeley.

→ Professor Morgan said to Jennifer, _____

_____

5 Alicia's mother told me that her daughter would no longer be allowed to go to my house unless she accompanied her.

→ Alicia's mother said to me, _____

_____

REVIEW

정답 및 해설 P. 27

A 다음 빈칸에 들어갈 가장 알맞은 것을 고르시오.

depressed 우울한

portable flash drive
휴대용 메모리 드라이브

1 A: What did your mother just say to you in Spanish?

B: She said that she _____ to thank Mr. Miller for the delicious meal.

① need   ② needs   ③ will need   ④ has needed

2 A: Have you decided when you are going to leave for Laos?

B: Well, actually, the problem is not when _____, but how to get there with five young children.

① go   ② would go   ③ will go   ④ to go

3 A: I wonder why Albert is looking so depressed lately. What's going on with him?

B: He told me that he _____ his portable flash drive yesterday. He had his final project on it.

① loses   ② lost   ③ has lost   ④ was losing

B 다음 대화를 읽고, 어법상 바르지 <u>않은</u> 문장을 고르시오.

anthropology 인류학

to be honest with
you 솔직히 말해서

lean toward ～쪽을
좋아하다, ～으로 기울어지다

vacancy 빈방, 빈 곳

used 중고의

stock ～을 갖추어 놓다

1 ① A: That was a pretty interesting anthropology lecture, don't you think?

② B: Well, to be honest with you, I didn't understand <u>what did Dr. Hahn</u> mean by "sporting behavior."

③ A: He meant that sports tell us a great deal about the kinds of basic survival skills humans have developed.

④ B: Right. Oh, I get it! Now it's starting to make sense.

2 ① A: I'd like to live in a smaller apartment. I'm thinking of moving next month.

② B: Have you decided where yet?

③ A: Not yet. I'm leaning toward Hockley Harbor, but I need more information. Is your uncle still working as a real estate agent?

④ B: Yes, he is. Let me ask him that there are any vacancies there.

3 ① A: I can't believe how much my books cost this semester! I've already spent over $300 at the bookstore!

② B: I heard that the university bookstore sells used copies of most textbooks. Why don't we go there?

③ A: I wonder if they have the math book I need. I need the fifth edition, not the fourth.

④ B: My professor said me that the bookstore stocks the latest editions.

REVIEW PLUS

정답 및 해설 P. 28

risk ~의 위험을 무릅쓰다
dormitory 기숙사
describe ~을 설명하다
throat 목구멍, 인후
lung 폐
act on
~에 따라서 행동하다
impulse 충동
instinct 본능
take over
이어받다, 인계받다, 우세해지다
obligation 의무
in need 어려움에 처한

 A 다음을 읽고, 어법상 바르지 <u>않은</u> 문장을 고르시오.

1

In the chaos of a late-night fire, Jeremy, a college student, risked his life to save others in the dormitory. ① During an interview, he tried to describe how much danger was he in. ② He said that there wasn't much air and that his throat and lungs were burning. ③ He added that he acted on impulse and that his instincts simply took over. ④ It was his obligation to help those in need.

barely 겨우, 간신히
sophomore 2학년
aside from
~은 별도로 하고, 이외에
occasional
가끔의, 때때로의
pickup game 자연스럽
게 모여서 시작되는 게임
strenuous 힘든
nagging (통증이) 계속되
는, 끊임없이 잔소리 하는

2

① David can barely remember the last time he took three months off playing basketball. ② However, that's what this sophomore forward did this past summer when he returned to his home in Columbia, South Carolina. ③ Aside from an occasional pickup game with his old friends, the most strenuous thing David did was to lift his fork to his mouth while putting away his mother's spaghetti. ④ He said that he was wanting to take time off to heal a nagging ankle injury.

richly 화려하게, 풍부하게
textured
특별한 질감을 살린
genre 장르
lay in ~에 있다
ancestor 조상
evolve
~을 발전하다, 발전시키다
commercial 상업의
blend 혼합

3

① The origins of jazz is as richly textured as the music itself. The term "jazz" covers many different kinds of music. ② In the late nineteenth century, African Americans created a new musical genre known as the blues, whose origins lay in the songs of their slave ancestors. ③ Within the African American community, blues evolved, and it grew into a popular form of commercial music. ④ Jazz, a blend of traditional African American folk music and blues, has been called "America's classical music."

B 다음 (A), (B), (C)에서 어법에 맞는 표현으로 가장 적절한 것을 고르시오. [기출 응용]

The highest lake with islands (A) _____ Orba Co in Tibet. This lake has a surface that is 5,209 meters above sea level. Tibet is also known as the "roof of the world." It is a rough, dry, cold plateau north of the Himalayas. It is bitterly cold in the winter and windy all year round. Rain and melted snow (B) _____ into dozens of lakes, four of which (C) _____ considered sacred by the local people. There is very little vegetation in the stark, rocky landscape. The only trees are in the most sheltered valleys, and even those are often small. Yet for all its barrenness, this land can be kind. Humans live near the lakes, where they grow healthy crops.

	(A)		(B)		(C)
①	is	⋯	flows	⋯	are
②	is	⋯	flow	⋯	are
③	are	⋯	flow	⋯	is
④	are	⋯	flows	⋯	is
⑤	are	⋯	flows	⋯	are

surface 표면
plateau 고원, 대지
bitterly 몹시
all year round
일 년 내내
melt 녹다
dozens of 수십의, 수많은
sacred 신성한, 성스러운
vegetation 식물
stark 황량한
rocky 바위가 많은
landscape 풍경
sheltered (비바람 등으로부터) 보호받고 있는
barrenness
불모임, 황량함
crop 곡물

C 다음 글의 밑줄 친 부분 중, 어법상 바르지 <u>않은</u> 것을 고르시오. [기출 응용]

① <u>My friend's family</u> had adopted a stray dog. Unable to trace his previous owner, they kept him and called him Toby. Perhaps a clue to his past was the fact ② <u>that</u> he got nervous if anyone smoked when he was around. As soon as they threw a cigarette butt down on the ground, Toby would jump ③ <u>and stamp on it</u> until the cigarette butt was extinguished. The family thought ④ <u>what</u> perhaps something related to fire had caused Toby to become lost. He seemed to recognize ⑤ <u>that</u> a cigarette meant fire, and he had taught himself how to put fire out.

adopt ~을 입양하다
stray 길 잃은, 임자 없는
trace ~을 추적하다
previous 이전의
clue 단서
nervous 긴장한
cigarette butt 담배꽁초
stamp on
~을 밟아 뭉개다
extinguish (불을) 끄다
recognize~을 인지하다
put out ~을 끄다

WRITING PRACTICE

정답 및 해설 P. 28

 A **Correct the errors and rewrite the sentences.**

1 I have no idea how <u>can a sugar pill</u> make sick people feel better.

→ _____

2 Uncle Danny <u>told</u> that the doctors don't expect Angelina's mother to live more than six months.

→ _____

3 When I came across Ian yesterday, he told me that he had not decided whether <u>subscribe</u> to the new cable service yet.

→ _____

_____

4 I asked him <u>remembers</u> that both trust and respect are qualities that have to be earned, they cannot be demanded from anyone.

→ _____

_____

B **Combine both sentences into a single, clear sentence.**

1 Elliot Hill is an Air Force engineer. He always plays the villain during military war games.

→ Elliot Hill, _____, always plays the villain during military war games.

2 Banks are very important institutions in our economy. They invest money as well as lend it.

→ Banks, _____, invest money as well as lend it.

3 "Earthshine" is faint sunlight. It is reflected from the Earth to the Moon and then back again.

→ "Earthshine," _____, is reflected from the Earth to the Moon and then back again.

4 RSI is repetitive strain injury. It is brought on by repeatedly moving a body part, for example your hand, in the same direction without rest.

→ RSI, _____, is brought on by repeatedly moving a body part, for example your hand, in the same direction without rest.

Rearrange the words. Follow the example.

「I think that+S+V」 ~하는 것이라고 생각한다

just like people / should / I think / pets / be given / that / love and attention,

→ _____ I think that pets should be given love and attention, just like people. _____

1 my roommate / a lot of / I think / tends to / things / take / for granted / that

→ _____

2 their children / human adults / enjoy making / laugh / everywhere in the world / I think / that

→ _____

3 to complete your experiment / I think / should / a logical series of steps / follow / that / you

→ _____

Rearrange the words. Follow the example.

「S+has[have] great difficulty (in) V-ing」 ~가 …하는 데 커다란 어려움이 있다

getting close / I / to other people / have great difficulty in

→ _____ I have great difficulty in getting close to other people. _____

1 balancing / nowadays / most people / family life and work / have great difficulty in

→ _____

2 adapting / has had great difficulty / to life / in America / the Sanchez family

→ _____

3 saying "goodbye" / all of my classmates / to each other / had great difficulty in / on the last day of school

→ _____

E Complete the dialogs using the words in parentheses.

1 A: You blew your whole allowance at the mall? That's going to make your mother furious.

B: I know, but I'll just promise her that I will never go _____(shop) again.

2 A: Excuse me, sir. I'd like to ask you whether you _____ (know) the young woman in this picture or not.

B: I know her, but not well enough to say that we're "friends."

3 A: Have you finished your chemistry project yet?

B: No. I'm having trouble coming up with a good idea. The teacher said it _____ (have to) be creative.

4 A: Henry and Karen had a quarrel about something during dinner.

B: I know because I was there. At that moment, I didn't know what _____ (do).

5 A: What should I do if I encounter a bear in the woods?

B: The best advice I can give you is never _____ (approach) a bear with its cub.

PART 8

Developing Writing Skills

Cleft Sentences & Inversion

Writers use several different strategies to focus their readers' attention on different parts of the sentence: **cleft sentences**, **there transformations**, and **inversion** techniques.

독자들의 관심을 문장의 다른 부분에 집중시키기 위해 분열문, there 변환, 도치법 등 여러 다른 방법을 사용한다.

FOCUS

1   *Declarative sentences — those that express statements — can usually be rewritten to focus a reader's attention on a specific part of the sentence. The* **cleft sentence** *— a sentence with two parts — focuses the reader's attention on the part that follows it is[was/has been], etc.*

독자의 관심을 문장의 특정 부분에 집중시키기 위해 서술문을 두 부분으로 분리할 수 있는데, 이를 "분열문"이라고 한다. 이때 강조하고 싶은 중요 요소를 it is[was/has been] 등의 바로 다음에 놓는다.

Form: It + be + focus + wh-/that clause

Carol shot a hole-in-one at Scarlet Woods last Saturday.①

→ It was <u>Carol</u> that[who] shot a hole-in-one at Scarlet Woods last Saturday.②

→ It was <u>last Saturday</u> that[when] Carol shot a hole-in-one at Scarlet Woods.③

→ It was <u>a hole-in-one</u> that[which] Carol shot at Scarlet Woods last Saturday.④

→ It was <u>at Scarlet Woods</u> that[where] Carol shot a hole-in-one last Saturday.⑤

2   *A similar type of inversion uses a* **what-clause** *as the* **subject**. *(NOTE: what-clauses are often used with verbs like adore, dislike, enjoy, hate, like, loathe, love, need, prefer, and want.)*

what절을 주어로 사용하는 것은 도치와 비슷한 유형이다. (주의: adore, dislike, enjoy, hate, like, loathe, love, need, prefer, want 등의 동사가 주로 what절과 함께 사용된다.)

Elizabeth <u>adores</u> her new puppy, Chip.①

→ <u>What Elizabeth adores</u> is her new puppy, Chip.②

→ Her new puppy, Chip, is <u>what Elizabeth adores</u>.③

A faulty circuit breaker <u>caused</u> the fire at the recycling plant.④

→ <u>What caused the fire at the recycling plant</u> was a faulty circuit breaker.⑤

→ It was a faulty circuit breaker <u>that caused the fire at the recycling plant</u>.⑥

The unseasonable warm temperature brought many people to Riverside Park today.⑦

→ <u>What brought many people to Riverside Park today</u> was the unseasonably warm temperature.⑧

→ It was the unseasonably warm temperature <u>that brought many people to Riverside Park today</u>.⑨

***All** can sometimes be used to replace what to focus attention on one particular thing.*

all은 특정한 것에 주의를 집중시키려고 할 때 종종 what 대신에 쓰일 수 있다.

I turned on the computer and suddenly the lights went out.⑩

→ **What I did was** turn on the computer and suddenly the lights went out.⑪

→ **All I did was** turn on the computer and suddenly the lights went out.⑫

Jessica wants a pair of gold earrings for her birthday.⑬

→ **All** Jessica wants for her birthday is a pair of gold earrings.⑭

→ A pair of gold earrings is **all** Jessica wants for her birthday.⑮

3 *Yet another type of inversion uses **there** as the (dummy) subject.*

there를 가주어로 사용하는 도치법도 있다.

Paul, a strange looking boy is knocking on the door!①

→ Paul, **there is** a strange looking boy knocking on the door!

No seats were left on the subway this morning. I had to stand all the way to Jamsil.②

→ **There were** no seats left on the subway this morning. I had to stand all the way to Jamsil.

Hundreds of angry demonstrators were protesting outside the company's headquarters.③

→ **There were** hundreds of angry demonstrators protesting outside the company's headquarters.

4 *Several other inversions of normal subject-verb-complement (object) order are also possible.*

일반적인 주어–동사–보어(목적어) 어순에도 여러 다른 도치법들이 있다.

a Subject-Verb Shift: *Move the subject after the verb. This effect helps the writer stress the important part of the sentence.*

주어–동사 도치: 주어를 동사 뒤로 옮겨 문장의 중요 부분을 강조시킨다.

Regular word order

Jenny sprinted <u>up the porch stairs and into the kitchen</u>, followed seconds later by her younger brother, Josh, beaming with excitement.①

Inverted word order

<u>Up the porch stairs and into the kitchen</u> sprinted Jenny, followed seconds later by her younger brother, Josh, beaming with excitement.②

b Subject-Verb-Direct Object Shift: *Move the object before the subject. This effect puts more emphasis on the object.*

주어–동사–직접목적어 도치: 목적어를 주어 앞으로 옮기면 목적어 강조 효과가 있다.

Regular word order

I cannot believe <u>that Joseph lost the race in the last three meters</u>.[1]

Inverted word order

<u>That Joseph lost the race in the last three meters</u>, I cannot believe.[2]

c **Adverb-Verb Shift**: *Clauses that begin with* **negative adverbs** *or* **adverb phrases** *(e.g.: barely, hardly, rarely, scarcely, seldom, never, no sooner, not for many months) use inverted word order. This effect makes the sentence sound both more formal and more dramatic.*

부사 −동사의 도치: 부정 부사(구) 또는 부사(구)로 시작하는 절은 어순이 도치되었을 때 더욱 격식 있고 극적으로 들린다.

Form: *Negative adverb + simple form of be (or first auxiliary) + subject*

<u>Never before</u> **was I** so happy to jump into my warm bed.[1]
← I was never before so happy to jump into my warm bed.

<u>Never before</u> **have we** witnessed such a fine display of sportsmanship.[2]
← We have never before witnessed such a fine display of sportsmanship.

<u>Very deliberately</u> **did they arrange** the Christmas presents beneath the tree.[3]
← They arranged the Christmas presents beneath the tree very deliberately.

d *So … that can also be used with inverted word order.*

so … that 또한 도치된 어순으로 쓸 수 있다.

<u>So exhausted</u> **were we** <u>that</u> we fell asleep at once.[1]
← We were **so** exhausted **that** we fell asleep at once.

<u>So strange</u> **was Steve's question** <u>that</u> I couldn't answer.[2]
← Steve's question was **so** strange **that** I couldn't answer.

<u>So difficult</u> **is the test** <u>that</u> students need a full year to prepare for it.[3]
← The test is **so** difficult **that** students need a full year to prepare for it.

EXERCISES

정답 및 해설 P. 29

A 우리말과 같은 뜻이 되도록 괄호 안에 주어진 단어를 알맞게 배열하시오.

1 부엌 바닥에 온통 포도 주스를 쏟은 것은 마크였지, 내가 아니야!
(Mark / it / not me! / all over the kitchen floor, / was / who spilled grape juice)

→ _____

2 기중기를 넘어뜨린 것은 강한 바람과 과도하게 무거운 짐의 결합이었다.
(was / the crane to topple over / a combination of high winds / what caused / and an excessively heavy load)

→ _____

3 당신의 집의 모든 표면에는 수백만의 작고, 안 보이는 병균들이 숨어서 포착되기를 기다리고 있다.
(lurking on every surface / there / just waiting to be picked up, / are / millions of tiny, / invisible germs / of your home)

→ _____

4 오늘 아침 나를 일찍 깨운 것은 내 호텔 창문 밖에서 과일을 파는 행상인들의 소리였다.
(woke me up / was / what / the noise from the fruit vendors / early this morning / hawking their wares outside my hotel window)

→ _____

> topple over
> 무너지다, 쓰러지다
> combination 결합
> excessively
> 과다하게, 지나치게
> lurk 숨다
> surface 표면
> tiny 작은
> invisible 보이지 않는
> vendor 노점상, 행상인
> hawk one's wares
> 돌아다니며 상품을 팔다

B 〈보기〉와 같이 밑줄 친 단어를 강조하는 문장으로 바꿔 쓰시오.

> **보기** Mark ordered a piping hot bowl of hearty beef stew <u>at a Korean restaurant in the mall</u>.
> → ___It was at a Korean restaurant in the mall that[where]___
> ___Mark ordered a piping hot bowl of hearty beef stew.___

> piping 아주 뜨거운
> ingredient 재료, 요소
> get in touch with
> ~와 연락하다
> choke collar 개 목걸이
> passerby 행인

1 Three billion humans eat <u>rice</u> as the main ingredient for their meals.

→ _____

2 Daniel finally got in touch with me <u>last week</u> about starting a photography club.

→ _____

3 The tiny black dog wearing a red choke collar suddenly bit the passerby <u>on the ankle</u>.

→ _____

offend ~을 화나게 하다
scarcely 겨우, 간신히
get out of ~에서 나오다
importance 중요성
step into ~에 들어서다

C 〈보기〉와 같이 밑줄 친 부분을 강조하는 문장으로 바꿔 쓰시오.

> 보기   I had <u>never</u> been so offended.
> → Never ＿＿＿＿＿＿＿ had I been so offended ＿＿＿＿＿＿＿.

1 I had <u>scarcely</u> got out of bed when the doorbell rang.
→ Scarcely ＿＿＿＿＿＿＿＿＿＿＿＿＿＿＿＿.

2 Samuel <u>rarely</u> hears such words of praise from his teacher.
→ Rarely ＿＿＿＿＿＿＿＿＿＿＿＿＿＿＿＿.

3 I <u>little</u> understood the importance of what my mother was saying at the time.
→ Little ＿＿＿＿＿＿＿＿＿＿＿＿＿＿＿＿.

4 I had <u>no sooner</u> made a bowl of noodles for myself when my sister walked into the kitchen.
→ No sooner ＿＿＿＿＿＿＿＿＿＿＿＿＿＿.

5 Ms. Park had <u>hardly</u> stepped into the classroom when her students jumped out of their seats and yelled, "Surprise!"
→ Hardly ＿＿＿＿＿＿＿＿＿＿＿＿＿＿
＿＿＿＿＿＿＿＿＿＿＿＿＿＿＿＿＿＿＿＿.

extremely 대단히, 몹시
celebrate 축하하다
experienced
노련한, 숙련된
surfer 파도타기하는 사람
dare ~할 용기가 있다
brave
~을 용감히 대면하다

D 〈보기〉와 같이 도치된 문장을 원래의 어순으로 바꿔 쓰시오.

> 보기   <u>An extremely handsome boyfriend</u> you have!
> → ＿＿＿ You have an extremely handsome boyfriend! ＿＿＿

1 <u>In first place</u> are the Boston Red Sox.
→ ＿＿＿＿＿＿＿＿＿＿＿＿＿＿＿＿＿＿＿

2 <u>So happy</u> was Mr. Kim that he took us all out to celebrate.
→ ＿＿＿＿＿＿＿＿＿＿＿＿＿＿＿＿＿＿＿

3 <u>Dry weather</u> it may be, but isn't it a nice change from all that rain?
→ ＿＿＿＿＿＿＿＿＿＿＿＿＿＿＿＿＿＿＿

4 <u>So high</u> were the waves that only the most experienced surfers dared to brave them.
→ ＿＿＿＿＿＿＿＿＿＿＿＿＿＿＿＿＿＿＿

Common Sentence Errors

Student writers often make mistakes in their first drafts that can be self-corrected through careful revising and editing. Be on the lookout for the following common sentence errors.

다음은 학생들이 자주 범하는 문장 오류들이다. 이런 실수들은 꼼꼼히 다시 읽고 교정하는 과정을 통해 스스로 고칠 수 있다.

FOCUS

1 *Student writers sometimes make mistakes using* **coordinating conjunctions**.

학생들은 등위 접속사 사용에 있어서 다음과 같은 실수를 한다.

a *Joining two main clauses with a comma, but without a coordinating conjunction. This is called a* **comma splice:**

콤마의 오용(誤用): 두 개의 주절을 등위 접속사를 사용하지 않고, 콤마로 연결한다.

Martin has won the World Championship since 2016, **and** he will win next year too.[①]

(✕) Martin has won the World Championship since 2016, he will win next year too.

b *Joining two main clauses with no punctuation at all. This is called a* **run-on sentence:**

무종지문(無終止文): 두 개의 주절을 아무런 문장 부호 없이 연결한다.

→ Professional athletes earn high salaries, **but** their careers are often very brief.[①]

c *Additionally, when you list three (or more) items in a series, it is generally a good idea to use a comma before the coordinating conjunction:*

셋 이상의 항목들을 나열할 경우, 일반적으로 등위 접속사 전에 콤마를 사용하는 것이 좋다.

Swamps are dominated by woody plants, small trees, **and** shrubs.[①]

2 *Student writers also make mistakes using* **subordinating conjunctions**.

학생들은 종속 접속사 사용에 있어서 다음과 같은 실수를 한다.

a *Punctuating a dependent clause as though it were a full sentence. This is called a* **fragment:**

단절된 문장: 마치 완전한 문장인 것처럼 종속절에 문장 부호를 붙인다.

A flock of birds will fly in a "V" shaped pattern **because** it is the most efficient way to travel.[①]

→ **Because** it is the most efficient way to travel, a flock of birds will fly in a "V" shaped pattern.

(✕) A flock of birds will fly in a "V" shaped pattern. ~~Because~~ it is the most efficient way to travel.

b *Using the wrong subordinator:* 잘못된 종속접속사를 사용한다.

Susan studied hard for her final exams **because** it is very important that she does well on them.[1]

(✗) Susan studied hard for her final exams ~~although~~ it is very important that she does well on them.

Because *introduces a dependent clause which must be connected to a full sentence.*

because로 시작하는 문장은 종속절이므로 반드시 주절과 연결되어야 한다.

3 *Good writers use* **parallel structure**; *that is, they put words, phrases, and clauses into a similar form. Using parallel structure will make your writing easier to read.*

단어와 단어, 구와 구, 절과 절을 같은 종류의 형태로 놓는 병렬 구조를 사용하면 독자들이 글을 더 쉽게 읽을 수 있다.

Stacey's new boyfriend is **tall, muscular, and handsome.**[1] (parallel adjectives)

(✗) Stacey's new boyfriend is ~~tall, muscular, and wears nice clothes.~~

The students were asked to dictate the passage **quickly, accurately, and thoroughly.**[2] (parallel adverbs)

(✗) The students were asked to dictate the passage ~~quickly, accurately, and in a detailed way.~~

My e-pal said that she likes **camping, cooking, and playing squash.** (parallel gerunds)

My e-pal said that she likes **to camp, (to) cook, and (to) play squash.**[3] (parallel infinitives)

(✗) My e-pal said that she likes ~~camping, cooking, and to play squash.~~

I will take either **the express bus** or **the KTX** to Busan this weekend.[4] (parallel noun phrases)

(✗) I will either ~~take the express bus or the KTX~~ to Busan this weekend.

Exercising and **eating** well will help you maintain a healthy complexion.[5] (parallel verb phrases)

(✗) ~~An exercise program and eating well~~ will help you maintain a healthy complexion.

As Jiho made more friends and **as he learned more English,** he began to love living in the UK.[6]
(parallel adverbial clauses)

4 *A* **dangling modifier** *is a phrase or clause that doesn't modify what it intends to because words are left out. A* **misplaced modifier** *is a word or phrase that causes confusion because it is not placed close enough to the word(s) it is supposed to modify.*

현수 수식어(dangling modifier): 단어가 생략되어 수식할 요소가 없는 구 또는 절
수식어 오류(misplaced modifier): 수식하고자 하는 말 가까이에 있지 않아 혼동을 주는 단어 또는 구

a *The subject of the main clause is the understood subject of the adverbial clause.*

부사절의 의미상 주어는 주절의 주어와 같아야 한다.

While talking on the phone with his mother, **Steve** heard the doorbell ring.[1]

(✗) While talking on the phone with his mother, the doorbell rang.

(Who was talking on the phone? *NOT* the doorbell)

b *When a verb phrase opens the sentence, the subject of the main clause is the understood subject of the opening verb phrase.*

동사구로 문장이 시작될 때도 동사구의 의미상 주어와 주절의 주어가 일치해야 한다.

Reaching the top of the mountain just before sunset, **we** enjoyed the spectacular view.①

(×) Reaching the top of the mountain just before sunset, the view was spectacular.

To succeed in college, **you** should maintain a regular study schedule.②

(×) To succeed in college, a regular study schedule is important.

c *Other modifiers — especially* **prepositional phrases** *and the words* **almost, even, just, nearly,** *and* **only** *— should be placed as close to the words they modify as possible to avoid confusion.*

전치사구 및 almost, even, just, nearly, only와 같은 부사는 혼동을 피하기 위해 대체로 수식하는 어구 가까이에 쓴다.

A young girl **in a blue skirt** was walking her dog.①

(×) A young girl was walking her dog in a blue skirt.

Here in the English Zone, students speak **only** English.②

(×) Here in the English Zone, students only speak English.

Samuel ate **nearly** a whole box of crackers after school today.③

(×) Samuel nearly ate a whole box of crackers after school today.

Chris gave us **only** one hour of writing homework to do this weekend.④

(×) Chris only gave us one hour of writing homework to do this weekend.

After I had written **almost** two pages, the buzzer sounded and I put down my pen.⑤

(×) After I had almost written two pages, the buzzer sounded and I put down my pen.

---

1 a ① 마틴은 2016년 이후로 세계 선수권 대회에서 우승해왔고, 내년에도 우승할 것이다. b ① 전문 운동선수들은 높은 연봉을 받지만, 흔히 그들의 선수 생활은 매우 짧다. c ① 늪은 울창한 나무, 작은 나무, 관목으로 가득 차 있다. 2 a ① 새의 무리는 이동하기에 가장 효율적이기 때문에 'V' 모양으로 난다. b ① 수잔은 시험을 잘 보는 것이 매우 중요하기 때문에 기말시험을 위해 열심히 공부했다. 3 ① 스테이시의 새 남자친구는 키가 크고, 근육질이며, 잘생겼다. ② 학생들은 문단을 빠르고, 정확하고, 완전하게 받아 적어야 했다. ③ 나의 이메일 친구는 캠프, 요리, 스쿼시 하는 것을 좋아한다고 말했다. ④ 나는 이번 주말에 부산까지 고속버스나 KTX를 타고 갈 것이다. ⑤ 운동하는 것과 잘 먹는 것은 건강한 피부를 유지하도록 도와줄 것이다. ⑥ 지호가 더 많은 친구를 만들고, 영어를 더 많이 배울수록 그는 영국에서 사는 것을 좋아하기 시작했다. 4 a ① 스티브는 어머니와 전화 통화를 하던 중에 초인종 소리를 들었다. b ① 해가 지기 바로 전에 산의 정상에 도달해서 우리는 멋진 경관을 감상했다. ② 대학에서 성공하려면 너는 학습 일정을 잘 지켜야 한다. c ① 파란 치마를 입은 어린 소녀가 자신의 개를 산책시키고 있었다. ② 여기 English Zone에서 학생들은 영어로만 말한다. ③ 사무엘은 방과 후 과자 한 상자를 거의 다 먹었다. ④ 크리스는 이번 주말에 한 시간 정도만 하면 되는 쓰기 숙제를 내주었다. ⑤ 나는 약 두 쪽을 쓰고서, 종료하는 벨이 울려서 펜을 내려놓았다.

EXERCISES

neat 깔끔한
accurately 정확하게
mow (잔디를) 깎다
lawn 잔디
trim ~을 다듬다
hedge 울타리
muscular 근육질의
barely 거의 ~않다
principal 교장 선생님
calm down 진정하다
come up with
~을 찾아내다, 생각해내다
disappear 사라지다

A 문장을 읽고 밑줄 친 부분을 바르게 고쳐 문장을 다시 쓰시오.

1 Tina's homework is always both neat and <u>accurately</u>.

→ _____

2 Jeff and I mowed the <u>lawn and</u> Luke trimmed the hedges.

→ _____

3 Grandpa is a slow <u>walker but</u> he is still quite muscular for his age.

→ _____

4 Ralph gave it all he <u>could but</u> he kicked the ball barely three yards.

→ _____

5 We didn't win the relay race at the track and <u>field meet but</u> we didn't care.

→ _____

6 The trip to Orlando and Tampa was a delight for <u>us for</u> we had a great time.

→ _____

7 The invitations will be sent tomorrow <u>but</u> the next day and will arrive in time for the event.

→ _____

8 The principal and the teachers were <u>shocked but</u> they soon calmed down and tried to come up with a solution.

→ _____

→ _____

9 The rabbit hopped and skipped about in the <u>yard, then</u> it squeezed its body under the fence and disappeared forever.

→ _____

→ _____

B 밑줄 친 부분을 바르게 고쳐 문장을 다시 쓰시오.

1 The goalie stood waving to the crowd in his net.

→ _____

2 Peter began separating the clothes piling up next to the washer.

→ _____

3 It was announced earlier in the week that IBM and Sun have together almost donated $500 million to the Gates Foundation this year alone.

→ _____

_____

4 The woman was carrying a French poodle and fiddling with her smartphone didn't even notice the taxi screech to a halt directly behind her.

→ _____

_____

C 밑줄 친 부분을 바르게 고쳐 문장을 다시 쓰시오.

1 Alexis exclaimed to everyone in earshot that her IQ was higher than Sue.

→ _____

2 Everyone in attendance agreed that the lecture was long and tediously.

→ _____

3 Barbara and Jeanne whispered and were giggling all night like schoolgirls on a sleepover.

→ _____

4 In her freshman composition class, Mina learned to read poems critically and appreciating good prose.

→ _____

5 After the first week, the student dorms were filled with torn banners, broken bottles, and the garbage bins overflowing.

→ _____

_____

Unit 33 Punctuation

KEY CONCEPTS

Punctuation helps writers control the rhythm and flow of their writing. When you use correct punctuation, your reader will be able to interpret your message clearly, as it was intended.

구두법은 글의 리듬과 흐름을 조절할 수 있도록 도와준다. 올바른 구두법을 사용하면 독자들은 작가가 의도한 대로 내용을 명확하게 알 수 있다.

FOCUS

1 **Periods**, **question marks**, *and* **exclamation points** *end sentences.* 마침표, 물음표, 느낌표는 문장을 끝낸다.

No actual black hole has ever been located or studied.①

Who was the first prime minister of England? Do you know?②

Don't put that hot frying pan down directly on the table. It will burn it!③

2 **Semicolons** *(;) connect two closely related sentences;* **colons** *(:) introduce explanations and lists.*

세미콜론(;)은 관계있는 두 문장을 연결하고, 콜론(:)은 설명이나 목록을 이끈다.

Jim took a part-time job; he needs the money to pay his college tuition.①

Some people prefer to write using a computer; others prefer to write by hand.②

The bedroom was painted three different colors: orange, blue, and green.③

James told his boss exactly what he wanted: a pay raise and two extra weeks of vacation.④

3 *In addition to joining two independent clauses with the help of a coordinating conjunction,* **commas** *are used.* 콤마는 두 독립절을 등위 접속사로 연결할 때 이외에도 사용된다.

a *to set off introductory words, phrases, and clauses:* 도입어, 구, 그리고 절을 구분하기 위해

Usually, American college students choose a major in their junior year.①

During a tornado's "mature" stage, the funnel reaches its greatest width.②

Although most archeologists believe that Native Americans originally came from Asia, many Native Americans themselves dispute this theory.③

b *to set off nonessential information and appositives:* 필수적이지 않은 정보와 동격을 구분하기 위해

The beaver, <u>which is one of Canada's national symbols</u>, is actually a large rodent.[1]

Leslie Snow, <u>a psychology professor</u>, wrote *The Science of Mind*.[2]

c *before transitional words and expressions:* 연결어와 연결 표현 전에

<u>For example</u>, Taylor is the old English spelling of the word tailor.[1]

d *between items in a series of three or more:* 셋 이상의 항목을 나열하기 위해

John and his brother quickly packed up their <u>tent</u>, <u>sleeping bags</u>, and <u>fishing poles</u>.[1]

---

1 ① 실제로 블랙홀의 위치가 발견되거나 연구된 적은 없다. ② 누가 영국의 최초 수상이었니? 너는 아니? ③ 그 뜨거운 프라이팬을 식탁에 바로 놓지 마. 탈거야! 2 ① 짐은 아르바이트를 구했다. 그는 자기의 대학 등록금을 내려면 돈이 필요하다. ② 몇몇 사람들은 컴퓨터를 사용해 글을 쓰는 것을 선호한다. 다른 이들은 손으로 쓰는 것을 선호한다. ③ 그 침실은 오렌지, 파랑, 초록의 세 가지 다른 색으로 칠해져 있었다. ④ 제임스는 그의 상사에게 그가 원하는 것인 월급 인상과 두 주의 추가 휴가를 정확히 말했다. 3 a ① 대개, 미국 대학생들은 3학년 때 전공을 선택한다. ② 토네이도는 '성숙' 단계에서 깔때기 모양이 최대의 넓이에 도달한다. ③ 고고학자 대부분은 미국의 인디언들이 원래 아시아에서 왔다고 믿지만, 많은 미국의 인디언들은 이 이론에 이의를 제기한다. b ① 캐나다의 국가적 상징 중 하나인 비버는 실제로는 정말로 큰 쥐이다. ② 심리학 교수인 레슬리 스노우는 '정신과학'이라는 책을 썼다. c ① 예를 들어, Taylor는 tailor(재단사)라는 단어의 고대 영어 철자이다. d ① 존과 그의 남동생은 자기들의 텐트와 침낭, 낚싯대를 재빨리 챙겼다.

EXERCISES

정답 및 해설 P. 31

A 필요한 곳에 콤마를 써넣어 문장을 다시 쓰시오.

exhaust ~을 몹시 지치다
journey 여행
relieve ~을 안심시키다
alumnus 졸업생
commencement
ceremony 졸업식

1 After the long and exhausting journey we were all so relieved to be finally home.

→ _____

2 Unlike in the past the people of India can now travel cheaply by rail water or air.

→ _____

3 I love a meal of fresh garden salad spaghetti and meat balls and chocolate cake for dessert.

→ _____

4 Steve Jobs an alumnus of the college spoke to the graduating class at the commencement ceremony.

→ _____
_____

B 밑줄 친 단어 뒤에 알맞은 문장 부호를 써넣어 문장을 다시 쓰시오.

silence 침묵
personality 성격
merit 장점
optimism 낙천주의
consideration 배려
decoration 장식

1 There was a sudden silence in the <u>classroom</u> everyone was shocked by the <u>news</u>

→ _____

2 My new girlfriend has three personality <u>merits</u> <u>optimism</u> <u>cheerfulness</u> and <u>consideration</u>

→ _____

3 A: How lovely your Christmas decorations <u>are</u>
B: Do you like <u>them</u> I made them <u>myself</u>

→ _____
_____

4 A: I heard on the radio that tomorrow will be a <u>sunny</u> warm <u>day</u>
B: <u>Great</u> Shall we go to the <u>pool</u>

→ _____
_____

170

REVIEW

정답 및 해설 P. 31

schedule 일정
tight 빡빡한
teenager 10대 청소년

A 다음 빈칸에 들어갈 가장 알맞은 것을 고르시오.

1 A: If you have time, visit your sister while you're in Busan.

B: My schedule is pretty tight, _____ I have a group project.

① but   ② and   ③ or   ④ nor

2 A: Justin, do you still have that golf training DVD I lent you?

B: Yes, I do. Sorry. _____ you don't mind, I'll return it to you next week. I haven't watched it yet.

① Because   ② Before   ③ If   ④ Unless

3 A: Is your friend Soojin still coming to visit this summer?

B: I hope so. She's like most teenagers. She likes _____.

① to hang out and watch movies   ② to hanging out and watching movies

③ to hang out and watching movies   ④ to hanging out and watch movies

B 다음 문장을 읽고, 어법상 바르지 <u>않은</u> 문장을 고르시오.

at a premium
구하기 힘든, 지나치게 비싼
patience 인내
crawl 기어가다
deliberately
조심성 있게, 신중하게
meow 야옹하고 울다
phonology 음운론
syntax 구문론
disorder 혼란, 장애
uptake 활용
inhibitor 억제제
contain ~을 포함하다
obscure
이해하기 힘든, 애매한
terminology 전문 용어
redundant 해고되는

1 ① To raise a pet in the city, where space is at a premium, patience is needed.

② Crawling slowly and deliberately across the floor, Carrie finally reached the toy.

③ After eating all of her cat food, Moxie meowed for more; she is such a little pig.

④ Having taught phonology every semester for the last five years, Daniel was eager to teach syntax.

2 ① Nancy called her boyfriend in Tokyo because she missed him.

② Both John and Roger wants to do really well on their history exam next week.

③ Most stress related disorders can be treated with serotonin-uptake inhibitors.

④ Even advanced learners' dictionaries do not contain obscure technical terminology; however, they do contain lots of other useful information for students studying a language.

3 ① After washing his new sports car, Steve waxed it.

② When taking a grammar quiz, concentration is everything.

③ To complete the project by the due date, you and your partners will have to begin at once.

④ Having worked for the company his whole life, Stuart was shocked to learn that he had been made redundant.

REVIEW PLUS

정답 및 해설 P. 32

 다음을 읽고, 바르지 <u>않은</u> 문장을 고르시오.

1

| consequently |
| 결과적으로 |
| extraordinarily |
| 엄청나게 |
| entertain |
| ~을 즐겁게 해주다, 접대하다 |
| unaware |
| ~을 눈치 못 채는 |
| burden 짐 |

My sister-in-law "Pat" works for the airlines, and she gets to fly for free. Consequently, she has been visiting us a lot lately. ① She stays in our house, never rents a car, and gives little notice of her visits. ② Pat's father lives near us, and he is getting older, so she wants to see him. ③ The problem is that both my husband and I live extraordinarily busy lives, we are taking care of Dad, too. And then Pat shows up, expecting to be entertained. ④ Don't get me wrong; Pat is very sweet, but I can't understand how she can be so unaware. How do I let Pat know she has become a burden without hurting her feelings?

2

| pandemic |
| 전국적인 유행병 |
| alert ~에 경보를 발하다 |
| measure 조치 |
| demonstrate |
| ~을 입증하다 |
| seriousness 심각함 |
| threat 위협 |
| swine 돼지 |
| contend ~와 논쟁하다 |
| slaughter 도살 |
| despite ~에도 불구하고 |
| ironically 풍자적으로 |

The World Health Organization recently raised its global pandemic alert from level five to its second highest level. ① While this measure demonstrates the seriousness of the threat facing the world from the spread of swine flu, others contend that countries have gone too far. ② For example, Egypt has ordered the slaughter of all 300,000 of its pigs despite there being no evidence that pigs spread the disease. ③ In Britain, with fewer than a dozen cases, health officials are planning to procure some 32 million masks. ④ And in Mexico, the government there are advising people to stop kissing. Ironically, world health experts say many of these measures may not stop the disease from spreading at all.

3

| overcome ~을 극복하다 |
| weigh 무게가 ~ 나가다 |
| shed (눈물 등을) 흘리다 |
| bride 신부 |
| traditional |
| 전통의, 전통적인 |
| indulge ~에 빠지다 |
| remain |
| 여전히 (~의 상태로) 남다 |

Have you ever faced a challenge that you thought was too big, too tough, or just too difficult to overcome? ① Before you throw in the towel or raise the white flag, consider the case of Manuel Uribe, who, until recently, held the Guinness World Records title of the Heaviest Man in the World. ② On October 26, he married his longtime sweetheart after years of diet, exercise, and to take medical care. ③ Uribe, who once weighed more than 1,200 pounds, lost more than 550 pounds before the wedding. ④ Shedding tears during the ceremony, Uribe and his bride later enjoyed the traditional "first dance," but he didn't indulge in any wedding cake, choosing instead to remain on his diet.

B 다음 (A), (B), (C)에서 어법에 맞는 표현으로 가장 적절한 것을 고르시오. [기출 응용]

Frodo woke and found himself lying in bed. At first he thought that he had slept late, after a long unpleasant dream that still hovered on the edge of memory. Or perhaps he had been ill? But the ceiling looked (A) _____ : it was flat, and it had dark, richly carved beams. He lay a little while longer looking at patches of sunlight on the wall and (B) _____ to the sound of the waterfall. "Where am I, and what is the time?" he said aloud to the ceiling. "In the House of Elrond, and it is ten o'clock in the morning," said a voice. There was the old wizard, (C) _____ in a chair by the open window.

(A)		(B)		(C)
① strangely	…	listened	…	sitting
② strangely	…	listening	…	sat
③ strangely	…	listened	…	sat
④ strange	…	listening	…	sat
⑤ strange	…	listening	…	sitting

C 다음 글의 밑줄 친 부분 중, 어법상 바르지 않은 것을 고르시오. [기출 응용]

Television has played a major role in the creation of adult-like children. ① Before the electronic age, children received much of their social information from the books they read. Children read children's books ② containing information appropriate to a child's level of understanding. Adult information was contained in adult books, ③ which children did not read. Today, children have access to adult information through television. Children are exposed to adult situations ④ and adult views of life. Many social scientists hold that the removal of the barriers between child information and adult information ⑤ have pushed children into the adult world too early.

WRITING PRACTICE

정답 및 해설 P. 32

A Rewrite the sentences focusing on the underlined words. Use the words in parentheses.

1 I listened to the whole album. What I heard sounded great! (almost)

→ _____

2 Because I am on a diet, I ate one donut and ignored the other three on the table. (only)

→ _____

3 The faulty alarm system in my apartment complex went off five times yesterday. (nearly)

→ _____

4 For homework, Professor Willis made us read three chapters that covered the entire history of the Art Deco movement. (almost)

→ _____

_____

B Combine the sentences using the given words in parentheses. Add commas if necessary.

1 Sue was running across the floor. The rug slipped and she lost her balance and fell. (as)

→ _____

2 I was walking along the beach. The hot sand burned my feet on my way to get a massage. (as)

→ _____

3 We watched the squirrels. They built their nests high up in the spruce trees that lined the street. (while)

→ _____

4 The nervous rookie pilot climbed into the cockpit. He adjusted his view finder. He attached his oxygen mask. He flashed a "thumbs-up" sign to the controller. (and)

→ _____

_____

C Rearrange the words in the correct order.

1 is / that / I / find / it / most enjoyable / learning English / nowadays

→ _____

2 most about your brother, / what I like / is / his dry sense of humor / Jeremy,

→ _____

3 have / as well informed as / never / thanks to / people / been / they are now, / the Internet

→ _____

4 and variety of fresh vegetables / we have grown / most about Korea / what / to love / is / the endless supply

→ _____

D Add punctuation marks where and if necessary.

1 Older television sets had tubes the newest models which take less space are digital

→ _____

2 My daughter Jean has solo backpacked throughout the world for example Australia Brazil Canada and Russia

→ _____

3 Your first draft is really quite good However I might suggest that you add a few more specific details to your second paragraph

→ _____

_____

4 The reason why so many young people go off to college is to gain knowledge to prepare for a career and to have a good time but not necessarily in that order

→ _____

_____

MEMO

이것이 THIS IS 시리즈다!

THIS IS GRAMMAR 시리즈

▷ 중·고등 내신에 꼭 등장하는 어법 포인트 분석 및 총정리

강남인강
강의교재

THIS IS READING 시리즈

▷ 다양한 소재의 지문으로 내신 및 수능 완벽 대비

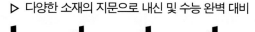

강남인강
강의교재

THIS IS VOCABULARY 시리즈

▷ 주제별로 분류한 교육부 권장 어휘

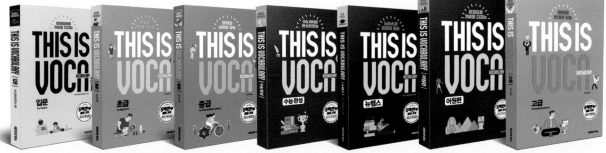

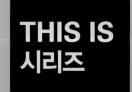

LEVEL CHART

NEXUS Edu

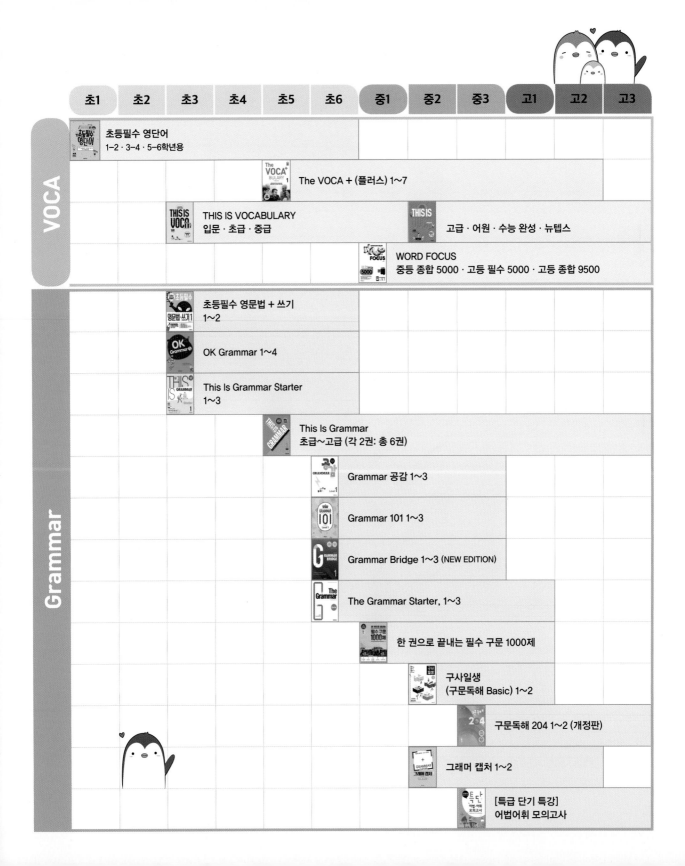

초1	초2	초3	초4	초5	초6	중1	중2	중3	고1	고2	고3

VOCA

- 초등필수 영단어 1-2 · 3-4 · 5-6학년용
- The VOCA + (플러스) 1~7
- THIS IS VOCABULARY 입문 · 초급 · 중급
- THIS IS 고급 · 어원 · 수능 완성 · 뉴텝스
- WORD FOCUS 중등 종합 5000 · 고등 필수 5000 · 고등 종합 9500

Grammar

- 초등필수 영문법 + 쓰기 1~2
- OK Grammar 1~4
- This Is Grammar Starter 1~3
- This Is Grammar 초급~고급 (각 2권: 총 6권)
- Grammar 공감 1~3
- Grammar 101 1~3
- Grammar Bridge 1~3 (NEW EDITION)
- The Grammar Starter, 1~3
- 한 권으로 끝내는 필수 구문 1000제
- 구사일생 (구문독해 Basic) 1~2
- 구문독해 204 1~2 (개정판)
- 그래머 캡처 1~2
- [특급 단기 특강] 어법어휘 모의고사

THIS IS GRAMMAR

Answers

넥서스영어교육연구소 지음

★원어민이 사용하는 생생한 문장들로 구성된 예문 ★내신, 토익, 토플, 텝스 등 각종 시험 완벽 대비, 이것이 **현대 영문법의 결정판**이다. ★단계별, 유형별로 구성된 연습문제와 리뷰문제

2

고급

NEXUS Edu

EXERCISES p. 9

A

1 on this bond at a rate of 7%
2 on location in the Swiss Alps
3 from your store the other day, properly
4 spontaneously, because of the high temperature and pressure
5 with the president, tomorrow morning at 10:15 a.m. Eastern Standard Time
6 quickly, to overtake the driver of the slow moving vehicle in front of him

해석

1 이 채권에 대한 이자는 7%가 붙을 것이다.
2 대부분의 모험 장면들은 스위스 알프스 산에서 야외 촬영으로 제작되었다.
3 일전에 당신의 가게에서 산 타일들은 제대로 붙지 않았어요.
4 높은 온도와 압력으로 인해 로켓 연료는 자연스럽게 점화되었다.
5 대통령과의 인터뷰는 동부 시간대로 내일 아침 열 시 십오 분에 방송될 것이다.
6 택시 운전사는 그의 앞에서 천천히 주행하는 운전자를 추월하기 위해 재빨리 속도를 냈다.

B

1 Could you fetch me a pair of scissors and some colored paper?
2 An immigration officer at the airport granted me an entry visa.
3 Our study group meeting is in the resource room on the third floor of the library.
4 This latest cross-border attack will exacerbate the already tense relations between the two countries.
5 The committee overseeing the selection process elected Dr. Reynolds Chair of the Physics Department.

 EXERCISES p. 12~13

A

1 but 2 or 3 and 4 and 5 but
6 or

해석

1 대부분의 농장 노동자들은 소를 계단에 오르게 하는 것은 가능하지만 다시 내려오게 하는 것은 가능하지 않다는 것을 안다.
2 이번 주 스콧을 보거나 그에게서 소식을 들었니? 난 그렇지 못해서 좀 걱정이 되기 시작해.
3 과학 실험실에서 위험한 화학물질은 조심스럽게 취급해야 하고, 사용 후에는 수납장에 넣어야 한다.

4 미야는 작문 주제를 읽고, 여러 아이디어를 브레인스토밍했으며, 45분 이내로 그녀의 답을 적었다.
5 우리는 휘발유가 다 떨어졌을 때 그 차를 버렸지만, 무슨 일이 있었는지를 설명하는 쪽지를 계기판에 확실히 남겨 두었다.
6 김 선생님께서 내게 실습실에 있는 컴퓨터나 여기에 있는 것을 사용해도 된다고 하셨다. 선생님께서는 내가 보고서를 정오까지 끝내기만 한다면 둘 중 어떤 방법이든 상관없다고 하셨다.

B

1 nor 2 so 3 nor 4 yet 5 for
6 yet

해석

1 헬렌도 그녀의 여동생도 나와 말하려고 하지 않는다.
2 크레이그가 아기들에게 아름다운 자장가를 불러주어서 아기들이 잠이 들었다.
3 내 남동생 게리는 운동하는 것을 싫어하고, 밖에서 시간을 보내는 것도 좋아하지 않는다.
4 수진이는 새로운 동료인 훈이를 알게 된 지 그렇게 오래된 것은 아니었지만, 그가 매우 친근하게 느껴졌다.
5 에버글레이즈 국립공원에서 하루 동안 트레킹을 한 후, 배가 고플 것을 알았기에 우리는 충분한 양의 점심을 쌌다.
6 쉐이키의 레스토랑은 동네에서 가장 맛있고, 가장 비싼데도 너는 항상 거기에서 점심을 먹고 싶어 하더라. 왜 그러니?

C

1 for 2 nor 3 and 4 yet

해석

1 콜린은 새 컴퓨터를 자기 힘으로 사고 싶기 때문에 열심히 일한다.
2 우리는 더 이상 우리의 고객에게 비닐봉지를 제공하지 않고, 주차권을 확인하지도 않을 것입니다.
3 허블 우주 망원경은 무게가 12톤에 길이가 43피트이며, 구축해서 지구 위의 궤도에 올리는 데 21억 달러가 들었다.
4 힘든 시기인 것은 알고 있었지만, 전 공장장인 미첼 씨가 예전 생산직 노동자들과 함께 실업 수당을 신청하는 것을 보고 매우 놀랐다.

D

1 but[yet] 2 but[yet] 3 and
4 and 5 yet[but] 6 but[yet]
7 yet[but]

해석

1 아까 누군가 전화로 헬렌을 찾았지만, 메시지를 남기려 하지는 않았다.
2 지금 당장 그의 이름이 생각나지는 않지만, 분명히 어디에선가 그를 본 적이 있다.
3 레슬리와 나는 일요일에 쇼핑을 가서 여름옷을 새로 살 예정이다.
4 광고업계는 속도감이 빠르고, 긴장을 요하며, 창의적인 아이디어를 끊임없이 요구하는 산업이다.
5 등대에서 강한 빛 한 줄기가 나왔지만, 그 배의 선장은 바위투성이 해안에서 배를 돌릴 수가 없었다.
6 직업이 목수인 존은 쉽게 오두막을 손수 개조할 수도 있었지만, 실직한 친구를 대신 고용했다.
7 종이를 일곱 번 이상 반으로 접을 수 없다는 것이 일반적인 통념이지만, 여러 경우에서 이 사실은 근거 없는 얘기로 밝혀졌다.

 A

1 when   2 but   3 and   4 or   5 than

해석

1 내가 일어서자마자 은행 창구 직원이 다음 손님에게 앞으로 오라고 했다.
2 캐서린은 지역 도서관에서 자원봉사를 할 뿐 아니라, 여러 어린이 자선단체에 아낌없이 기부한다.
3 주식과 채권 모두 올해 실적이 저조하다. 미래를 위해 돈을 투자할 적기이다.
4 오늘 밤의 특선 영화는 '마다가스카' 또는 '찰리와 초콜릿 공장'이야. 시간표를 확인해 보지 그래?
5 내가 새 컴퓨터를 사자마자 그 회사는 더 최신식의 빠른 모델이 다음 주부터 판매될 것이라고 발표했다.

 B

1 is   2 are   3 are   4 has to 5 have

해석

1 너나 제니퍼 둘 중 한 명은 이 프로젝트를 끝내야만 한다.
2 이 모델을 완성하기 위해서는 풀과 쇠줄 둘 다 있어야 한다.
3 그 신문의 칼럼니스트들과 편집자 모두 파업을 할 것이다.
4 환경 또는 경제적 자극 중 하나가 우선 순위가 되어야 한다.
5 동네에 있는 도서관과 서점 모두 내가 읽고 싶은 소설책이 없다.

 C

1 or   2 but also   3 whether
4 nor   5 had I

해석

1 우리는 더 빨리 걷거나 택시를 타야 한다.
2 그날은 아름다운 날이었을 뿐만 아니라 겨울의 첫날이었다.
3 나는 샘이 그 영화를 전에 봤는지 안 봤는지 모르겠어.
4 호텔 밖에서 기다리는 관중은 많지도 그다지 열정적이지도 않았다.
5 내가 창문을 열자마자, 큰 땅벌이 방 안으로 날아들어 왔다.

 D

1 or   2 nor   3 and   4 but

해석

1 나의 사촌 니콜은 가을에 UC버클리나 하버드에 갈 것이다.
2 매니저와 주위를 돌아다니고 있는 웨이터들 중 그 누구도 우리의 주문을 받으려고 하지 않는 것처럼 보인다.
3 환경 파괴를 막고 싶다면 개인과 국가 모두 에너지를 어떻게 쓰는지에 대해 다시 생각해봐야 할 것이다.
4 잘 만들어진 관광 지도는 A에서 B까지 가는 방법을 알려 줄 뿐 아니라, 가는 길에 있는 흥미로운 장소도 표시해 주어야 한다.

 E

1 not only develops a child's curiosity but also fosters a sense of responsibility

2 Either help us put up these posters for the school dance, or stop pestering us and let us finish before we run out of time.
3 both invented the telephone and set a world water-speed record of over seventy miles an hour
4 neither smart enough to perform complex operations nor disciplined enough to remain focused on the task at hand

해석

1 애완동물을 키우는 것은 어린이의 호기심을 발달시켜 준다. 이는 또한 책임감을 키워 준다.
→ 애완동물을 키우는 것은 어린이의 호기심을 발달시켜줄 뿐 아니라 책임감을 키워 준다.
2 학교 댄스파티에 포스터 붙이는 것을 도와줘라, 아니면 시간이 다 되기 전에 끝마칠 수 있도록 방해하지 마라.
→ 학교 댄스파티에 포스터 붙이는 것을 도와주든가 시간이 다 되기 전에 끝마칠 수 있도록 방해하지 마라.
3 생전에, 알렉산더 그레이엄 벨은 전화기를 발명했다. 그는 또한 시속 70마일이 넘는 세계 수상 스피드 기록을 세웠다.
→ 생전에, 알렉산더 그레이엄 벨은 전화기를 발명했고 시속 70마일이 넘는 세계 수상 스피드 기록을 세웠다.
4 포괄적인 훈련에 앞서, 이 개들은 복잡한 활동을 할 정도로 똑똑하지 않다. 또한 그들은 지시된 일에 집중할 정도로 훈련되어 있지도 않다.
→ 포괄적인 훈련에 앞서, 이 개들은 복잡한 활동을 할 정도로 똑똑하지도 않고 지시된 일에 집중할 정도로 훈련되어 있지도 않다.

 A

1 ⓒ, how he can get one of those new electronic passports
2 ⓐ, even though they had not seen each other for many years
3 ⓒ, that International Business Machines (IBM) coined the term word processor in 1964
4 ⓑ, which stands stoically atop a small hill overlooking the village
5 ⓑ, whose new product won the industrial design competition held last month in Geneva

해석

1 박 씨는 새로운 전자 여권을 어떻게 발급받을 수 있는지 알아내야 한다.
2 두 형제는 여러 해 동안 서로를 본 적이 없었지만, 단번에 서로를 알아보았다.
3 오늘 수업에서 우리는 국제 사무기기(IBM)가 1964년에 "워드 프로세서"라는 단어를 만들었다는 것을 배웠다.
4 무너져 가는 중세 성은 마을이 내려다보이는 작은 언덕 위에 의연히 서 있는데, 몇 마일 떨어져서도 보인다.
5 새로운 제품으로 지난달 제네바에서 개최된 산업 디자인 대회에서 상을 받은 그 회사는 직원들에게 특별한 저녁을 제공하며 이 일을 축하하고 있다.

B

1 You would not believe me even if I told you the truth.
또는 Even if I told you the truth, you would not believe me.

2 Do you know whether the stores at the mall are open today?

3 You cannot become an expert diver until you dive professionally for several years.
또는 Until you dive professionally for several years, you cannot become an expert diver.

4 Although it was well past 2:00 a.m., neither Mark nor his wife, Kate, felt the least bit tired.
또는 Neither Mark nor his wife, Kate, felt the least bit tired although it was well past 2:00 a.m.

5 After she earned her degree in education, Ms. Mills started teaching high school geography at Centennial Collegiate.
또는 Ms. Mills started teaching high school geography at Centennial Collegiate after she earned her degree in education.

해석

1 너는 나를 믿으려 하지 않았다. 나는 너에게 사실을 말했다.
→ 내가 사실을 말했지만, 너는 나를 믿으려 하지 않았다.

2 너는 아니? 오늘 쇼핑몰에 있는 상점들이 문을 열었니?
→ 오늘 쇼핑몰에 있는 상점들이 문을 열었는지 아니?

3 너는 전문 잠수부가 될 수 없다. 너는 몇 년간 전문적으로 잠수해야 한다.
→ 너는 몇 년간 전문적으로 잠수할 때까지는 전문 잠수부가 될 수 없다.

4 새벽 두 시가 훨씬 넘은 시간이었다. 마크나 그의 아내 케이트는 전혀 피곤하지 않았다.
→ 새벽 두 시가 훨씬 넘었지만, 마크나 그의 아내 케이트는 전혀 피곤하지 않았다.

5 그녀는 교육학 학위를 받았다. 밀즈 양은 센테니얼 콜레지에이트 고등학교에서 지리학을 가르치기 시작했다.
→ 교육학 학위를 받은 후, 밀즈 양은 센테니얼 콜레지에이트 고등학교에서 지리학을 가르치기 시작했다.

 EXERCISES p. 23

 A

1 moreover
2 Likewise
3 However
4 Nonetheless
5 Hence
6 Nevertheless

해석

1 맷 데이먼은 미국의 실력 있는 배우이며 똑똑하기까지 하다.

2 음식은 맛있었다. 이와 마찬가지로, 서비스도 뛰어났다.

3 제인의 새로운 사무 보조원은 친절하다. 하지만 그녀는 약간 건망증이 있다.

4 우리 할아버지는 아흔 살이 다 되셨다. 그럼에도 불구하고, 그의 정신은 여전히 활동적이고 그의 나이 절반 정도 되는 남자와 같은 평안한 마음을 가지고 있다.

5 에베레스트 베이스캠프에서는 흔한 흐린 날이 또다시 찾아왔다. 그래서 우리는 산의 맑은 풍경을 볼 수 없었다.

6 스미스 씨가 크리스틴이 해주었으면 하는 일은 그녀에게 완전히 낯설었다. 그렇지만, 그렇게 어려워 보이지는 않았다.

 B

1 Maria studied for many months. Consequently, she knew the material thoroughly.

2 I would rather travel to Canterbury by train. However, the bus leaves earlier, and it's cheaper.

3 This smartphone has more storage capacity. Moreover, it also comes with a built-in Bluetooth headset.

4 Nell applied herself conscientiously during practice. As a result, she performed well at the recital.

5 Namhee is well-educated. Besides, she has very good manners.

해석

1 마리아는 몇 달간 공부해서 자료들을 완벽히 알았다.
→ 마리아는 몇 달간 공부했다. 그 결과, 그녀는 자료들을 완벽히 알았다.

2 나는 차라리 기차로 캔터베리에 가겠지만, 버스가 더 일찍 출발하고 더 저렴하다.
→ 나는 차라리 기차로 캔터베리에 가겠다. 하지만 버스가 더 일찍 출발하고 더 저렴하다.

3 이 스마트폰은 저장 용량이 더 크고, 내장된 블루투스 헤드셋도 딸려 있다.
→ 이 스마트폰은 저장 용량이 더 크다. 게다가, 내장된 블루투스 헤드셋도 딸려 있다.

4 넬은 연습에 성실하게 전념해서 연주회에서 훌륭히 공연했다.
→ 넬은 연습에 성실하게 전념했다. 그 결과, 그녀는 연주회에서 훌륭히 공연했다.

5 남희는 교육을 잘 받았고, 매우 예의 바르다.
→ 남희는 교육을 잘 받았다. 게다가, 매우 예의 바르다.

REVIEW
p. 24

 A

1 ③
2 ④
3 ②

해설/해석

1 "공부를 마친 후에 무엇을 하고 싶니?"라는 의미로 문맥상 after가 가장 적절
A: 공부를 마친 후에 무엇을 하고 싶니?
B: 나는 해외로 나가서 영국이나 호주에서 공학을 공부하고 싶어.

2 루브르 박물관은 파리에 있는 것이므로 '파리에 있는 동안'의 의미를 갖도록 while이 적절
A: 지난달에 파리에 있는 동안 루브르 박물관을 방문했었니?
B: 응! 레오나르도 다빈치의 모나리자를 본 것은 내 여행의 하이라이트였어.

3 "기름값이 상승했기 때문에 자전거 타는 사람들이 많다."라는 의미로 문맥상 이유를 나타내는 접속사 because가 적절
A: 네가 사는 곳에서 자전거 타는 것은 인기 있니?
B: 응. 요즘, 기름값이 너무 올라서 많은 사람들이 자전거로 출근을 해.

1 ④   2 ③   3 ③

해설/해석

1 ④ 사서가 죄송하다고 하는 것으로 보아 둘 다 대출이 불가능한 것으로 추정. 그러므로 의미상 「neither A nor B」이 적절. 「neither A nor B」는 'A도 B도 아닌', 「either A or B」는 'A와 B 둘 중 하나'

A: 실례합니다만, 이 DVD들은 대여 기간이 얼마나 되나요?
B: 도서관 방침상 7일 후에 반납하셔야 해요.
A: 7일밖에 안 돼요? 별로 길지 않네요. 음, 그렇다면, 이 두 개만 빌릴게요.
B: 정말 죄송하지만, 신작이나 인터넷 학습 DVD는 대출이 되지 않습니다.

2 ③ 문맥상 '햄버거에 넣을 조미료와 아이들 음료수 둘 다'라는 의미가 되어야 하므로 「both A and B」가 적절. 「both A and B」는 'A와 B 둘 다'

A: 내가 너에게 부탁한 대로 소풍에 필요한 것은 다 챙겼니?
B: 물론이지. 네가 하라고 한 것 모두 부엌 식탁 위에 있는 바구니에 있어.
A: 제리! 햄버거에 넣을 조미료와 아이들을 위한 음료수가 없어졌어.
B: 오, 그것들은 내가 아이스박스에 넣어서 이미 차에 실었어.

3 ③ 문맥상 '늦게까지 남거나 주말에 올 수 있다'라는 의미가 되어야 하므로 「either A or B」가 적절. 「either A or B」는 'A와 B 둘 중 하나'

A: 이런 말을 하게 돼서 유감이지만, 토마스 씨는 네가 초안을 작성한 제안에 만족스러워하지 않으셨어.
B: 이런, 어떻게 하지? 수정하는 것 좀 도와줄 시간 있니?
A: 음, 난 이번 주는 일 끝나고 늦게까지 남거나 주말에 올 수 있어.
B: 우리 아들이 오기로 해서 주말엔 올 수 없어. 이번 주 늦게까지 남아줄래?

REVIEW PLUS
p. 25

1 ④   2 ③   3 ②

해설/해석

1 ④ 「neither A nor B」는 'A도 B도 아닌'이라는 의미로 either를 neither로 고치는 것이 적절

동결 건조는 진공을 이용해 음식에서 수분을 제거하는 과정이다. 음식을 동결 건조하면 많은 이점들이 있다. 예를 들어, 고기와 야채, 또는 과일과 같이 부패하기 쉬운 식품들을 동결 건조하면 냉동하지 않고 실온에서 보관할 수 있다. 더구나, 동결 건조한 음식은 무게가 70~90% 덜 나간다. 이러한 두 이점을 가진 동결 건조 제품들은 식량을 시원하게 유지할 수 없거나, 저장할 공간이 충분치 않은 야영객들이나 등산객들에게 알맞다.

2 ③ 앞 문장과 내용이 상반되는 것이 아니라, 추가 설명이 연결되므로 but을 and로 고치는 것이 적절

지난 100년간 미국은 많은 변화를 겪었다. 예를 들어, 한 세기 전에는 욕조가 있는 집이 15%가 안 되었다. 대부분의 여자들은 머리를 한 달에 한 번만 감았고, 샴푸로 보락스라고 불리는 세제를 사용하거나, 이따금 달걀 노른자를 사용하였다. 또 다른 예로, 나라 전체를 통틀어 자동차는 8,000대 이하였고, 도로는 144마일만이 포장되어 있었으며, 대부분의 도시들은 최고 제한 속도가 고작 시속 10마일이었다.

3 ③ 「either A or B」는 'A와 B 둘 중 하나'라는 의미로 and를 or로 고치는 것이 적절

말하기와 쓰기의 또 다른 중요한 차이는 말하기는 실시간으로 일어난다는 것이다. 그 결과, 화자들은 요점이 잘 전달되지 않았거나 잘못 해석된 경우 거의 항상 자신들을 설명할 기회가 있다. 이와 반대로, 작가들은 그러한 사치를 누릴 수 없다. 세심한 작가는 두 번의 기회가 없다는 것을 알기에, 그들은 처음부터 자신이 전하고자 하는 바를 가능한 한 정확하고 명확하게 하도록 크게 주의해야 한다.

④

해설/해석

(A) 선행사 willow bark를 받는 주격관계대명사는 which가 적절하며, what은 계속적 용법에 사용될 수 없음 (B) 앞 문장과 거리가 있는 내용을 서술하기 위해 역접의 의미를 갖는 연결어 however가 적절 (C) company는 이름을 스스로 짓는 것이 아니라, 사람들에 의해 이름이 지어지는 것이므로 수동의 의미를 갖는 named가 적절

약 2,400년 전, 히포크라테스는 천연의 아스피린이 함유된 버드나무 껍질을 처방했다. 하지만 19세기 초반이 되어서야 화학자들은 그 원료보다 간단한 원료를 만들었다. 불행히도, 그것은 위장의 내벽을 갉았다. 1880년대 후반, 화학자 펠릭스 호프만은 한층 더해진 실험을 행했다. 그는 부작용이 더 적은 효과적인 해열 진통제를 만들었다. 1899년 1월, 바이엘이라는 이름의 한 독일 회사는 이 새로운 약을 "아스피린"으로 상표 등록했다.

⑤

해설/해석

⑤ 문맥상 어른들이 왜 체리를 먹지 않는지 그 이유에 대해 궁금해 한 것이므로 의문사 why가 적절

내가 자랄 때, 가장 즐겨 찾은 장소 중 하나는 뒤뜰의 체리나무였다. 매년 여름, 체리가 익기 시작했을 때, 나는 나무 높은 곳에 올라 달콤하고, 햇볕으로 따뜻해진 체리들을 따 먹으며 시간을 보내곤 했다. 어머니는 항상 내가 나무에서 떨어질까 봐 걱정했지만 나는 결코 그런 적이 없었다. 그러나 나는 체리에 대해 약간의 경쟁심이 있었다. 새 떼들도 나만큼 체리를 좋아해서, 내가 없을 때마다 나무에 모여서 재빨리 그리고 열성적으로 열매들을 먹곤 했다. 나는 어른들이 왜 체리들을 안 먹는지 궁금해 했다.

WRITING PRACTICE
p. 27~28

1 The bola is a rope which is used to catch animals, and it has weights on the end of it.

2 The young boy who is playing the piano is my cousin from Canada, and he will be staying with us for the whole summer.

3 After the tornado moved on, my house was gone; however, my neighbor's house remained as it was – seemingly oblivious to the maelstrom that had passed.

4 Although Jill and her sister searched the entire neighborhood, their pet Dachshund, Doxie, was nowhere to be found, and the girls couldn't help but feel that she was lost forever.

1 볼라는 동물을 잡을 때 사용하는 줄이며, 끝에 추가 있다.

2 피아노를 치고 있는 어린 소년은 캐나다에서 온 내 사촌이고, 그는 여름 내내 우리와 있을 것이다.

3 토네이도가 지나간 후, 우리 집은 사라졌다. 하지만 내 이웃의 집은 지나간 대혼란을 모르는 듯 그대로 남아 있었다.

4 질과 그녀의 여동생이 온 동네를 뒤졌지만 그들의 애완견 닥스훈트 독시는 어디에서도 찾을 수가 없어서, 소녀들은 개를 영원히 잃어버린 것처럼 느낄 수밖에 없었다.

B

1 After the long hike through Lynn Canyon, the kids were hot, sweaty, and a bit cranky.

2 Neither Susan nor her husband will be able to attend the family reunion next month.

3 Miley wasn't in the backyard, nor was she upstairs.

4 As the lions approached the dead elk, the jackals and buzzards retreated to a safe distance to wait.

5 I can't be sure because I was trying to find my camera.

1 린 캐니언에서 오랫동안 하이킹을 한 후, 어린이들은 덥고, 땀나고, 다소 짜증이 난 상태였다.

2 수잔 또는 그녀의 남편은 다음 달 가족 모임에 참석할 수 없을 것이다.

3 마일리는 뒷마당에도, 위층에도 없었다. 솔직히, 나는 그녀가 어디로 갔는지 모르겠다.

4 사자들이 죽은 엘크에 다가가자, 자칼들과 말똥가리들은 안전한 거리만큼 뒤로 빠져 기다렸다.

5 여우는 구멍 속으로 도망갔거나 저 바위들 뒤로 도망갔다. 나는 카메라를 찾는 중이었기 때문에 확실히는 모르겠다.

C

1 I didn't get to see the end of the game, nor did anyone else.

2 Has Jessie decided whether she will come to see us

3 Scarcely had John and his friend Larry set off toward the summit

4 This new model is not only more powerful but also more fuel efficient

5 My great grandfather was neither rich nor famous

6 humans have created and stored more information than in the previous 5,000 years

7 only one hundred years ago that 95% of births took place at home

1 나는 경기의 후반부를 보지 못했고 다른 사람들도 역시 그러했다. 경기는 비가 와서 중단되었다.

2 이번 여름에 제시가 우리를 보러 올지 말지 결정했니?

3 존과 그의 친구 래리가 정상을 향해 출발하자마자 매섭게 눈이 내리기 시작했다.

4 이 새로운 모델은 더 강력할 뿐 아니라, 연비도 효율적이어서 도시 차로 적합하다.

5 우리 증조할아버지는 부자도 아니고 유명하지도 않았지만, 전체적으로 그는 인생을 즐겁게 살았다.

6 1970년대 초반부터, 사람들은 5,000년 전보다 더 많은 정보를 창조하고 저장해 왔다.

7 요즘, 비교적 편안하고 안전하게 병원에서 아이를 낳는 것이 일반화되었지만, 100년 전만 해도 출산의 95%는 집에서 이루어졌다.

 Unit 06 EXERCISES  p. 33~34

A

1 takes	2 is taking
3 goes	4 is preparing
5 connects	6 is learning
7 am walking	

1 태양에서 지구까지 빛이 도달하는 데 8분 3초가 걸린다.

2 너는 지금 당장 화장실에 들어갈 수 없어. 제시카가 샤워를 하고 있어.

3 필립은 매주 월요일, 수요일, 그리고 금요일에 입시 학원에 간다.

4 지수는 내일 있을 중요한 입사 면접을 준비하고 있어. 그녀를 방해하지 마.

5 브루클린 다리는 맨해튼 섬과 브루클린을 연결한다.

6 캐서린은 8월에 이탈리아에 갈 예정이다. 요즘 그녀는 이탈리아어를 조금씩 배우고 있다.

7 나는 학교에 갈 때 주로 버스를 탄다. 하지만 이번 달에는 운동 삼아 걸어 다니고 있다.

B

1 often wears, is wearing

2 is eating, never eats

3 often meet, are meeting

4 always travels, is traveling

5 always has, is having

6 usually snows, is snowing

7 often calls, is calling

1 사라는 청바지를 자주 입지만, 오늘은 파티에 가려고 드레스를 입고 있다.

2 우리 고양이가 당근을 먹다니 너무 놀라워! 우리 고양이는 야채를 절대 먹지 않거든.

3 그들은 종종 만나 점심을 함께 하지만, 요즘에는 업무 시간이 길어져서 저녁에 만난다.

4 올랜도는 항상 일반석을 타지만, 오늘은 좌석을 업그레이드 받아 비즈니스 석을 타고 간다.

5 패트릭은 아침 식사로 항상 과일을 먹지만, 장 보는 것을 깜박해서 오늘 아침에는 토스트를 먹고 있다.

6 주로 11월 말경에 첫눈이 오지만, 아직 10월 말인데도 밖에 눈이 오고 있다.

7 크레이그는 미국에 있는 그의 친구에게 휴대 전화로 자주 전화하지만, 비용 때문에 이번 달에는 유선 전화로 하고 있다.

C

1 is fishing
2 am taking
3 is sleeping
4 spends
5 believe
6 cause

해석

1 봐! 저스틴이 친구들과 강에서 낚시하고 있어.
2 오늘 출근이 늦을 거예요. 여동생을 병원에 데리고 가고 있어요.
3 이번 주에 내 남동생은 시험 때문에 매우 적게 자고 있어.
4 매주 피터는 금요일이 되기 전에 그의 용돈을 다 쓴다.
5 이슬람교도들은 신이 예언자 모하마드를 통해 말씀하셨다고 믿는다.
6 토네이도는 매년 미국에 수백만 달러의 피해를 준다.

D

1 ① is weighing ② weighs
2 ① smells ② is smelling
3 ① think ② is thinking
4 ① are feeling ② feel
5 ① see ② are seeing

해석

1 ① 판매 사원이 지금 나를 위해 바나나의 무게를 재고 있다.
　② 이 피아노는 내가 들기에는 너무 무거워요. 무게가 너무 많이 나가요.
2 ① 우리 오빠의 방에 들어갈 때마다, 약간 이상한 냄새가 난다.
　② 니콜의 향수가 방 전체에 진동하고 있어 속이 메스껍다.
3 ① 결정을 내리기 전에 시간이 조금 더 필요한 것 같다.
　② 요즘 ABC 은행은 고객들이 업무 시간 이후에 ATM기를 이용할 때 서비스 요금을 올리는 것을 고려 중이다.
4 ① 우리가 먹은 이 음식이 이상해. 왜냐하면, 우리 모두 약간씩 속이 좋지 않기 때문이야.
　② 자화상은 훌륭했지만, 나는 그 풍경화가 상을 받았어야 한다고 느낀다.
5 ① 네가 그 영화가 그다지 재미있지 않다고 한 것이 무슨 말인지 알겠다.
　② 올해 심사 위원들은 엄격하다. 그래서 그들은 참가자들이 범하는 실수들을 다 보고 있다.

Unit 07 EXERCISES

p. 38~39

A

1 was jogging
2 discovered
3 rotates, creates
4 was already having, found

해석

1 메리는 오늘 아침 조깅을 하다가 고등학교 때 친구와 마주쳤다.
2 아이작 뉴턴은 중력을 발견했을 때 사과나무 아래에 앉아 있었다.
3 지구는 24시간마다 한 번 지축을 중심으로 회전한다. 이로 인해 하루 24시간이 만들어진다.
4 에릭은 자신이 시험에서 낙제한 것을 알았을 때 이미 안 좋은 하루를 보내고 있었다.

B

1 laid
2 raised
3 sat
4 rose, risen
5 set

해석

1 그가 닭고기 수프를 데우는 동안 나는 식탁을 차렸다.
2 석유 가격이 올랐기 때문에 가게 주인은 물건 가격을 올렸다.
3 제니스가 시험을 보기 위해 자리에 앉았을 때 그녀의 어머니는 그녀가 시험에 합격하도록 기도했다.
4 해가 떴을 때 많은 사람들이 이미 일을 시작하기 위해 일어나 있었다.
5 사람들이 불평을 했기 때문에 정부는 식품 제조에 대한 새로운 기준을 만들었다.

C

1 would[used to], used to[would]
2 would[used to], used to[would]
3 would[used to], used to[would]
4 used to, used to

해석

1 캐리는 절대 시금치를 먹지 않았다. 그녀는 엄마가 보고 있지 않을 때 시금치를 항상 개에게 주곤 했다.
2 한국에 오기 전에 나는 점심으로 기름진 패스트푸드를 많이 먹었다. 나는 정기적으로 햄버거와 감자튀김을 먹었다.
3 켄의 남동생은 학교에서 집으로 오는 도중에 책을 읽곤 했다. 그는 최소한 일주일에 세 번씩 도서관에 가곤 했다.
4 내 여동생은 어렸을 때 마빈 윌리엄스의 팬이었다. 그녀는 그의 콘서트 티켓을 사기 위해 맨 앞에 줄 서 있던 사람들 중 하나였다.

D

1 preferred
2 existed
3 belonged to
4 was looking
5 became
6 created

해석

1 어렸을 때 나는 포도보다는 오렌지를 좋아했다.
2 공룡들은 지구를 지배하기 오래전부터 존재했다.
3 미국의 일부가 되기 전, 텍사스는 멕시코에 속했었다.
4 토마스는 자신의 휴대 전화를 찾던 중 다른 방에서 자신의 휴대 전화가 울리는 것을 들었다.
5 아놀드 스왈츠제네거는 캘리포니아 주지사가 되기 오래전부터 유명했다.
6 마야 족은 콜럼버스가 신대륙에 도착하기 오래전에 정확한 달력을 만들었다.

E

1 traveled[was traveling]
2 was baking, was decorating
3 was, spoke
4 was vacuuming
5 was returning

해석

1 A: 이 이야기책들은 모두 어디에서 났니?
　B: 우리 아버지가 런던을 여행하실 때 나를 위해 사신 거야.
2 A: 내가 정오에 전화했을 때 너희 둘은 무엇을 하고 있었니?
　B: 내가 아빠 생신 케이크를 굽는 동안, 랄프는 거실을 꾸미고 있었어.

3 A: 제니랑 마지막으로 이야기한 게 언제야? 어젯밤에 그녀에게서 전화가 왔었어.
   B: 오, 그거 놀라운걸! 그녀랑 이야기한 지 너무 오래됐어. 그녀가 너에게 왜 전화했니?
4 A: 어젯밤에 집에 없었어? 문을 여러 번 두드렸지만, 아무도 대답을 안 하더라고.
   B: 집에 있었는데. 아마 내가 진공청소기로 카펫을 청소하고 있을 때 네가 문을 두드렸나 봐.
5 A: 어제 너를 가게에서 봤는데, 너는 나를 못 본 것 같더라.
   B: 오, 그래? 그때 내가 산 재킷을 환불하고 나서 엄마를 만나기 위해 서두르고 있었어.

  EXERCISES p. 42~43

Ⓐ

1 has worked
2 have worn
3 has cleaned
4 have played
5 has spent
6 has raged

해석

1 리사는 세 시간 동안 그녀의 프로젝트를 하고 있다. 그녀는 아직도 도서관에 있다.
2 나는 이 신발을 2015년부터 신었다. 이런 스타일은 더 이상 찾기 힘들다.
3 훈이는 집 안 대청소를 했다. 이제 끝마쳤기 때문에 그는 편히 긴 휴식을 취해도 된다.
4 어린이들이 공원에 있다. 그들은 지난 두 시즌 동안 같은 야구팀에서 뛰어왔다.
5 폴은 그의 용돈 전부를 만화책에 썼다. 이제 그는 버스를 탈 충분한 돈도 없다.
6 시리아 내 갈등이 심화된 지 7년이 넘었다. 지금은 아무도 그 나라에 평화가 언제 올지 말할 수 없다.

Ⓑ

1 have been studying
2 has been playing
3 has been writing
4 have been building
5 has been working
6 has been cleaning
7 have been waiting

해석

1 나는 몇 년 동안 한국어를 공부해왔지만, 매우 어렵다.
2 2시간 동안 글렌은 친구들과 농구를 하고 있다.
3 캐리는 2년간 신문에 칼럼을 써왔다.
4 그들은 10년 넘게 빅토리아 댐을 짓고 있다.
5 사라는 회사에서 5년간 일했다. 그녀는 승진할 예정이다.
6 상우는 내일 파티를 열기 때문에 오늘 온종일 집을 치우고 있다.
7 이번 운송 파업은 심각한 문제들을 일으키기 시작했다. 우리는 한 시간 이상 기다렸지만, 기차는 아직도 오지 않고 있다.

Ⓒ

1 have been waiting
2 already bought
3 has eaten
4 have started
5 has been studying

해석

1 A: 존, 어디 갔었니? 몇 시간이나 기다렸어.
   B: 정말? 너희가 아직 여기 있는지 몰랐어. 정말 미안해.
2 A: 넬슨, 봐! 이 노트북 컴퓨터가 할인판매 중이야. 하나 사고 싶지 않니?
   B: 오, 아니. 이미 어제 하나 샀는데 훨씬 비싸게 샀어.
3 A: 누가 내 참치 샌드위치를 먹었니? 점심때 먹으려고 아껴두고 있었는데.
   B: 미안해, 댄. 네가 먹을 거였는지 전혀 몰랐어.
4 A: 나는 운전 강습을 받기 시작했어. 이렇게 재미있다니 믿어지지 않아!
   B: 우와! 너 차를 살 거니? 정말 부럽다.
5 A: 존은 몇 년 동안 일어를 공부해왔지만, 여전히 한자에 어려움을 느끼고 있어.
   B: 나는 전적으로 그의 상황을 이해해. 나도 일어를 잘하지 못해.

Ⓓ

1 haven't[have not] visited
2 has been
3 hasn't[has not] tasted
4 has been helping[has helped]
5 has been looking for
6 Have, been watching

해석

1 나는 2015년 크리스마스 이후로 캐나다를 방문한 적이 없다.
2 피터는 3개월간 우리 반의 반장이었다.
3 에드먼드는 11월에 한국을 떠난 이후 김치를 먹어본 적이 없다.
4 인수는 내가 기억하는 한 아주 오랫동안 나의 일을 도와줘 왔다.
5 오스카는 거의 두 시간 동안 자신의 강아지를 찾고 있지만, 찾을 수가 없다.
6 내가 나간 이후에도 계속 TV를 보고 있었니? TV 앞에 하루 종일 앉아 있으면 안 돼.

  EXERCISES p. 46

Ⓐ

1 had already finished
2 had dreamed
3 had been traveling
4 had been studying
5 had been playing
6 struggled

해석

1 비가 오기 시작했을 때 경기는 이미 끝나 있었다.
2 베르사유 궁전은 내가 꿈꿔온 것보다 더 화려했다.
3 니콜이 도착했을 때 그녀는 24시간 이상 여행하고 있었다.
4 은지는 그녀의 오빠가 도와주러 오기 전 몇 시간 동안 공부를 하고 있었다.
5 어린이들은 조지가 그들을 데리러 오기 전 몇 시간 동안 놀고 있었다.
6 작년에 영주는 한국 평화봉사단을 위해 자원봉사할 수 있도록 그녀의 부모님을 설득하려고 애썼다.

Ⓑ

1 had gone, took
2 visited, hadn't[had not] crossed

3 was, hadn't[had not] taken
4 confessed, had received
5 had existed, conquered
6 got, had eaten
7 missed, had forgotten

해석

1 내가 한 모금 마셨을 때 커피는 식어 있었다.
2 호주를 방문하기 전에 나는 적도를 가로질러 간 적이 없었다.
3 질리안은 제주도에 가게 되어 매우 신났다. 그녀는 몇 년간 휴가를 간 적이 없었다.
4 조이스는 엄마에게 자신이 과학 시험에서 나쁜 성적을 받았다고 실토하였다.
5 기자의 대(大) 피라미드는 로마가 이집트를 정복한 2,000년 전부터 존재해 왔다.
6 나는 그저께 내 생일에 먹은 블루베리 치즈 케이크 때문에 어제 아팠다.
7 마빈은 알람시계를 맞추는 것을 잊어서 버스를 놓쳤다. 그는 학교까지 달렸지만 이미, 수업은 시작해 있었다.

Unit 10 EXERCISES
p. 48

A

1 were eating
2 has decided
3 have been playing
4 had been raining
5 hasn't eaten
6 died, came
7 had had

해석

1 어제저녁에 우리가 밥을 먹고 있을 때 언니가 전화했다.
2 돈을 좀 더 벌기 위해, 케이트는 아르바이트를 구하기로 결심했다.
3 스코틀랜드인들은 스코틀랜드에서 수 세기 동안 골프를 해왔다. 그것은 그들의 국민 스포츠이다.
4 우리가 런던에 도착했을 때 비가 왔던 것처럼 보였다. 거리가 여전히 젖어 있었다.
5 윤미는 내일 저녁에 탕수 돼지갈비를 먹고 싶다. 그녀는 몇 주간 중국 요리를 먹지 못했다.
6 다이애나비는 1997년 여름에 끔찍한 자동차 사고로 죽었다. 많은 영국인들이 나와서 그녀의 죽음을 애도하였다.
7 웬디는 방금 병원에서 의사를 만나고 돌아왔다. 그녀는 3일 동안 딸꾹질을 했다. 하지만 의사의 치료를 받고 이제 더 이상 딸꾹질을 하지 않는다.

B

1 have been posted
2 have told[have been telling]
3 has already pulled out
4 has been attending[has attended]
5 had been talking[had talked]
6 had been living[had lived]

해석

1 이번 주만 해도 100개가 넘는 메시지가 내 블로그에 올라왔다.
2 아메리카 인디언들은 자신들의 문화에 대한 전설들을 수백 년 동안 전해왔다.

3 우리는 너무 늦었어. 멜버른으로 가는 기차가 이미 역을 빠져나갔어.
4 지나는 지난달부터 근처 학원에서 영어 수업을 받고 있다.
5 나는 오랫동안 아프리카에 가는 것에 대해 이야기해왔고, 마침내 지난 겨울에 다녀왔다.
6 1492년 크리스토퍼 콜럼버스가 미국을 발견했을 때 아메리카 인디언들은 거기서 수천 년 동안 살고 있었다.

REVIEW
p. 49

 A

1 ① 2 ④ 3 ③

해설/해석

1 "우리 만난 적 없나요?"라는 의미로 과거부터 현재까지 만난 경험이 있는지 묻는 것이므로 현재완료인 Haven't we met이 적절
A: 우리 만난 적 있지 않나요? 매우 낯이 익은데요.
B: 어쩌면요. 하지만 확실하지 않아요. 어느 대학을 나오셨어요?

2 과거의 비슷한 시점에 일어난 일 중에서, 더 먼저 시작되어 진행되고 있던 일은 과거진행형으로, 그 사이에 갑자기 일어난 일은 과거 시제로 씀, 자전거를 먼저 타고 있었으므로 was riding이 적절
A: 소미의 행운에 대해 들었니?
B: 응, 자전거 타고 학교 가는 길에 10달러를 발견했대. 나도 그런 행운이 있으면 좋겠다.

3 발표가 예상했던 것보다 길어졌다는 것은 발표하기 이전에 일어난 일이므로 과거완료 시제를 써야 함, 또한 주어 I가 예상한 것이므로 과거완료 능동태인 had expected가 적절
A: 어디 갔었니, 대런? 몇 시간 동안 너에게 전화했었어.
B: 회사에서 발표하고 있었는데, 내가 예상했던 것보다 길어졌어.

 B

1 ② 2 ④ 3 ③

해설/해석

1 ② have가 '~을 가지고 있다'의 소유를 나타내는 상태동사로 쓰였을 때는 진행형이 불가능하므로 am not having을 don't have로 고치는 것이 적절
A: 안녕, 제이슨. 내일 무슨 계획 없니?
B: 아직 계획은 없어. 같이 뭐 할래? 영화 보러 가는 건 어때?
A: 새로운 코미디 영화를 보고 싶어. 낮 시간 영화는 몇 시에 시작하니?
B: 확실히 모르겠어. 보통 두 시쯤 시작하는 것 같아.

2 ④ 습관적, 반복적인 행동은 단순현재 시제를 사용하며, 빈도부사는 일반동사의 앞에 위치하므로 am always meeting을 always meet로 고치는 것이 적절
A: 안녕, 칼. 아트센터에서 새로운 유럽 미술 전시회를 봤니?
B: 아니, 안 봤어. 어제 그것에 대한 서평을 읽었어. 정말 좋다고 하더군.
A: 그렇대. 내일 아침에 가볼래? 미술관은 주로 오전 9시에 열어.
B: 오, 이런! 월요일 아침 9시에 항상 교수님과 만나서 내 연구 프로젝트에 대해 논의를 하거든.

3 ③ decide는 상태동사로 진행형으로 쓸 수 없음, 이미 결정을 내린 상태이므로 was deciding을 과거 시제인 decided로 고치는

것이 적절, 또한 이미 과거에 결정을 내렸고, 그 결정에 따라 현재 공항에 있게 된 상황이므로 have decided도 적절

A: 어이, 민수! 세상이 좁구나! 너를 여기서 볼 줄은 몰랐어.
B: 스콧, 이렇게 만나다니 놀라운걸! 공항에서 뭐 하고 있니?
A: 아, 드디어 휴가를 가기로 결정했어. 오늘 오후에 호주로 떠나.
B: 정말? 나는 막 호주에서 오는 길이야. 즐거운 여행이 되길 바랄게.

REVIEW PLUS

p. 50~51

1 ②   2 ④   3 ③

해설/해석

1 ② from 2004 to 2006은 과거의 특정 시점이므로 has been을 단순과거 시제 was로 고치는 것이 적절

반기문은 많은 한국 청년들에게 역할 모델이다. 그는 유엔 사무국의 수장에 오르기까지 매우 열심히 일했다. 그는 2004년부터 2006년까지 한국에서 외무 장관을 지냈다. 2006년 2월에는, 사무총장직을 위한 선거전을 시작했다. 그는 선출된 이후로 지구 온난화와 다르푸르에 특별히 강경한 견해를 보였다.

2 ④ for decades는 과거부터 현재까지 계속되는 행동을 나타내는 시간 표현이고, 이 글을 쓰고 있는 순간에도 여전히 계속되는 행동이므로 현재완료진행인 has been building이 적절

세계 야생 동물 보호 기금 협회는 세계 생물 다양성을 지원하는 무정부 단체이다. 1961년 시작부터 세계 야생 동물 보호 기금 협회는 멸종 위기의 생물들을 보호하기 위해 노력해왔다. 그들은 미래의 세계에 코끼리, 고래, 자이언트 판다, 그리고 다른 야생 생물들이 포함되도록 노력을 하고 있다. 요즘 서식지 파괴와 오염은 많은 동물들을 멸종으로 몰아넣고 있다. 수십 년간 세계 야생 동물 보호 기금 협회는 인간의 필요 요건이 자연과 조화를 이루어 충족될 수 있는 미래를 건설해왔다.

3 ③ every year는 어떤 행동이 1년 주기로 반복적으로 일어나고 있음을 나타내는 시간 표현이므로, 현재 시제인 visit가 적절

찰스 다윈은 19세기 영국의 동식물학자였다. HMS 비글호를 타고 떠난 5년간의 여행은 그를 존경받는 과학자로 만들었다. 1835년 9월에 다윈은 그의 사상에 가장 크게 영향을 준 섬, 갈라파고스에 도착했다. 이 섬은 심지어 오늘날까지도 과학자들의 흥미를 돋우는 섬이다. 게다가, 매년 수천 명의 관광객들이 갈라파고스 섬을 방문한다. 2007년에는 유네스코에서 갈라파고스 섬을 세계 유산 중 요주의 리스트에 올려 놓았다. 후손들을 위해 이 섬들을 보존하려고 에콰도르는 갈라파고스의 동물들을 밀렵꾼들과 관광객들로부터 보호하는 법안을 내놓을 것이다.

④

해설/해석

(A) 과거에 있었던 일을 기술하고 있는 글이므로 과거 시제인 stood가 적절 (B) 과거의 특정 시점에 진행 중인 행동으로 과거진행 시제인 was talking이 적절 (C) 말하는 순간 진행되고 있는 일에 대해 언급하는 것이므로 현재진행 시제인 are playing이 적절

아버지께서는 내가 미식축구 시합을 할 때마다 경기를 보러 오셨다. 아버지는 사이드라인에 서서 주의 깊게 경기를 지켜보셨다. 나는 경기장에 오는 방법을 아버지께 말씀드린 적이 없었지만, 아버지는 어쨌든 나타나셨다. 1쿼터가 끝나고 내가 운동장에서 나오면 아버지는 나를 부르시곤 했다. 자신의 말에 대한 확신도 없으면서, 아버지는 "론, 잘하고 있어. 무릎을 조금

더 굽혀."라는 항상 똑같은 말만 하셨다. 나는 다시 경기에 들어가서 무릎을 더 굽히고 더 빨리 달리는 것으로 아버지의 말에 응답하곤 했다.

②

해설/해석

② for hundreds of years는 과거부터 현재까지 계속되는 행동이나 상태를 나타내는 시간 표현이므로 현재완료 시제가 적절하며, 주어인 Gullah는 동사 speak의 행위의 주체가 아니므로, 이 경우 동사를 수동태로 써야 함, 현재완료시제의 수동태는 [have/has+been+p.p]의 형태이므로 has been spoken이 옳은 표현

걸러어는 서아프리카에서 무역 언어로 시작되었다. 나중에 그것은 아프리카에서 끌려 온 노예들에 의해 카리브 해와 미국으로 퍼져나갔다. 걸러어가 수백 년 동안 사용되었지만, 최근까지 문자화하려는 시도는 거의 없었다. Sea Island 번역 위원회는 현재 이 언어를 보존하기 위해 작업하고 있다. 걸러어 사용자들은 과거에 걸러어가 조악한 영어라는 말을 들을 때가 많았다. 그들은 걸러어를 사용하는 것을 부끄럽게 여겼다. 언어학자들은 오늘날 걸러어를 실제적인 언어로 인정한다. 그 위원회는 어린이들이 자신들의 언어를 더 잘 이해하고 나중에 더 쉽게 영어로 바꾸어 사용할 수 있도록 걸러어로 쓰인 교수 자료를 개발하고자 한다.

WRITING PRACTICE

p. 52

1 Hojun was drinking coffee when I saw him at the cafe.
2 By the time Timothy came home, we had finished the laundry.
3 We haven't been able to afford a new car since last year.
4 While I lay[was lying] on the couch watching TV, someone kept buzzing the intercom.
5 Most of Europe was experiencing the Dark Ages when the Aztecs built the Pyramid of the Sun.

해석

1 내가 호준이를 카페에서 보았을 때 그는 커피를 마시고 있었다.
2 티모시가 집에 왔을 때쯤 우리는 빨래를 마친 상태였다.
3 작년부터 우리는 새 차를 살 여유가 없다.
4 내가 TV를 보며 소파에 누워 있는 동안, 누군가 계속해서 인터폰을 눌렀다.
5 아즈텍인들이 태양의 피라미드를 지었을 때 대부분의 유럽은 암흑 시대를 겪고 있었다.

1 Scientists' experiences have shown that wearing protective eyewear is necessary in the laboratory.
2 The dancer's experiences have shown that taking adequate rest is needed before a performance.
3 Daniel's recent experience has shown that a passport should be photocopied when you travel.

1 과학자들의 경험으로 미루어 보건대 실험실에서 보안경을 쓰는 것이 필수적이다.
2 무용수의 경험으로 미루어 보건대 공연 전 적당한 휴식을 취하는 것이 필요하다.
3 다니엘의 최근 경험으로 미루어 보건대 여행 시 여권을 복사해서 가지고 다녀야 한다.

PART 3

Unit 11 EXERCISES
p. 56

1 is going to rain
2 am going to visit, Will you join
3 is going to come
4 is going to start
5 is going to fly, will be exhausted

해석

1 먹구름이 몰려오고 있는 것 좀 봐. 비가 올 것 같아. 우리 빨래를 걷는 게 좋겠어.
2 재스민이 오늘 아침 교통사고가 났대. 오늘 밤 병문안을 가려고 하는데 너도 같이 갈래?
3 이 복사기가 또 고장 났어. 내가 벌써 서비스 센터에 전화했어. 내일 수리기사가 와서 수리할 거야.
4 진희는 가을에 대학이 시작되기 때문에 요즘 정말 들떠 있다. 그녀는 산업디자인을 공부하기로 결심했다.
5 다음 주, 그레타가 스위스에서 비행기로 들어올 것이다. 틀림없이 그녀는 여행으로 지칠 테니까 관광시켜 주기 전에 쉬게 놔두자.

B

1 am going to give, are going to do
2 will be, will have
3 am going to visit, will do

해석

1 A: 무슨 일이야, 애론? 좀 창백해 보이는데.
  B: 오늘 이따가 발표를 해야 해.
  A: 너무 긴장하지 마. 네가 잘할 거라 확신해.
  B: 응원해줘서 고마워. 어떻게 됐는지 내일 알려줄게.
2 A: 안녕하세요. 저는 트래비스이고, 오늘 여러분의 담당 웨이터입니다.
  B: 안녕하세요, 트래비스 씨. 저에게는 소갈비와 가든 샐러드를 주세요.
  A: 좋은 선택이십니다. 더 필요하신 건 없으신가요?
  B: 지금은 됐어요, 감사합니다.
3 A: 케이시, 토요일에 농구 경기 가니?
  B: 가고 싶지만, 시간이 없을 것 같아. 토요일에 할머니 댁에 갈 거야..
  A: 정말 멋진 게임이 될 거래. 정오에 시작한대. 오도록 해봐.
  B: 좋아. 최선을 다해볼게. 거기서 널 만났으면 좋겠다.

Unit 12 EXERCISES
p. 59

A

1 will have been living
2 will have arrived
3 will have been acting
4 will have finished
5 will have been
6 will have won

해석

1 6월이면 나는 서울에서 산 지 8년이 된다.
2 다음 주 이맘때면 크리스가 토론토에서 돌아와 있을 것이다.
3 유진은 10월이 되면 브로드웨이에서 연기한 지 10년이 된다.
4 희주는 오늘 저녁 7시까지 그녀의 프로젝트를 끝낼 것이다.
5 내일 우리 부모님은 결혼하신 지 25년이 된다.
6 그가 오스카상을 받으면 다른 어떤 배우보다 더 많은 영화 상을 받게 될 것이다.

1 will, have, perfected
2 will, be, eating
3 will, be, studying
4 will, have, been, traveling
5 will, have, completed

해석

1 A: 리즈가 또 클라리넷을 연습하고 있니? 정말 열심히구나.
  B: 응. 다음 주 연주회에는 그녀가 저 곡을 완벽하게 숙달하게 될 것이라고 확신해.
2 A: 개리야, 내일 수학 시험과 관련해서 이따가 전화로 물어봐도 되니?
  B: 물론, 괜찮아. 하지만 여섯 시에서 일곱 시 사이에는 전화하지 말아 줘. 나는 그때 저녁을 먹고 있을 거야.
3 A: 줄리야, 집에 오면 제발 조용히 있어 줘. 네 오빠가 시험공부를 하고 있을 거야.
  B: 네, 엄마. 오빠를 방해하지 않겠다고 약속할게요.
4 A: 토마스야, 우리 곧 착륙할 거 같아?
  B: 그러면 좋겠는데, 수. 우리가 요하네스버그에 도착할 때쯤 되면 거의 24시간을 여행한 것이 돼.
5 A: 진주야, 이번 주말에 영화 보러 갈래? 시간이 되니?
  B: 물론이지. 그거 좋겠다. 토요일쯤에는 내 발표 준비를 끝냈을 거야.

Unit 13 EXERCISES
p. 61

1 when
2 when
3 As soon as
4 until
5 As soon as
6 before
7 After

해석

1 빌리는 여행 경비를 충분히 모으면 한국을 방문할 것이다.
2 용준이는 농구 시즌이 끝나면 일본에서 돌아올 것이다.
3 우리가 집에 도착하자마자, 나는 네가 곧장 위층으로 가서 샤워를 했으면 해.
4 새로운 발전소가 완성될 때까지는 정전은 계속 문제가 될 것이다.
5 극장에 도착하자마자, 우리는 자리를 찾아야 해. 우리는 거의 늦었어.
6 차에 타기 전에 화장실 가는 것 잊지마. 우리는 긴 여행을 앞두고 있어.
7 물, 밀가루, 그리고 이스트를 같이 섞은 후, 반죽은 30분간 부풀도록 둔다.

B

1 gets	2 grow	3 stop
4 saves	5 are, enjoying	6 leave

해석

1 지민이는 다음 주 그녀의 오빠가 제주도에서 돌아올 때까지 그의 개를 돌볼 것이다.

2 수박이 충분히 자라자마자, 농부는 그것들을 시장으로 가져가 팔 것이다.

3 우리가 대기를 오염시키는 것을 멈추지 않는 한, 지구의 온도는 매년 계속 오를 것이다.

4 우리 아버지는 노후에 자신을 부양할 충분한 돈을 모은 후 은퇴하실 것이다.

5 네가 이 아름다운 봄 날씨를 즐기고 있는 동안, 나는 과학 시험을 준비하고 있을 거야. 인생은 참 불공평해.

6 하와이로 떠나기 전에 새 수영복을 사는 것 잊지 마. 그곳의 해변들은 멋지거든.

Unit 14 EXERCISES
p. 64

A

1 is harvested	2 will die
3 disappeared	4 can be stored
5 can be taught	6 will be expected
7 have helped	8 are growing

해석

1 일반적으로, 밀은 가을에 추수한다.

2 물을 충분히 주지 않으면 꽃들이 죽을 것이다.

3 갑자기, 그 이상한 남자가 내 눈 앞에서 사라졌다.

4 이 새 휴대 전화에는 3,000개 이상의 번호를 저장할 수 있다.

5 몇몇 동물들은 굉장히 똑똑해서 그들에게 많은 놀라운 재주들을 가르칠 수 있다.

6 이 수업을 듣는 모든 학생들은 영어로 쓰여진 소설책 몇 권을 읽게 될 것이다.

7 유니세프와 세계보건기구와 같은 단체들은 전 세계의 수백만의 사람들을 도와왔다.

8 일반 시민들에게 위협이 되는 바이러스의 공격, 피싱 사기, 그리고 사이버 폭력은 인터넷이 확장되면서 늘어나고 있다.

B

1 is known	2 was hired
3 has evolved	4 was born
5 resembles	6 will be conducted
7 has been translated	

해석

1 북극 여우는 눈여우 또는 흰여우로도 알려져 있다.

2 그는 아시아까지의 북서 항로를 알아내기 위해 무역회사에 채용되었다.

3 그것은 지구상에서 가장 추운 기온 속에서도 살아남도록 진화했다.

4 위대한 영국의 탐험가 헨리 허드슨은 영국 런던에서 태어났다.

5 글랜 씨의 세 아들 중, 가장 어린 톰이 아버지를 가장 많이 닮았다.

6 인터뷰는 이번 달 말에 교수진 중 한 명과 진행될 것이다.

7 그의 최신 소설은 그가 2017년에 초판을 출간한 이후 열 개의 언어로 번역되었다.

A

1 ③	2 ③	3 ①

해설/해석

1 질문을 받은 시점 전에 생각하던 중이었으므로 과거진행인 was thinking이 적절

A: 저녁 먹으러 어디로 가고 싶니?

B: 나는 중국 음식을 먹을까 생각하고 있었어. 어때?

2 과거에 일어난 어떤 일보다 먼저 일어난 사건은 과거완료를 써야 하므로 had planned가 적절

A: 제리야, 작년에 휴가는 어디에서 보냈니?

B: 음, 우리는 타히티에 가기로 계획했었지만, 마지막 순간에 안가기로 결정했어. 그래서 우리는 발리에 갔어.

3 현재를 포함한 일정 기간, 즉 이번 학기 동안만 진행될 일을 나타낼 때는 현재진행 시제로 미래를 대신할 수 있으므로, are you taking이 적절

A: 현정아, 이번 학기에는 어떤 과목들을 듣니?

B: 나는 영문학과 한국 역사 두 과목만 수강해.

B

1 ②	2 ①	3 ③

해설/해석

1 ② two days ago는 과거의 명확한 시점을 나타내는 시간 표현이므로 단순과거 시제인 moved로 써야 함

A: 헤더, 네 새 룸메이트는 어때?

B: 그녀는 상냥해. 이틀 전에 이사 왔는데 서로 잘 지내고 있어.

A: 잘 됐네. 좋은 룸메이트는 찾기 어려운데.

B: 응, 맞아. 그리고 우리는 둘 다 한국어 공부에 관심 있어서 서로를 도와줄 수 있어.

2 ① last week는 과거의 명확한 시점을 나타내는 시간 표현이므로 과거 시제를 써야 함, find의 과거형은 found

A: 미셸, 정말 좋은 소식이 있어. 지난주에 의사한테 갔었는데 나 임신했대.

B: 그거 정말 좋은 소식이다! 네 남편이 정말 기뻐하겠는걸.

A: 응. 그와 시부모님 모두 매우 기뻐하셔. 이 아이가 그분들의 첫 손자가 될 거야.

B: 그거 정말 잘 됐다! 축하해! 너와 네 가족에게 좋은 일만 있기를 바랄게.

3 ③ for almost a month는 과거부터 현재까지를 포함하는 시간 표현이고, 수리가 아직 다 끝나지 않고 대화가 이루어지는 시점에서도 진행되고 있으므로 현재완료진행인 have been working 또는 계속의 의미를 지닌 현재완료 have worked가 적절

A: 오늘 저녁 교통은 정말 끔찍했어. 고속도로는 여전히 폐쇄되어 있어.

B: 아직도 보수가 안 끝났다는 것이 믿어지지 않아.

A: 그러니까 벌써 작업한 지 거의 한 달이 되어 가는데.

B: 다음 주까지는 완료될 거야. 그러면 다시 정상으로 돌아올 거야.

1 ④ **2** ② **3** ①

[해설/해석]

1 ④ it이 World Wide Web을 지칭하고 있고 우리가 쉽게 정보에 접근할 수 있도록 허용하는 주체가 되므로 능동태로 써야 함. allows가 옳은 표현

인터넷은 전 세계 사람들의 삶을 극적으로 변화시켰다. 컴퓨터를 사용함으로써, 우리는 전 세계 사람들과 몇 초 안에 연락이 가능하다. 이메일의 사용은 인터넷에 있어 중대한 부분이다. 이는 빠르고 저렴하게 서로 의사소통을 할 수 있게 한다. 이메일과 더불어 월드 와이드 웹은 인터넷의 중요한 기능이다. 이는 거의 모든 주제에 관한 정보에 쉽게 접근하도록 해준다. 월드 와이드 웹은 사용하기 쉽다. 웹 브라우저와 인터넷 연결만 있으면 된다.

2 ② 주어인 classes가 라틴어로 가르치는 주체가 아니고, 다른 행위자에 의해 가르침을 받는 것이므로 동사를 수동태로 써야 함. were taught가 옳은 표현

중세에는 많은 학교들이 있었다. 하지만 대부분은 남학교였다. 교회가 많은 학교들을 운영하였고, 기독교에서도 기도를 라틴어로 했기 때문에 수업은 라틴어로 이루어졌다. 이러한 학교에 다니는 소년들은 적당한 나이가 되면 성직자나 수도사가 될 것으로 기대되었다. 몇몇 마을에서는 상인이 되고자 하는 소년들을 위해 상인들이 학교를 세웠다. 이 상인 학교들은 교회 학교들과 마찬가지로 항상 여학생들에게 열려 있던 것은 아니었다.

3 ① solar energy가 미래의 에너지 문제를 해결하는 것이므로 will을 사용한 것은 맞지만, 미래의 특정 시점에 진행되고 있을 것은 아니므로 미래 진행으로 쓰는 것은 어색함. will solve가 옳은 표현

많은 사람들이 태양 에너지가 미래의 에너지 문제를 해결할 것이라고 생각한다. 화석연료는 많은 양의 해로운 배기물을 만들어낸다. 게다가, 화석연료 대부분이 빠른 속도로 고갈되고 있다. 태양 에너지를 화석 연료의 실용적 대체물로 만들기 위해 과학자들은 밤과 흐린 날에 사용할 전력을 저장하는 더 나은 방법을 찾아야 한다. 배터리 기술을 향상시킬 수 있다면, 태양 에너지는 곧 석탄과 석유와 같이 오염이 심한 연료들을 대체할 것이다.

⑤

[해설/해석]

(A) 원급 비교 구문인 as dangerous에 연결될 수 있는 구로 as it is가 적절 (B) 동명사 주어 keeping the lens covered라는 행동은 권장하는 것이 아니라 권장되는 것이므로 수동태인 is recommended가 적절 (C) The lens는 단수 명사이므로 is similar to가 적절. 「be similar to」는 '~와 비슷하다'

밝고, 더운 날 사진을 찍는 것은 당신에게 위험한 만큼 카메라도 위험하다. 당신이 햇볕에 살짝 타는 것에 대처하는 동안, 당신의 카메라는 과도한 햇빛 노출로 영구적인 손상을 입는다. 사용하지 않을 때는 렌즈를 덮는 것이 권장된다. 일출과 일몰 사진은 찍고 나중에 보는 재미가 있지만, 렌즈를 직접 태양을 향하게 하면 렌즈에 손상이 갈 수 있다. 렌즈는 사람의 눈과 비슷해서 햇빛을 똑바로 바라보면 둘 다 손상을 입게 된다.

④

[해설/해석]

④ it은 동명사구 mourning a dead pet을 대신하며, 그러한 행동은 부적절한 것으로 간주하는 것이 아니라 간주되는 것이므로 it is not considered로 쓰는 것이 적절

동물의 죽음에 대한 슬픔을 규제하는 사회적 관습은 없다. 고양이의 사체를 쓰레기통에 넣어도 되고 묻어준 후 비석을 세워줘도 된다. 어느 정도의 애도가 필요한 가까운 가족 일원의 죽음과는 사뭇 다른 상황이다. 하지만 일반적으로 동물의 죽음에 대한 슬픔의 표시는 어린이들에게는 적절하지만, 어른들에게는 그렇지 않다는 개념이 있다. 죽은 애완동물을 애도하는 것은 어린이들에게 사람, 가족 일원을 잃었을 때의 '리허설'로 유용하다. 하지만 그러한 슬픔을 겪는 성인을 위한 사회적인 지지는 부족하기에 이는 어른들에게는 적절하지 않다고 여겨진다.

1 This time next year, we will have known each other for ten years.
2 This time next month, we will be backpacking around Europe. I'm so excited.
3 New York City will be repairing lower Manhattan for several years to come.
4 By the time Dr. Rogers retires, he will have been working at this university for 30 years.
5 Sean will have been dating Carrie for seven years when they get married.

[해석]

1 내년 이맘때쯤 우리는 서로를 알고 지낸 지 10년이 된다.
2 다음 달 이때쯤 우리는 유럽을 배낭여행 중일 거야. 난 너무 신이 나.
3 뉴욕 시는 향후 몇 년간 맨해튼 남부를 보수할 것이다.
4 로저 박사님이 은퇴할 때쯤에 그는 이 대학에서 30년간 일하신 것이 된다.
5 션은 캐리와 결혼할 때쯤 그녀와 사귄 지 7년이 된다.

1 It is believed that the earth was formed more than four billion years ago.
2 It is believed that a unified Korea would be a global scientific powerhouse.
3 It is believed that many illnesses are actually caused by the human mind.

[해석]

1 지구는 40억 년 전보다 더 오래전에 형성되었다고 여겨진다.
2 통일된 한국은 세계적인 과학 강국이 될 것으로 여겨진다.
3 많은 질병이 실제로는 사람들의 생각에서 발생되었다고 여겨진다.

PART 4

Unit 15 EXERCISES p. 71

A

1 ⓑ   2 ⓕ   3 ⓓ   4 ⓔ   5 ⓒ
6 ⓐ

해석

1 내 첫 아르바이트는 프랑스 식당에서 바닥 청소를 하는 것이었다.
2 그 탐정은 지문을 찾기 위해 문의 손잡이를 꼼꼼하게 살폈다.
3 너한테 내 휴대용 디스크를 빌려준 것을 완전히 잊고 있었어. 잃어버린 줄 알았어.
4 내가 떠나기 전에 우리가 이 일을 끝낼 시간이 충분할지 확실하지 않아.
5 질은 팔목이 부러졌지만 계속해서 태권도 수업을 받았다.
6 빗속에서 한 시간 넘게 친구들을 기다린 제이크는 무척 화가 났다.

B

1 to have   2 disappointed
3 to use   4 to find
5 growing   6 covering
7 to improve

해석

1 너는 나와 진지한 대화를 나누기 싫지, 그렇지 않니?
2 내가 도착했을 때 크리스는 이미 공항으로 떠나 있었어. 매우 실망스러웠어.
3 수학 선생님은 학생들이 시험 도중에 계산기를 사용하는 것을 허용하지 않는다.
4 밴쿠버에서 숙박 업체를 찾으려던 마이크의 시도는 별로 성공적이지 못했다.
5 나는 지난 몇 달간 네가 블로그에 단 댓글들을 읽고 있는데 점점 화가 치민다.
6 내 방을 둘러싼 벽을 바꾼 다음에는 분위기가 완전히 밝아졌다. 정말 좋은 생각이었어!
7 나는 항상 내 스마트폰으로 음악을 듣지만, 오늘은 듣기를 향상하기 위해 영어 강의를 듣고 있다.

Unit 16 EXERCISES p. 74~75

A

1 Many senior high school students
2 most people
3 Eugene
4 The audience
5 carved images of clan symbols
6 the professions

해석

1 많은 고등학교 3학년생들은 진로를 결정하느라 힘든 시기를 보내고 있었다.

2 심각한 병을 대면할 때, 대부분의 사람들은 그들의 삶에서 희망하고 소망할 것들이 많다는 것을 알게 된다.
3 지친 유진은 이렇게 늦은 시간에 설거지를 시작하는 것은 어리석은 짓이라고 중얼거렸다.
4 강당에 드문드문 앉아 있는 관객들은 숨죽이며 농구 경기를 지켜보았다.
5 집 앞에는 그 안에 사는 가족을 대표하는 씨족의 상징이 새겨진 상들이 있었다.
6 최고 지위의 직업들은 수년의 교육과 훈련이 필요한 전문직 즉, 의사, 변호사, 교수, 그리고 성직자이다.

B

1 transplanted   2 released
3 stimulating   4 fixed
5 pleased   6 tiring
7 colored

해석

1 신장은 가장 흔히 이식받는 장기가 되었다.
2 새롭게 개봉되어 상영 중인 영화는 내가 본 것 중 최고였다.
3 우리는 대중들의 관심을 사로잡을 매우 자극적인 마케팅 전략이 필요하다.
4 만약 로렌스의 가족이 정해진 날짜까지 빚을 갚지 못하면 그들은 집을 잃게 될 것이다.
5 입학시험은 완전히 성공적이었고, 맥키는 당연히 매우 기뻤다.
6 일은 지치고 지루했다. 내가 해야 했던 일은 온종일 벤치에 앉아서 수영하는 사람들을 지켜보는 것이었다.
7 남동생은 그날 저녁에 자기 애를 돌봐 달라고 내게 부탁했다. 나는 그의 아들과 색종이로 종이비행기를 접으며 시간을 보냈다.

C

1 disturbed   2 disconcerting
3 confusing   4 bewildering
5 satisfied   6 embarrassed

해석

1 소피아는 자신의 아버지가 병에 걸리셨다는 이야기를 듣고 불안했다.
2 아이작이 무대에서 연달아 실수하는 것을 보는 것은 당혹스러웠다.
3 이 TV 프로그램은 현 상황이 혼란스러울 뿐 아니라 위험할 수도 있다는 것을 보여 준다.
4 선생님은 새로운 학생의 태도가 당혹스러웠다. 그녀는 그 학생의 부모님을 부르기로 결심했다.
5 내 남자 친구와는 달리, 나는 아무것도 안 하며 하루하루를 보내는 것에 만족하지 못한다. 그래서 나는 종종 그와 싸운다.
6 제인은 호주 친구들에게 자신을 영어로 잘 표현하지 못할 때 쉽게 당황스러워 한다.

D

1 ① conflicting   ② conflicted
2 ① admiring   ② admired
3 ① captivated   ② captivating
4 ① astounding   ② astounded

해석

1 ① 그가 사형 선고를 받았는지에 대해서는 엇갈리는 보고가 있었다.
　② 앤은 종종 두 소년을 향한 자신의 마음 때문에 누구를 선택할지에 대해 갈등을 느낀다.
2 ① 브래들리는 그를 매력적으로 여기는 여자들로부터 사랑을 고백하는 편지를 많이 받았다.
　② 그녀는 미국의 최초 영부인으로서 우아함과 따스함으로 널리 사랑받았다.
3 ① 해리는 밴드의 음악 소리에 너무 사로잡힌 나머지 그들의 콘서트를 두 번이나 봤다.
　② 로란은 매혹적인 목소리로 인해 가수로서 큰 성공을 했다.
4 ① 데이비드는 배가 고파서 투덜거렸지만, 곧 평소와 같은 놀라운 속도로 다시 일하기 시작했다.
　② 내 가장 친한 친구가 내 비밀을 모든 사람이 다 들을 수 있게 말했을 때 나는 너무 놀랐다.

 Unit 17 EXERCISES p. 78

A

1 visiting	2 Holding[To hold]
3 asking	4 disturbed
5 having lost	6 receiving

해석

1 존과 나는 둘 다 미술관 가는 것을 매우 좋아한다.
2 이 섬에서 회의를 개최하는 것은 매우 비쌀 것이다.
3 나한테 돈을 달라고 하는 것만 아니면 어떤 부탁도 들어줄 수 있어.
4 당신을 둘러싼 사람들로부터 방해받는 것을 피하고 당신의 일에 집중하세요.
5 콜리는 내가 그녀와 마주칠 때마다 자신의 남동생을 잃어버렸던 기억이 떠오른다고 하였다.
6 여러분의 지원서를 받게 되어서 감사드립니다만, 선택되신 지원자들께만 연락이 갈 것입니다.

B

1 Squinting[To squint]	2 offering
3 leaving	4 Implying[To imply]

해석

1 밝은 빛에서 눈을 가늘게 뜨면 얼굴과 눈가에 주름이 생긴다.
2 이 공원은 방문객들에게 조용한 환경을 제공하는 것으로 높이 평가된다. 그곳에는 잘 가꾸어진 몇 개의 정원이 있다.
3 존은 지문을 남기지 않으려고 장갑을 꼈지만, 난간에 있는 그의 지문은 그의 범행에 대한 결정적인 증거였다.
4 다른 식으로 돌려 말한 것은 끔찍한 실수였다. 나는 그러한 말을 한 것에 대해 네가 사과하길 바란다.

 Unit 18 EXERCISES p. 82~83

A

1 to have	2 perform
3 keep, to keep	4 to quit
5 be	6 to give

7 affecting, to affect		8 appreciate	
9 buying		10 mention	
11 to close		12 decide	
13 to be		14 to immigrate	

해석

1 제이미가 팀을 저녁 식사에 초대했을 때 그는 매우 기뻤다.
2 그 밴드가 콘서트에서 공연하는 것을 보는 것은 놀라웠다.
3 강한 바람과 건조한 상태로 인해 불길이 계속됐다.
4 그가 너에게 2주 안에 관두라고 한 것은 불합리하다.
5 오늘부터 저희는 여러분의 주문품을 예전만큼 빨리 배달할 수 없을지도 모릅니다.
6 켈리는 일주일 안에 내 전자사전을 돌려주겠다는 약속을 어겼다.
7 강한 황사는 이번 주말에 계속 우리나라에 영향을 줄 것이다.
8 그 쇼는 마티나 맥브라이드가 얼마나 대단한 가수인지 감탄하게 했다.
9 나는 컴퓨터 게임기를 살 준비가 거의 되어 있지만, 산 후에 후회할까 봐 두렵다.
10 이 일은 이미 진행되고 있기 때문에 더는 언급하지 않는 것이 좋을 것 같다.
11 토네이도가 도시 남쪽 끝을 강타했다. 강한 바람으로 인해 고속도로 다리도 폐쇄되었다.
12 나는 학생들에게 그들이 필요한 모든 정보를 제공하고, 그들 스스로 결정하게 둔다.
13 그 이야기 속 여자 주인공은 20년 이상 더 살 수 있을 거란 의학검사 결과에도 불구하고, 치명적인 병을 가진 척했다.
14 안타깝게도 로라는 1983년 5월 14일, 미국으로의 이민 허가를 받던 바로 그 날, 생을 마감했다.

B

1 ① to include	② switching, locking
2 ① to mention	② hearing
3 ① to locate	② doing
4 ① having	② to say

해석

1 ① 여행을 위해 작은 담요를 여행 가방에 넣는 것을 잊지 마라.
　② 우리가 나오기 전에 불 끈 거 기억나니? 문을 잠근 것은 기억하는데.
2 ① 우리가 어디서 만날지 얘기하는 것을 잊었어. 그녀에게 다시 가야 해.
　② 매우 멋진 날이었어. 나는 대통령의 연설을 들은 것을 절대 잊지 못할 거야.
3 ① 내가 친부모를 찾으려고 노력하면 그들의 마음이 다칠까 봐 두렵다.
　② 네가 제일 좋아하는 음악에 맞춰 춤을 추거나 친구들과 놀러 나가는 등 너에게 동기 부여가 될 수 있는 활동적인 뭔가를 하도록 해봐.
4 ① 나는 실패로 끝난 어떤 일을 시작한 것을 뒤돌아보고 후회하고 싶지 않다.
　② 유감스럽게도 우리는 본질적으로 해결책과 전략을 논의하고 있지, 문제점을 논의하고 있지 않다고 말씀 드리고 싶어요.

C

1 The website would not allow me to copy and paste the text.
2 Both my brothers tend to dread and postpone cleaning the house.
3 After you have finished reading the magazine, put it

back where it was.

4 Eric was relieved to discover that at least one person enjoyed the food he made.

5 I'd better stop asking you questions. Let's just get started with the easiest part of the process.

6 Remember that as dogs enjoy human company, they will not appreciate being left alone for long periods.

해석

1 그 웹사이트는 글을 복사하고 붙여넣는 것을 허용하지 않을 것이다.

2 우리 오빠들은 둘 다 집을 청소하는 것을 끔찍해 하고 미루는 경향이 있다.

3 잡지를 다 읽은 후에는 제자리에 갖다 놓아라.

4 에릭은 최소한 한 사람은 자기가 만든 음식을 맛있게 먹었다는 것을 알고는 안심했다.

5 너에게 질문하는 것을 그만하는 게 낫겠다. 과정 중 가장 쉬운 부분부터 시작하자.

6 개들이 사람과 함께 있는 것을 즐거워하는 만큼 장기간 홀로 남겨지는 것을 좋아하지 않는다는 것을 기억하라.

REVIEW

p. 84

1 ③   2 ④   3 ②

해설/해석

1 After I had retired from engineering이라는 문장으로 만든 분사구문이므로 Having이 적절

   A: 마치 엔지니어같이 말씀하시네요. 선생님이 되기 전에 어떤 일을 하셨나요?
   B: 공학에서 은퇴한 후 교편을 잡았어요.

2 미안한 감정의 원인을 나타내기 위해서는 to부정사를 사용해야 하고, 과거에 가지 않았던 것을 현재 미안해하는 것이므로 완료형 부정사인 to have come이 적절

   A: 지난 주말에 네가 우리 집 파티에 올 줄 알았는데. 무슨 일 있었니?
   B: 못 가서 정말 미안해. 그날 저녁 내 조카를 돌봐야 했어.

3 앞의 명사를 수식할 수 있는 동사 형태는 현재분사, 과거분사, to부정사, 이때, 현재분사는 '~하고 있는', 과거분사는 '~된', to부정사는 '~할'의 의미, '피로연에 초대된 대부분의 사람들'이라는 뜻이 되어야 하므로 과거분사인 invited가 적절

   A: 비키와 관련된 사람들은 여기에 하나도 안 보여. 이 사람들은 누구인 것 같니?
   B: 피로연에 초대된 대부분의 사람들은 그녀의 옛날 친구들이야. 그래서 우리가 아무도 낯익지 않은 거야.

1 ③   2 ①   3 ④

해설/해석

1 ③ postpone은 동명사를 목적어로 취하는 동사, 따라서 traveling이 적절

   A: 나는 시드니에 있는 오페라 하우스 앞에 가보고 싶어.
   B: 이번 여름방학에 호주에 가지 그래?
   A: 못 가. 의학 시험 때문에. 시드니 여행은 연말까지 미뤄야 해.
   B: 행운을 빌게.

2 ① 「forget+to부정사」는 '~할 것을 잊다'이고, 「forget+동명사」는 '~했던 것을 잊다'라는 의미, 아버지께 전화해야 하는 것을 잊은 것이므로 calling이 아니라 to call로 써야 함

   A: 벌써 열한 시야. 늦을 거라고 아버지에게 전화하는 것을 잊었어.
   B: 괜찮을 거야. 우리가 졸업 파티에서 재미있게 보내고 있다고 이해하실 거야.
   A: 아버지에게는 예외가 없어. 전화 없이 열 시까지 집에 안 가면 문이 잠겨서 못 들어갈 거야.
   B: 우와, 정말 엄격하시구나.

3 ④ 두 문장을 접속사를 사용하지 않고 한 문장으로 나타낼 때 접속사를 포함하고 있는 종속절을 분사구문으로 줄여 쓸 수 있음, After I have been a father for many years라는 문장에서 비롯된 분사구문이므로 Having been a father가 적절

   A: 어린 시절에 대해 여쭤보고 싶은데요. 어떠셨나요?
   B: 어릴 때는 매우 외로웠습니다. 부모님은 의사여서 일하느라 바쁘셨거든요.
   A: 어린 시절이 아버지가 된 후 어떤 영향을 주었습니까?
   B: 오랜 시간 아버지로 살아보니, 아이들과 보내는 시간이 얼마나 소중한지 이제 알게 되었죠.

REVIEW PLUS

p. 85~86

1 ③   2 ②   3 ①

해설/해석

1 ③ encouraged는 '격려를 받은', encouraging은 '격려가 되는, 힘을 북돋아 주는'이라는 의미, 연구 결과가 사람들에게 힘을 북돋아 주는 것이므로 encouraging이 적절

   미국인들이 살찌는 것은 놀랄 일이 아니다. 새로운 연구에 의하면 쿠키와, 사탕, 그리고 베이컨이 2% 더 싸진 반면에 야채와 신선한 과일의 가격은 20% 올랐다. 메릴랜드 대학에서 발견한 희망적인 한 자료에 의하면 통조림 및 냉동된 야채와 과일의 가격은 고정적인데, 영양적 가치를 거의 그대로 유지한다. 계절에 맞는 농산물을 사는 것과 농산물 직판장에서 제품을 사는 것이 도움이 될 것이다.

2 ② 문장의 주어인 Dreaming of something you're worried about은 동명사구로 단수 취급해야 하기 때문에 are가 아니라 is가 적절

   꿈은 무의식이 의식과 의사소통하는 방법이다. 당신이 걱정하는 것에 대해 꿈을 꾸는 것은 뇌가 당신에게 불행이 닥칠 경우에 대비해 준비시켜 주는 것이다. 수영 대회나 학교에서 발표하는 것과 같은 도전에 관한 꿈은 당신의 성과를 향상할 수 있다. 인지 신경 과학자들은 또한 꿈과 당신이 자는 사이에 일어나는 빠른 안구의 움직임이 학습 능력 및 기억 능력과 연관 있다는 것을 발견하였다.

3 ① 추상명사의 내용을 보충 설명하기 위해서 to부정사를 사용할 수 있음, 그러므로 opportunity의 상세 내용을 담으려면 taking을 to take로 바꿔야 함

   캐나다 국립공원에서 북극곰 생물학자들과 늦겨울 현장 연구에 동행하던 중, 다니엘은 석 달이 된 새끼 곰 한 쌍이 굴 안에서 꼭 껴안고 있는 장면을 사진으로 포착할 정말 이례적인 기회를 잡았다. 그는 곰들을 놀라게 하지 않기 위해 매우 천천히 움직였다. 굴 벽의 무늬는 엄마 곰이 발톱을 이용해 땅을 판 데에서 생겼다. 동상에 걸렸지만, 그는 그것이 정말 가치 있는 일이었다고 믿었다.

⑤

(A) 전치사 뒤에는 명사 또는 동명사 형태를 써야 하므로 communication 또는 communicating 둘 다 가능 (B) 단어 '웨비나'가 유래를 찾는 것이 아니라 단어의 유래가 찾아지는 것이므로 수동태로 써야 함, 「be derived from ~」은 '~로부터 유래하다, 비롯되다'라는 의미 (C) the web and conferencing software를 사용하는 세미나이므로 능동형인 using이 적절

"웨비나"는 무엇이며, 이것이 회사를 위해 어떠한 이로움을 주는가? 더 많은 사업들이 통신비용을 줄이는 것뿐만 아니라 새로운 고객에게 다가갈 참신한 방법들을 찾으면서 웨비나가 종종 거론되고 있다. 웨비나라는 말은 웹과 세미나라는 두 개의 뿌리 단어에서 나왔다. 웨비나는 웹과 회의 소프트웨어를 이용한 세미나이다. 웨비나의 가장 즉각적인 이점 중 하나는 회사 출장 경비의 상당 부분을 없앨 수 있다는 데 있다. 항상 얼굴을 마주 대하는 회의가 필요할 때도 있겠지만, 많은 사업 교환들이 웹 회의를 통해 처리될 수 있다.

③

③ tofu's protein은 알고 있는 것이 아니라 알려지는 것이므로 수동의 의미를 지닌 과거분사형 known이 적절, 분사구문에서 Being이 생략된 형태 「be known as ~」는 '~으로 알려지다'

전설에 의하면, 중국 당나라 때 한 가난한 공무원이 너무 정직해서 뇌물을 받지 않았다. 그는 가족에게 먹일 고기를 사지 못해서 그는 두부를 발명했다. 오늘날까지 몇몇 중국인들은 정직한 공무원을 "두부 공무원"이라고 부른다. "중국의 소고기"라고 알려진 두부의 단백질은 품질에 있어서 고기의 단백질과 비슷하다. 하지만 두부는 제조 방법상 치즈와 더 비슷하다. 두유는 미네랄 소금으로 걸쭉하게 해서 덩어리를 만들어서 두부의 다른 유명한 이름이 "콩 덩어리"인 것이다.

WRITING PRACTICE

p. 87~88

1 It is sometimes a difficult task to please
2 It is not good for your health to study all day
3 is interested in working for
4 she's still poor at speaking Spanish

1 부모님을 기쁘게 하는 것은 가끔 힘든 일이다.
2 온종일 도서관에서 공부하는 것은 건강에 좋지 않다.
3 내 친구 재키는 온라인 회사에서 일하는 것에 관심이 있다.
4 캐시는 스페인에서 1년간 살았지만, 여전히 스페인어를 잘하지 못한다.

1 Go down these stairs and keep on walking across until you reach the other side.
2 We already own many of the things that we need to clean a house and to mend household items.

3 I consider Tanya's ideas not as established facts, but rather as provocative ideas that stimulate others.
4 I have been hoping to become a member of the Korean national team. I will put a great deal of effort into doing so.
5 Listening to the tremendous ovation, I was ushered into Seoul Stadium along with the other members of my team.

1 이 계단을 내려가서 반대편에 다다를 때까지 계속 가로질러 가세요.
2 우리는 집을 청소하고 살림살이를 고치는 데 필요한 것들을 이미 많이 가지고 있다.
3 나는 타냐의 생각을 기정사실로 생각하지는 않지만, 오히려 다른 사람들을 자극하는 도발적인 의견이라고 생각한다.
4 나는 한국 국가 대표 팀의 일원이 되기를 희망해 왔다. 나는 그렇게 되기 위해 엄청난 노력을 할 것이다.
5 엄청나게 큰 박수갈채를 받으면서 나는 우리 팀의 다른 멤버들과 함께 서울 경기장 안으로 인도되었다.

1 cannot help raising serious concerns with our school administration
2 couldn't help wondering whom my sister was conversing with on the Internet
3 of the surrounding mountains in Germany couldn't help impressing me

1 그러한 사실은 학교 행정에 대한 심각한 우려를 낳을 수밖에 없다.
2 나는 내 여동생과 인터넷으로 대화를 나누는 사람이 누구인지 궁금해하지 않을 수 없었다.
3 독일에서 주변 산들의 웅장한 광경에 나는 감탄하지 않을 수 없었다.

1 To tell the truth, I have little interest in my professor's lectures.
2 To tell the truth, rumor has it that several workers including you will be laid off.
3 To tell the truth, the kidnappers have put him in solitary confinement for a month.

1 솔직히 말해서, 나는 우리 교수님의 강의에 별로 관심이 없다.
2 사실은, 너를 포함한 여러 명의 직원이 해고될 것이라는 소문이 있더라.
3 사실대로 말하자면, 납치범들은 그를 한 달 동안이나 홀로 감금해 왔다.

PART 5

Unit 19 EXERCISES
p. 92

A

1 quite
2 predictable
3 old enough
4 surprisingly
5 highly
6 extremely

1 길 아래 새로 생긴 인도 식당의 카레는 정말 맛있다.
2 최근 몇 년간 공포 영화들은 너무 뻔한 내용이 되었다.
3 너는 네가 어른으로서 책임을 질만 한 충분한 나이라고 생각하니?
4 네가 오늘 산 여행 가방은 놀랄 만큼 가볍고 가지고 다니기에 편하다.
5 향신료와 담배는 과거에 매우 높은 가치를 지녔고 무역 상품으로 사용되었다.
6 상미는 지하철에서 강도를 당했지만, 운 좋게도 정말 비싼 것은 아무것도 잃어버리지 않았다.

B

1 at the station almost two hours late this morning
2 regularly at the gym every evening to tone his body
3 carefully on icy roads in winter to prevent accidents
4 loudly in the hall last week to celebrate Foundation Day
5 the playground in a hurry last night to have a shower
6 south quickly when the winter approaches to escape the cold

Unit 20 EXERCISES
p. 95

A

1 over the table: jumps, behind the chair: hides
2 happy
3 run
4 by an hour: was delayed, in the morning: early

1 그 장난기 많은 새끼 고양이는 항상 식탁 위로 뛰어오르고 의자 뒤에 숨는다.
2 모든 유치원 어린이들이 놀이 공원에 가는 것에 대하여 기뻐했다.
3 햄스터는 좋은 애완동물이긴 하지만, 주의하지 않으면 작은 공간으로 재빨리 숨어버릴 수도 있다.
4 비행기 이륙이 한 시간 정도 늦어졌지만, 그들은 아침 일찍 도착하였다.

B

1 out to sea at five in the morning
2 at a fashion event ten years ago
3 in the playground on Wednesdays and Thursdays
4 across the street before they went into the bank

1 부산에서는 숙련된 어부들만이 새벽 다섯 시에 바다로 나간다.
2 데이비드와 빅토리아는 10년 전 한 의류 행사에서 서로 처음 만났다.
3 빌리는 주로 수요일과 목요일에 운동장에서 축구를 한다.
4 그 곤충들은 어두운 창 밑에서 살았었다.

C

1 because of his good review
2 because of her hard work and studying

1 우리 학교 신문의 편집자인 호준이는 새로운 학교 연극에 관해 좋은 평론을 썼다. 연극의 공연 첫날 밤, 많은 학생들과 교사들이 참석했다.
2 우리 언니는 해외에 있는 대학에 가기 위해 많은 학원들을 다니고 자습도 많이 했다. 지난주 언니는 유명한 프랑스 대학에 입학 허가를 받았다.

Unit 21 EXERCISES
p. 99~100

A

1 while
2 If
3 Although
4 because
5 before
6 whereas

1 교장 선생님이 연설하는 동안 몇몇 학생들은 잠이 들었다.
2 우리가 오늘 밤 일찍 출발하고 운이 좋다면 콘서트에서 앞줄에 있는 좌석을 잡게 될거야.
3 스위스가 시계 제조로 유명하지만, 내가 좋아할 만한 것을 찾지 못했다.
4 딘은 다리가 부러져서 병원에 있어야 했기 때문에 2주간 결석했다.
5 지난주에 잡지에 실린 한 기사에서 자기 바로 전에 고기를 먹는 것은 건강에 좋지 않다고 했다.
6 한국에서 집에 들어갈 때는 신발을 벗어야 하는 반면에 남아프리카에서는 그러지 않아도 된다.

B

1 ⓑ
2 ⓔ
3 ⓓ
4 ⓒ
5 ⓐ
6 ⓓ

1 케빈은 그다지 수다스럽지 않지만, 영어를 매우 잘한다.
2 택배 회사는 내가 개를 산책시키는 동안 소포를 배달했다.
3 존은 이미 17개 나라를 여행한 반면, 제시카는 10개 나라밖에 여행하지 않았다.
4 근로조건이 적절하면 나는 그 회사의 영입 제안을 받아들일 것이다.
5 이제 기말 프로젝트가 다 완료되어서 모든 학생들은 긴장이 풀려 활기차 보인다.
6 박 선생님의 예전 방법은 지루했던 반면에, 발음 강습에 대한 새로운 방법은 흥미롭고 재미있다.

C

1 By the time he realized his spelling mistakes
2 while the sleeves were made of satin
3 as long as you complete your homework

4   If we find cheap plane tickets
5   whereas the boys are good at geography

해석

1   잭이 철자를 잘못 썼음을 깨달았을 때 이미 이메일을 보낸 상태였다.
2   그녀가 입고 있던 드레스는 실크로 만들어진 반면, 소매는 공단으로 만들어졌다.
3   네가 숙제를 다 마치기만 하면 컴퓨터 게임을 해도 된다.
4   우리가 값싼 비행기 표를 찾으면 우리는 올해 여름에 태국에 갈 것이다.
5   우리 반 여자 아이들은 수학을 잘하는 반면, 남자 아이들은 지리학을 잘한다.

1   Although many guests complained about the food
2   If summer is really hot this year
3   because nobody laughed at his jokes that night
4   whereas his classmates wanted to make a
     presentation

해석

1   많은 손님들이 음식에 대해 불평했다. 그들은 파티에서 즐거운 시간을 보냈다.
     → 많은 손님들이 음식에 대해 불평했지만, 그들은 파티에서 즐거운 시간을 보냈다.
2   올해 여름은 정말 덥다. 나는 대부분의 시간을 수영장에서 보낼 것이다.
     → 올해 여름이 정말 덥다면, 나는 대부분의 시간을 수영장에서 보낼 것이다.
3   그 코미디언은 비참하고 실망스러웠다. 그날 밤 아무도 그의 농담에 웃어주지 않았다.
     → 그 코미디언은 그날 밤 아무도 그의 농담에 웃어주지 않아서 비참하고 실망스러웠다.
4   아담은 평가 방법으로 시험을 보는 것을 선호한다. 그의 학우들은 발표를 하고 싶어했다.
     → 아담은 평가 방법으로 시험을 보는 것을 선호하는 반면, 그의 학우들은 발표를 하고 싶어했다.

Unit 22 **EXERCISES**   p. 103~104

1   looking   2   watching
3   Having raised   4   reading
5   Having seen   6   going
7   having seen

해석

1   신발 가게를 찾던 중, 나는 많은 옷 가게들이 할인판매 하는 것을 보았다.
2   TV를 보기 전에 바이런은 숙제를 마치고 애완동물에게 먹이를 주었다.
3   고양이를 10년간 기른 후 제니퍼는 수의사가 되기로 결심했다.
4   기사를 읽는 동안 윌리엄은 익숙하지 않은 단어들을 사전에서 찾아보았다.
5   그가 체육관에 정기적으로 다니는 것을 보았기 때문에 사람들은 그의 몸매가 좋고 건강하다고 생각한다.
6   스페인어를 전공하기 위해 대학에 가기 전, 데니스는 남미에서 2년을 보냈다.
7   사고를 목격한 후 무리 중의 한 사람이 즉시 경찰을 불렀다.

1   singing   2   Having broken
3   (Because) Having   4   (While) Talking

해석

1   우진은 노래를 부르기 전에 무대 뒤에서 목을 가다듬고 발성 연습을 하였다.
     → 노래를 부르기 전에 우진은 무대 뒤에서 목을 가다듬고 발성 연습을 하였다.
2   새로 산 안경을 실수로 부러뜨렸다. 나는 어제 안과에 갔었다.
     → 새로 산 안경을 실수로 부러뜨려서 나는 어제 안과에 갔었다.
3   에밀리오는 패션 감각이 뛰어나기 때문에 그는 신부를 위해 드레스를 골라 달라는 부탁을 받았다.
     → 패션 감각이 뛰어나기에 에밀리오는 신부를 위해 드레스를 골라 달라는 부탁을 받았다.
4   조셉이 전화 통화를 하던 중에 고양이가 비싼 중국 화병을 깨는 것을 보았다.
     → 전화 통화를 하던 중에 조셉은 고양이가 비싼 중국 화병을 깨는 것을 보았다.

1   Having no confidence
2   (After) Having completed the form
3   Not having a lot of money
4   (Before) Going out

해석

1   벤은 자신감이 전혀 없었기 때문에, 반에서 발표하겠다고 지원한 적이 한 번도 없다.
     → 자신감이 전혀 없었기에, 벤은 반에서 발표하겠다고 지원한 적이 한 번도 없다.
2   양식을 완성한 후 이 주소로 모든 필요한 문서들과 같이 보내 주세요.
     → 양식을 완성한 후 이 주소로 모든 필요한 문서들과 같이 보내 주세요.
3   제이미는 돈이 별로 없었기에, 가게에서 가장 싼 펜을 사기로 결정했다.
     → 돈이 별로 없었기에, 제이미는 가게에서 가장 싼 펜을 사기로 결정했다.
4   베티는 나가기 전에, 모든 불을 끄고 창문들이 닫혀 있는지 확인했다.
     → 나가기 전에, 베티는 모든 불을 끄고 창문들이 닫혀 있는지 확인했다.

1   After I had finished work on the weekend
2   Because[As] Franklin was disturbed by his noisy
     neighbors
3   As soon as Sangjun had heard that he passed the
     entrance exam
4   After they had met in Rome, they got married.

해석

1   주말에 일을 마친 후, 나는 너무 피곤해서 침대에 쓰러졌다.
2   시끄러운 이웃들 때문에 방해를 받아서, 프랭클린은 그들에게 음악을 줄여 달라고 부탁하기로 했다.
3   입학시험에 합격했다는 소식을 듣자마자 상준이는 어머니께 바로 전화 드렸다.
4   로마에서 만난 후 그들은 결혼했다. 결혼기념일을 축하하기 위해 그들은 매년 그곳으로 간다.

1 ①   **2** ①

 해설/해석

1 타동사 뒤에는 목적어가 와야 하고, 목적어 뒤에 부사구가 위치, 또한, 부사구 뒤에 전치사구가 위치하므로 our house every summer for three weeks가 적절

A: 이번 여름에 우리는 제주도에 갈 거야. 너는 방학 동안에 무엇을 할 거니?

B: 우리 할머니는 대개 여름마다 3주 동안 우리 집에 와 계셔.

2 의미상 '열악한 근로 조건과 낮은 임금 때문에 파업을 하고 있다'가 되어야 하므로 이유를 나타내는 because of, since, now that 중에서 poor conditions and low salaries라는 명사구를 뒤에 쓸 수 있는 because of가 적절

A: 뉴스 봤니? 자동차 노동자들이 또 파업한대.

B: 응. 그들은 열악한 근로 환경과 낮은 임금 때문에 파업을 하고 있어.

1 ④   **2** ③   **3** ④

 해설/해석

1 ④ 식당에 가기 전에 예약을 하는 것이므로 after가 아니라 before가 적절

A: 이번 주 열리는 음식점 페스티벌에 대해 들었어?

B: 아니, 하지만 재미있을 것 같아. 어떤 건데?

A: 음, 다양한 음식점이 참여를 해서 세계 각지의 다양한 음식을 먹어 볼 수 있어.

B: 좋아. 그럼 이런 음식점에 가기 전에 예약해야겠네.

2 ③ 어려운 상황에서도 성공에 이른다는 것은 예상치 못한 결과를 나타내는 것이므로 Because 대신 양보의 접속사 Even though 또는 Although를 쓰는 것이 적절

A: 우와, 나는 인생에서 가장 힘든 시험을 이겨낸 사람들이 정말 존경스러워.

B: 응, 나도 그래. 그들의 결단력과 강인함을 보면 놀라워.

A: 그들은 끔찍한 상황을 겪는데도 불구하고 여전히 성공하잖아.

B: 나도 내 인생에서 그러한 자질들을 개발할 수 있으면 좋겠어.

3 ④ 스위스와 다른 나라들이 좋은 이유를 각각 자연적 측면과 음식적인 측면에서 대조하고 있으므로 even though 대신 대조의 접속사 whereas 또는 while을 쓰는 것이 적절

A: 나는 우리가 유럽으로 여행하게 되어 정말 신나. 정말 재미있을 것 같아.

B: 당연하지! 유럽은 특히 여름에 매혹적이야. 어느 나라들을 방문할 거니?

A: 우선 프랑스에 가서 일주일을 보낸 뒤, 이탈리아, 스위스, 그리고 독일에 갈 거야.

B: 다른 곳들은 음식 때문에 좋은데, 스위스는 그 경치 때문에 좋은 것 같아.

1 ①   **2** ④   **3** ②

 해설/해석

1 ① 아픈 것이 진찰을 받은 것보다 더 먼저 일어난 것이므로 완료 부사구를 써야 함. 완료부사구는 「Having+p.p.」의 형태이므로 Having suffered가 적절

몇 주 동안이나 요통에 시달린 나는 동네 병원에 가서 진찰받기로 결심했다. 의사는 침술 요법을 해 주었고, 등 근육을 늘려 주기 위해 요가를 할 것을 내게 제안했다. 나는 그의 조언을 기꺼이 받아들여 사무실 근처 체육관에서 요가 수업을 찾았다. 나는 이제 아침 7시부터 8시 반까지 매일 요가 수업에 참여하고 훨씬 나아졌다.

2 ④ 셔틀콕의 깃털들이 치는 것이 아니라, 선수들에 의해 타격이 가해지는 것이므로 수동태 분사구를 써야 함. Having been hit이 적절

신나는 라켓 운동인 배드민턴은 올림픽에서의 위상 때문에 상당한 인기를 누리고 있다. 배드민턴은 셔틀콕을 사용하는데 셔틀콕은 대부분의 다른 라켓 운동에서 사용하는 공들과는 매우 다르게 날아간다. 셔틀콕은 원뿔 모양의 깃털이 달린 기구이기 때문에 배드민턴을 특별하게 만든다. 맞으면, 셔틀콕의 깃털들은 셔틀콕을 강하게 잡아당겨 공보다 훨씬 더 빨리 속도를 잃게 한다.

3 ② 문맥상 필요한 것은 아니지만 매일 해주는 것이 좋다라는 의미가 되어야 하므로 양보의 접속사 Although, Even though, Though가 적절

말을 손질하는 것은 시합에 나가는 말의 외모를 향상시키기 때문에, 말을 키우는 데 있어 중요하다. 반드시 필요한 것은 아니지만, 말에게 많은 도움이 되므로 날마다 손질할 것을 권한다. 정기적으로 손질을 받으면 말의 피부는 더 건강해지고 건강 문제의 위험이 줄어든다. 말 손질은 또한 말과 주로 주인인, 손질하는 사람 사이에 가까운 관계가 빨리 형성되도록 도와준다.

②

 해설/해석

(A) 주절의 주어인 I가 직접 찾아다니는 것이므로 능동 분사구인 searching이 적절 (B) 부사의 역할을 하는 전치사구를 연이어 나열할 때는 장소에서 시간 순으로 써야 하므로 to class on time이 적절 (C) 주절의 주어인 I가 설명을 하는 것이므로 능동 분사구인 explaining이라 써야 하고, 'while I explained'라는 문장에서 접속사를 남겨두고 분사구문을 만든 것으로 볼 수 있음, during은 전치사이므로 뒤에 문장이 올 수 없고, 명사만 올 수 있음

어느 날 저녁 일과 후에 캠퍼스에 도착해보니 주차장이 꽉 차 있었다. 주차 공간을 찾다가 맏딸인 마가렛을 발견했는데 그 아이는 나와 같은 학교에 다니는 학생이었다. 딸은 그날 마지막 수업을 마치고 집으로 가기 위해 차 있는 곳으로 걸어가고 있었다. 딸이 떠나는 자리를 맡으려고 하는 몇 명의 운전자들이 그녀를 따라가고 있었다. 수업 시간에 맞추기 위해 필사적이었던 나는 차를 세워 놓고 뛰쳐나와 딸에게로 달려갔다. 나는 나의 수업이 끝난 후에 딸의 차를 가지고 가겠다고 설명하면서 딸과 자동차 열쇠를 바꾸고 내 차를 몰고 집으로 가라고 말했다. 내가 다른 운전자들을 지나 교실로 달려갈 때 딸은 입을 딱 벌리고 놀란 모습으로 나를 쳐다봤다.

④

주절의 주어인 you가 스스로 기대하는 것이므로 능동형 분사인 expecting이 적절

테디 베어는 솜을 채운 장난감 곰이다. 정말 이상하게도, '테디 베어 효과' 는 수동적인 청자가 듣는 것 외에는 어떤 것도 하지 않고 화자에게 지혜를 주는 것처럼 보이는 현상을 가리킨다. 여러분이 누군가로부터 대답을 듣고 거기서 뭔가를 배울 것이라고 예상하면서 질문을 한다고 생각해 보라. 여러분은 종종 단지 질문을 말로 표현하는 행동만을 통해서 스스로 답을 발견하게 된다. 이 상황에서, 청자는 테디 베어에 비유되는데, 그 이유는 분명히 장난감 곰을 갖다 놓아도 같은 역할을 할 것이기 때문이다.

WRITING PRACTICE

p. 108~110

1 (Before) Joining the gym, James was terribly overweight and got tired easily.
2 (After being) Sent to the dry cleaners, the suit looked good as new and it smelled great.
3 Feeling really ill, Janet quickly decided to postpone her birthday picnic at the riverside.
4 (While) Excavating the site, the archeologists discovered the ruins of an unknown civilization.
5 Not having received any news about her university application, Kay was very worried about next year.

1 체육관에 등록하기 전에 제임스는 심한 과체중이었고 쉽게 지쳤다.
2 드라이클리닝 하러 맡긴 후, 정장은 새것처럼 보이고 냄새도 좋았다.
3 몸이 정말 안 좋았기 때문에, 자넷은 재빨리 강변에서의 생일 피크닉을 연기하기로 결정했다.
4 유적지를 발굴하는 동안 고고학자들은 알려지지 않은 문명의 유적을 발견하였다.
5 대학 지원서에 대해 아무런 소식도 받은 것이 없기에, 케이는 내년이 매우 걱정됐다.

B

1 The teacher makes an announcement in class every morning.
2 My mother likes Italian food, whereas[while] my father prefers Chinese food.
3 If it rains tomorrow, I'll wear my black coat and take an umbrella.
4 Having mixed the chemicals, they observed the chemical reaction.
5 The children were happy because their father bought them gifts overseas.

1 선생님은 아침마다 교실에서 공지를 한다.

2 우리 어머니는 이탈리아 음식을 좋아하시는 반면 우리 아버지는 중국 음식을 선호하신다.
3 내일 비가 온다면 나는 검은 코트를 입고 우산을 가져갈 것이다.
4 화학 약품을 섞은 후, 그들은 화학 반응을 관찰했다.
5 아이들은 아버지가 해외에서 선물을 사다 주셨기 때문에 기뻤다.

1 because of the locked hall
2 because of the gorgeous weather
3 because of her frozen computer

1 학교 밴드와 합창단은 연주회장이 잠겨서 어제 연습을 할 수 없었다.
2 화창한 날씨 때문에 놀이동산은 토요일에 사람들로 매우 붐볐다.
3 오늘 제니퍼는 고장 난 컴퓨터 때문에 이메일 계정에 접속할 수 없었다.

1 during the summer vacation
2 during the director's speech
3 during the game show on television

1 우리 가족은 여름방학 동안 하와이에 머물렀다.
2 웨이터들과 요리사들은 임원이 연설하는 동안 음식을 준비하였다.
3 우리 어머니와 아버지는 우리가 TV에서 게임 쇼를 보는 동안 저녁을 하셨다.

1 before reaching a decision, they mulled it over for a week
2 because you never ate red meat
3 that's why he sits quietly at the back of the class every day
4 Having worked as an intern, she learned the skills
5 How was the concert last night?

1 A: 세금에 대한 정부의 새 정책에 관한 뉴스 읽었니?
   B: 응, 결론에 도달하기 전, 정치인들은 일주일 넘게 이에 대해 논쟁을 했어.
2 A: 나는 네가 붉은 고기를 안 먹어서 채식주의자인 줄 알았어.
   B: 정말? 난 붉은 고기는 안 먹지만, 닭과 생선은 먹어. 하지만 주로 야채를 먹지.
3 A: 그는 생동감 있게 이야기하는 것을 정말 잘하지만, 그렇게 자신감이 넘치진 않아.
   B: 오, 그래서 그가 날마다 교실 뒤에 조용히 앉는 거구나.
4 A: 우와! 티나는 정말 회사에서 일을 잘하고 항상 사장님께 칭찬을 듣는구나.
   B: 응, 인턴으로 일해 오면서, 그녀는 일에 필요한 기술들을 매우 빨리 익혔어.
5 A: 어젯밤 콘서트는 어땠어? 가수가 한 시간 늦었다고 들었어.
   B: 가수가 늦게 도착했지만, 관중은 그녀가 시작하기를 침착하게 기다렸어.

PART 6

Unit 23 EXERCISES
p. 115~116

A

1 aglow 2 alive 3 alike 4 afloat 5 alight

해석

1 그 아이는 그의 아버지가 오랜 시간 떨어져 있다가 집에 돌아온다는 것에 신이 나서 얼굴이 붉게 달아올랐다.
2 화면이 켜진 다음에 컴퓨터 시스템을 재시동하려면 시스템이 재시동될 때까지 F8키를 계속 눌러라.
3 특정한 종류의 새들은 그들이 조류라는 점에서만 같다. 펭귄과 독수리가 그 훌륭한 예이다.
4 오직 선원의 전문성과 끈기만으로 망가진 배는 폭풍 속에서도 떠 있을 수 있었다.
5 지난주 토요일, 소방관들은 화재 현장으로 출동했다. 도착하자마자 그들은 불붙은 건물을 발견하였다. 화재의 원인은 사고로 추정되었다.

B

1 portable 2 beautiful 3 tiny
4 traditional 5 wooden

해석

1 우리가 산에 야영을 갈 때 아빠는 우리가 식사 준비를 할 수 있도록 항상 휴대용 가스레인지를 가져오신다.
2 나는 전통 한국 한복이 매우 아름답다고 생각한다. 그것들은 대부분의 서양 옷보다 훨씬 색감이 풍부하다.
3 내가 나의 새 강아지를 집에 데려왔을 때 그가 얼마나 작은지 믿을 수가 없었다. 나는 그를 손바닥에 들고 있을 수 있었다.
4 엄마는 추석을 위해 많은 다양한 종류의 음식을 준비하고 계시고, 아이들 모두는 전통 의상을 입고 있다.
5 우리 형 방의 벽에는 커다란 나무 가면이 걸려 있다. 원래, 그것은 서아프리카 부족원의 것이었다.

C

1 old black leather jacket
2 The most dangerous electrical storm of the year
3 Those two celadon vases
4 many precise mathematical questions
5 those mouth-watering smells wafting up
6 vivid, brightly colored frescos covering the walls
7 exhausting physical agility test
8 very well-designed precision
9 the extreme bone-chilling cold

해석

1 내 낡은 검은 가죽 재킷이 내가 가진 것 중 가장 따뜻한 외투이다.
2 어젯밤에 올해 중 가장 위험한 뇌우가 일어났다.
3 저 두 청자는 고려 왕조의 매우 값진 유물들이다.
4 내 공학 시험에는 정밀한 수학 문제들이 많았다.
5 길거리를 떠도는 이 군침 도는 냄새는 무엇이지?

6 나는 선명한 밝은 색상의 프레스코가 교회 벽을 메우고 있는 것을 보았다.
7 소방관이 되기 전에 모든 지원자들은 매우 힘들고 지치는 신체 민첩성 시험에 참여해야 한다.
8 그 우주선은 우주여행을 위해 사용되는 매우 잘 설계된 정밀한 비행 물체이다.
9 캐나다 북부를 여행하던 중 우리는 툰드라의 뼛속까지 에이는 극심한 추위를 경험했다.

Unit 24 EXERCISES
p. 118

A

1 ⓑ   2 ⓐ   3 ⓐ   4 ⓐ, ⓐ   5 ⓑ
6 ⓐ, ⓑ   7 ⓐ   8 ⓑ, ⓑ   9 ⓑ, ⓑ

해석

1 메리는 뒷마당에서 줄넘기를 하고 있다.
2 제가 옷장에서 담요를 가져다 드릴까요?
3 스티브 잡스는 신상품에 대한 프리젠테이션을 했다.
4 원 안에 있는 좌석들이 극장 1층 정면의 특별 좌석들보다 싸다.
5 매튜는 잃어버린 보물을 찾아 산으로 들어갔다.
6 크리스마스 전에 매출에 놀랄 만한 성장이 있었다.
7 한라산 반대쪽에는 철쭉들이 좀 피어 있다.
8 나는 6년 동안 집에 가지 못했다. 그 사이에 우리 가족은 이사를 갔다.
9 이 길을 따라 세 블록 내려가신 다음 모퉁이에서 왼쪽으로 돌면 쉽게 찾으실 수 있을 거예요.

B

1 has   2 are   3 are
4 are not   5 is   6 are
7 was   8 was cleaned 9 insists

해석

1 네 명의 회원은 각자 다른 배경을 가지고 있다.
2 식물원의 꽃들은 아름답다.
3 케이트와 나는 둘 다 자동차 공장에서 일한다.
4 이 동네 집들의 절반은 비어 있다.
5 면세점의 향수는 다른 가게보다 싸다.
6 계속해서 증가하는 박사학위 소지자들은 직업을 찾는 데 어려움을 겪고 있다.
7 학생들을 위한 모든 추가 재료들은 학교에서 제공되었다.
8 바닥에 있는 카펫은 어제 가사 도우미가 청소했다.
9 골드스카이항공의 탑승 수속 카운터는 관광객들에게 최소 출발 두 시간 전에 탑승 수속을 할 것을 요구하고 있다.

Unit 25 EXERCISES
p. 122~123

A

1 which, that   2 whom
3 which, that   4 whose
5 which   6 who
7 which, that

해석

1 우리는 최근 지은 새집으로 이사했다.
2 아기 때 내가 돌봐줬던 저스틴 킹은 유명한 극작가가 되었다.
3 내 이웃이 내게 뭔가를 말해 줬는데, 이는 분명 너를 엄청나게 놀라게 할 거야.
4 쿼터백은 미식축구팀을 이끄는 책임 있는 선수이다.
5 부드럽게 이륙한 비행기 5340편은 난기류로 인해 곧바로 심하게 흔들리기 시작했다.
6 승객의 이상한 휴대 전화 벨소리 때문에 정신이 흐트러진 그 택시 운전사는 교통사고를 냈다.
7 캐리의 개인 운동 트레이너가 고안한 새로운 기본 운동 프로그램은 그녀의 몸매 유지에 도움이 안 되었다.

B

1 who 2 whose 3 which 4 which 5 who
6 whom 7 whose

해석

1 계단에서 구른 소년은 팔이 부러졌다.
2 이미 꽃망울이 핀 장미는 사지 마라.
3 그 집은 2층이고, 앞과 뒤로 두 개의 큰 테라스가 있다.
4 제인이 우리에게 추천해준 이탈리아 레스토랑에서 진짜 토스카나 요리가 나왔다.
5 우리를 도와준 한국 객실 승무원은 스페인어와 영어에 능통했다.
6 모든 학생들이 존경하고 동경한 윌콕스 선생님은 화학 선생님이었다.
7 UN에서 일하는 것이 꿈인 세현은 그의 대부분의 시간을 외국어를 배우는 데 쓴다.

C

1 Venus is one whom we would call a natural beauty.
2 My brother turned out his light, which means he is ready to sleep.
3 Donald Trump was the candidate who won the presidential election.
4 An architect, who designs and draws buildings, is often confused with an archeologist.

해석

1 비너스는 자연 미인이라 불렸던 사람이다.
2 내 남동생이 불을 껐는데, 이는 그가 잘 준비가 됐다는 뜻이다.
3 도널드 트럼프는 대통령 선거에서 이긴 후보자였다.
4 건물을 디자인하고 그리는 건축가는 종종 고고학자와 헷갈린다.

D

1 an influx that   2 an improvement that
3 an occurence that

해석

1 매년 봄에 연간 강변 달리기 대회가 네바다, 레플린에서 열리는데, 이 행사로 이만 명 정도의 인구가 유입된다.
2 최근에 컴퓨터들은 과거보다 더 작고 휴대가 더 쉬워졌는데, 이는 판매 증가에 큰 도움이 되었다.
3 매년 수천 마리의 돌고래들이 어부들의 그물에 실수로 걸리는데, 이는 그 종을 위태롭게 하고 있다.

 **EXERCISES** p. 126

A

1 Paris, the City of Lights, is my hometown.
2 The suit hanging in the closet belonged to my uncle.
3 The wall encircling the embassy is for the security of the workers inside.
4 Canadians traveling across the border to the U.S. are now required to show their passports.

해석

1 빛의 도시, 파리는 나의 고향이다.
2 옷장에 걸려 있는 양복은 우리 삼촌 것이다.
3 대사관을 둘러싸고 있는 벽은 내부 직원들의 안전을 위한 것이다.
4 국경을 넘어 미국으로 여행하는 캐나다인들은 이제 여권을 제시해야 한다.

B

1 The woman who is holding the sign is waiting for my mother to arrive.
2 Young people should not sit in seats which are reserved for the elderly.
3 The cruise ship which is departing from pier 11 is en route to the island of Tahiti.
4 This documentary is about the ecological damage which is being caused by pollution.
5 Substances which are poisonous should not be left out where children can reach them.

해석

〈보기〉 자기 지갑을 찾고 있는 저 남자를 아니?
1 팻말을 들고 있는 여자는 우리 어머니가 도착하기를 기다리고 있다.
2 젊은 사람들은 노약자석에 앉으면 안 된다.
3 11번 부두를 떠나고 있는 관광선은 타히티 섬에 가는 중이다.
4 이 다큐멘터리는 오염으로 야기되고 있는 생태계 파괴를 다루고 있다.
5 독성이 있는 물질들은 어린이들의 손이 닿을 수 있는 곳에 두면 안 된다.

REVIEW p. 127

A

1 ④   2 ③   3 ①

해설/해석

1 「all of the 복수명사」는 복수 취급하며, 과거 일에 대한 대답이므로 과거형 복수 be동사를 사용한 were sold가 적절
  A: 피겨 스케이팅 결승전 표를 샀니?
  B: 불행하게도 아니야. 모든 좌석이 다 매진이야.

2 선행사 anyone의 이름이므로 소유격 관계대명사 whose가 적절
  A: 아직도 이름 안 부른 사람 있나요?
  B: 저기요, 샌더슨 씨. 제 이름을 안 부르셨는데요.

3 형용사의 어순은 「형태 → 나이/신구(新舊) → 목적」

A: 오래되고 낡은 중고 컴퓨터에 포토샵 프로그램을 설치하느라 고생을 좀 했어.

B: 새로 하나 사지 그래? 예전만큼 비싸지 않아.

1 ③ 2 ④ 3 ②

해설/해석

1 ③ 명사 job을 수식하기 위해 형용사를 사용해야 하므로 stress가 아니라 stressful이 적절

A: 많은 사람들이 조종사가 멋진 직업이라고 생각해.

B: 어째서? 꽤 힘든 직업 같은데.

A: 매우 고되고 스트레스가 많은 직업이지만, 공짜 여행이나 높은 연봉 같은 보상도 있어.

B: 그렇구나. 조종사를 직업 후보로 넣어 놓는 것도 괜찮겠다.

2 ④ 선행사가 older people로 사람이고, 관계대명사가 주어의 역할을 하므로 who 또는 that이 적절

A: 안녕, 줄리아. 한동안 못 본 것 같아. 그간 잘 지냈니?

B: 안녕, 에릭! 정말 오랜만이다. 나는 노인 자원봉사를 하느라 계속 바빠.

A: 대단하네. 어떤 종류의 일을 하는데?

B: 나는 독거노인들을 돕고 있어. 그들에게 음식이나 잡지를 가져다 드리고 집안일도 도와 드려.

3 ② 명사 산토리니를 수식하는 형용사가 뒤따르는 것이 적절. 따라서 elegant and romantic이 옳은 표현

A: 신혼여행을 어디로 갈 예정이니?

B: 내 약혼자는 우아하고 로맨틱한 산토리니를 가고 싶어 하는데 나는 아시아에 있는 어딘가를 가고 싶어.

A: 오, 아니야! 이건 네 신혼여행이잖아. 특별한 곳이어야만 해!

B: 나도 알아. 하지만 너무 멀리 가고 싶지는 않아. 나는 장거리 비행이 정말 싫어.

REVIEW PLUS

p. 128~129

1 ② 2 ② 3 ④

해설/해석

1 ② 선행사 people은 뒷문장에서 주어 역할을 하므로 whose가 아니라 주격관계대명사 who가 적절

한 저명한 교수가 농담이 다른 사람들과의 관계를 개선하는 무해한 방법이라고 말했다. 많은 사람들은 긴장과 불안을 해소하기 위해 농담을 한다. 더 나아가, 그룹의 일원들도 종종 그들의 그룹 일원이 아닌 사람들에 대해 농담을 한다. 이러한 종류의 농담은 그룹을 묶는 데 도움이 되면서 개인의 정체성을 정립해준다. 사람들은 계속해서 농담을 하는 이유가 무엇이든, 여전히 많은 이들이 웃음이 최고의 약이라고 느낀다.

2 ② 선행사 this product와 purpose의 소유 관계가 성립되어야 하므로 what이 아니라 소유격 관계대명사인 whose가 적절

인공 근육을 만드는 방법을 연구해온 연구원들은 최근 인조 실크의 한 종류를 사용하는 방법을 발견하였다. 손상된 근육을 대체하거나 고치는 것이 목적인 이 제품에 대한 발견은 의학 분야에 급격한 변화를 가져왔다. 이 물질을 만드는 데 사용되는 방법은 다소 복잡하다. 연구원들은 인조 실크인 올론을 가지고 실험을 했는데 올론을 고무 재질이 될 때까지 끓였다. 올론이 식으면 인간의 근육 조직의 인공 대체물로 사용할 준비가 되는 것이다.

3 ④ 선행사 villagers는 뒷 문장에서 주어 역할을 하므로 whose가 아니라 주격관계대명사인 who가 적절

칠레 북부 연안 마을의 상당수가 충분한 양의 안개와 구름에도 불구하고 물 부족으로 고통받고 있다. 그러나 해가 너무 뜨거워서 안개와 구름들이 비로 발전하기 전에 증발해 버린다. 한 마을은 해결책을 가지고 실험 중이다. 마을 사람들도 삼각형으로 짜인 폴리프로필렌 그물을 두 개의 나무 막대 사이에 매달아서 구름과 안개로부터 물방울들을 포획한다. 이 방법을 쓰는 마을 사람들은 매일 그물 하나당 약 40갤런의 물을 모을 수 있다. 이 마을은 하루에 2,500갤런의 물을 만들 수 있게 되었고, 이는 모두가 마시고, 요리하고, 청소하고, 심지어 작은 정원에 물을 줄 만큼 충분한 양이다.

⑤

해설/해석

(A) 명사 names를 수식해야 하므로 형용사가 필요. 동사 mislead의 형용사는 분사 형태인 misleading을 사용함 (B) 선행사가 athletes로 복수 형태이므로 복수 동사 형태를 써야 함 (C) 선행사 a metal ball이 제시되어 있고, 관계대명사절 hangs의 주어 역할을 하므로 주격관계대명사인 that이 적절

하계 올림픽 경기에는 오해를 불러일으키는 명칭을 가진 종목들이 많이 있다. 예를 들어, 3단 뛰기 종목은 육상 경기이다. 이 종목의 명칭을 보면 이것이 세 번의 점프를 포함하고 있다고 생각할 수 있지만 이것은 hop, skip, jump로 구성되어 있다. 이 종목에서 경기하는 선수들은 도움닫기할 때 마치 춤을 추는 것처럼 보인다. 또 다른 경기는 해머던지기이다. 이 종목의 명칭은 해머가 목수의 도구와 전혀 다르기 때문에 오해를 일으킨다. 올림픽 경기에서의 해머는 철사로 된 손잡이에 연결된 금속 공이다. 선수는 양손으로 손잡이를 잡고서 힘을 모으기 위해 빙빙 돌리고 나서 공중으로 해머를 던진다.

②

해설/해석

② '그들이 지방을 저장하는 곳'이므로 why가 아니라 장소가 포함된 관계부사 where이 적절

힐러몬스터는 세계에서 독이 있는 단 두 종류의 도마뱀 중 하나이다. 그들의 독은 거의 방울뱀의 독만큼이나 독성이 있다. 그들은 식사 후 두꺼워지는 굵은 꼬리를 가지고 있는데 이 꼬리가 그들이 지방을 저장하는 곳이기 때문이다. 이 도마뱀들은 한 끼에 그들 몸무게의 3분의 1만큼이나 먹는다고 알려져 있다. 그것은 마치 몸무게가 60파운드인 아이가 무게가 4분의 1파운드인 햄버거를 80개나 먹는 것과 같다. 그들은 대개 작은 새, 알 그리고 곤충을 먹는다. 힐러몬스터는 냄새를 맡아 먹이를 추적한다. 힐러몬스터는 때때로 carrion(죽은 고기)도 먹는데 이것은 이미 죽어 있는 동물을 뜻한다.

WRITING PRACTICE

p. 130~132

1 I'm looking for the book which[that] you gave me.

2 The orchard where Jimmy grows oranges is very large.

3 The child who[that] is playing over there is my neighbor's son.

4 The dinner includes a special dance performance

and a feast of traditional Maori food.

5 I want to speak to the woman whose job is to make reservations.

해석

1 네가 나에게 준 책을 찾고 있어.
2 지미가 오렌지를 키우는 과수원은 매우 크다.
3 저기서 놀고 있는 어린이는 내 이웃집 아들이다.
4 저녁 식사에는 특별 춤 공연과 마오리 전통 음식 연회가 포함되어 있다.
5 예약을 담당하는 여자 분과 이야기하고 싶은데요.

1 The cars we saw at the auto show were really nice.
2 The woman wearing the baseball cap looks very kind.
3 The manuscripts written by the author were sent to the publisher.
4 Four hours and thirty minutes is an extremely long time to be talking on the phone.
5 In ancient Rome, gladiators, who were highly trained, fought to the death.

해석

1 자동차쇼에서 우리가 본 차들은 정말 훌륭했다.
2 야구모자를 쓴 여자는 매우 친절해 보인다.
3 작가가 쓴 원고가 출판사로 보내졌다.
4 4시간 반은 전화 통화하기에 매우 긴 시간이다.
5 고도의 훈련을 받은 고대 로마의 검투사들은 죽을 때까지 싸웠다.

C

1 The baby who is crying is my niece, Amber.
2 Today I met a woman whom I had never met before.
3 Neither of these couches is very attractive nor comfortable.
4 Those two enormous gray elephants helped the tsunami victims.
5 The old man's dream was to return to the town where he was born.

해석

1 울고 있는 아기가 나의 조카 앰버입니다.
2 오늘 나는 한 여인을 만났는데 나는 전에 그녀를 만난 적이 없다.
3 이 두 소파 모두 그렇게 예쁘지도 편하지도 않다.
4 그 엄청 큰 회색 코끼리 두 마리가 해일 피해자들을 도왔다.
5 그 할아버지의 꿈은 자신이 태어났던 마을로 다시 돌아가는 것이었다.

1 She moved to Reno, where she became a social studies teacher.
2 The restaurant needs a chef who is capable of managing the kitchen staff.
3 Many people in Africa live in abject poverty, a situation that saddens me.
4 The young man, who graduated at the top of his law class, is working as a public defender.

E

| 1 | has | 2 | has | 3 | was | 4 | is | 5 | was |

해석

1 A: 집의 4분의 1이 개조되었어.
   B: 집의 나머지 부분들은 언제 끝날 것 같니?
2 A: 야생에 있는 호랑이 수가 감소했어.
   B: 응, 알고 있어. 매우 슬픈 일이야.
3 A: 길 아래쪽에 사시는 노부인이 길에서 지갑을 발견하셨대.
   B: 내가 잃어버린 게 아닌가 싶은데.
4 A: 검은 바지에 선글라스를 낀 남자는 유명한 작가야.
   B: 정말? 몰랐는걸. 무슨 책들을 썼는데?
5 A: 그를 놀라게 한 것은 큰 갈색은둔거미였어. 그것이 그의 팔을 타고 올라갔어.
   B: 팔을 타고 올라갔다고? 나 같아도 무서웠겠어. 난 거미를 매우 싫어하거든.

PART 7

Unit **27** EXERCISES   p. 136

A

| 1 | ⓒ | 2 | ⓒ | 3 | ⓑ | 4 | ⓒ | 5 | ⓐ |
| 6 | ⓓ | 7 | ⓓ |

해석

1 너는 돈을 물 쓰듯 쓰는 것을 그만두는 것이 좋겠어.
2 탐정은 그 강도 사건을 내부자의 소행으로 믿는 것 같다.
3 문제는 이 동네의 집값이 비싸다는 것이다.
4 월터가 계속 우리를 방해하고 있다. 누군가 그에게 가라고 해야 할 것이다.
5 인터넷에 가짜 소문을 퍼뜨리는 것은 범죄이고, 그렇게 다뤄질 것이다.
6 나는 타블로이드판 신문을 읽지 않는다. 나는 그저 그들이 말하는 것을 그다지 믿지 않는다.
7 뇌물 수수와 횡령 소문이 회사의 이미지를 손상하는 데 일조했다.

B

1	living	2	to be	3	what
4	ending	5	Decorating[To decorate]
6	planting

해석

1 시간이 갈수록, 나는 대도시에 사는 것이 싫다.
2 현장 학습은 선생님이 수업 시간에 말한 것에 대하여 학생들이 더욱 흥미를 느끼도록 장려할 것이다.
3 알렉스는 선생님이 다윈의 자연 선택 이론에 대해 말한 것에 매료되었다.
4 2주 전 심하게 다툰 이후, 윤희는 훈과의 관계를 끝낼 생각을 해왔다.
5 유령과 악귀 사진으로 집을 꾸미는 것은 북미의 많은 지역에서 행해지는 전형적인 핼러윈 전통이다.
6 봄이 코앞으로 다가왔기 때문에 지역사회는 도시 전역에 야생화 심기를 기념하기 위한 행사를 열 것이다.

A

1 Here comes Mr. Campbell, our school's new math teacher and athletic coach.
2 John Styth Pemberton, an Atlanta-based pharmacist, created the original recipe for Coca-Cola in 1886.
3 When I saw the insect, a large, multi-legged creature, scurrying toward me across the kitchen floor, I screamed.

해석

〈보기〉 정확한 진단을 하기 위해, 심리학자는 개인 인터뷰와 가계보고서 두 가지 기본적인 수단을 사용한다.

1 우리 학교 새로운 수학 선생님이자 체육 코치인 캠벨 선생님이 오신다.
2 애틀랜타의 약학자 존 스타이스 펨버튼은 1886년에 코카콜라의 원조 제조법을 창조했다.
3 크고, 다리가 여러 개인 생물인 곤충이 부엌 바닥을 가로질러 나에게 달려오는 것을 보고 나는 소리를 질렀다.

B

1 the former home of Elvis Presley
2 carbon, nitrogen, air, and water
3 a descendant of the infamous Spanish flu virus

해석

〈보기〉 미치 앨봄은 '모리와 함께한 화요일'의 저자이다. 그는 신문 칼럼니스트이자 방송인으로 일한다.
→ '모리와 함께한 화요일'의 저자인 미치 앨봄은 신문 칼럼니스트이자 방송인으로 일한다.
1 그레이스랜드는 앨비스 프레슬리의 고향이다. 그곳은 미국에서 가장 인기 있는 관광지 중 하나이다.
→ 앨비스 프레슬리의 고향인 그레이스랜드는 미국에서 가장 인기 있는 관광지 중 하나이다.
2 유기 합성물은 네 가지 기본적인 요소가 필요하다. 그 네 가지 기본요소는 탄소, 질소, 공기 그리고 물이다.
→ 유기 합성물은 탄소, 질소, 공기 그리고 물이 네 가지 기본적인 요소가 필요하다.
3 돼지 독감의 발병은 멕시코를 드나드는 항공 여행에 차질을 주고 있다. 이는 악명 높은 스페인 독감 바이러스의 후손이다.
→ 악명 높은 스페인 독감 바이러스의 후손인 돼지 독감의 발병은 멕시코를 드나드는 항공 여행에 차질을 주고 있다.

A

1 ⓒ   2 ⓐ   3 ⓑ   4 ⓑ   5 ⓐ

해석

1 그 도둑은 판사가 그에게 경고만 주고 놔줘서 안심하는 듯 보였다.
2 핵심은 우리는 아직도 화재를 일으킨 원인이 무엇인지 여전히 모른다는 것이다.
3 5만 달러의 상금은 지명 수배자들을 먼저 체포하는 사람에게 갈 것이다.

4 우리는 돈과 옷, 그리고 다른 기증품을 요구하는 어느 구호 기관이든지 그것들을 보내줄 것이다.
5 또 다른 흥미로운 사실은 브리티시컬럼비아주의 캠루프스는 그 지역의 원주민들인 슈스왑프 인디언들에 의해 "쿰클롭스"라고 불리었다는 것이다.

B

1 to stay   2 drink   3 to make
4 be   5 to deal with

해석

1 네가 집을 떠나기 전에 도쿄 어디에서 묵을지 결정해야 한다.
2 하루에 한 캔 이상 탄산음료를 먹지 말 것을 권한다.
3 학생들은 이 드문 기회를 어떻게 최대한 활용할지 계속 의논했다.
4 모든 학생들이 영어와 수학을 배울 필요가 있다는 것은 중요하다.
5 기자들에게 질문 공세를 받자 신참 지방 검사는 그 상황을 어떻게 할지 몰랐다.

C

1 if[whether]   2 that   3 that
4 whether   5 whether

해석

1 그녀의 사과로 이제 어떻게 달라질지가 의문이다.
2 로버트는 지원 마감일이 이미 지나갔음을 곧 알아차렸다.
3 리차드는 그의 공인중개사가 매개자 역할을 해주기를 기대했다.
4 A: 찰리는 항상 나를 놀려. 개인적으로 받아들여야 하는 건지 아닌지 알기 쉽지 않아.
  B: 너무 심각하게 받아들이지 마. 그냥 너를 놀리는 것을 즐기는 거야.
5 A: 캐리라는 여자를 아세요? 이 미용실에 가끔씩 오는 것 같던데요.
  B: 그녀가 단골인지는 모르겠어요. 이름이 익숙하지 않아요. 저도 새로 왔거든요.

D

1 it cost   2 who capitalized
3 discuss   4 whether to change
5 my children became 6 if[whether (or not)]
7 be   8 the banks would

해석

1 영국을 왕복하는 데 비용이 얼마가 들었었는지 잊어버렸다.
2 지난달 합병에서 누가 가장 많이 투자를 했는지 명확히 해야 한다.
3 나는 에스더가 이 상황에 대해 먼저 그녀의 부모님과 논의할 것을 권한다.
4 한 씨 가족은 그들의 가게 이름을 변경할지에 대해 생각 중이다.
5 나는 내 아이들이 언제부터 병따개를 모으는 것에 흥미를 가졌는지 기억이 나질 않는다.
6 우리는 켄에게 그가 내년에 학교를 떠나는지 물어봐야 해. 이것은 소문임에 틀림없어!
7 범죄 심리학자는 범죄자들을 특수 장비가 갖춰진 교도소에 넣자고 제안하였다.
8 여러분은 은행들이 경제가 계속해서 성장하도록 하기 위해 어떻게 충분한 돈을 빌려줄 수 있는지 궁금할 것입니다.

E

1 It upsets me that
2 It was my mother's idea that
3 It shocked me that
4 It doesn't surprise me that
5 It amazed us that
6 It is no big surprise that

해석

1 너희 둘 다 너희 세상인 양 행동하는 것이 나를 언짢게 한다.
2 이 이상한 머리 모양을 하라고 한 것은 우리 엄마의 생각이었지 내 생각은 아니었다.
3 줄리안의 남자 친구가 교통사고 이후 기억 상실증에 걸렸다는 것을 알고 나는 무척 놀랐다.
4 장기간 소음에 노출되는 것이 청각 손실로 이어질 수 있다는 것은 별로 놀랍지 않다.
5 많은 새들이 날에 죽임을 당하는 것이 풍력의 단점 중 하나라는 것은 우리를 깜짝 놀라게 했다.
6 TV 산업이 문화보다는 소비자 중심주의를 장려하는데 더 흥미가 있는 사람들에 의해 통제되고 있다는 점은 크게 놀랄 일이 아니다.

  EXERCISES p. 148~150

A

1 was preparing   2 there was
3 told   4 need
5 would be studying 6 would
7 had requested

해석

1 그의 아버지는 나에게 자신이 아들을 위해 깜짝 파티를 준비하고 있다고 속삭였다.
2 일기 예보관은 오늘 비가 올 확률이 50%라고 발표했다.
3 그 유명한 사진작가는 그 건물이 큰 상선의 앞부분같이 생겼다고 말했다.
4 안내자가 우리에게 바로 저 버스를 타라고 했어! 하루에 한 번만 왕복한대.
5 스테파니는 그해 여름에 이 교수님과 오보에를 공부할 것이라고 말했다.
6 필립은 직업 워크숍에서 연설하는 상담사와 상담하기 위해 거기 간다고 말했다.
7 우리 삼촌은 나에게 그가 사건 2주 전에 경찰청에 더 조사해 보라고 요청했었다고 말씀하셨다.

B

1 While Chris was in Korea, he was often asked where he came from.
2 Garry had promised his wife that he would cut down eating burgers and fries.
3 When Ryan told me that Wendy had stood him up twice, I knew that something was wrong.
4 My neighbor admitted that she had forgotten to feed my dogs while I was away on vacation.
5 Todd asked me whether I was the famous child actor in the Kellogg's television commercials.

해석

1 크리스가 한국에 있는 동안 그는 어디에서 왔느냐는 질문을 종종 받았다.
2 개리는 그의 아내에게 햄버거와 프렌치프라이 먹는 것을 줄일 것이라고 약속했다.
3 라이언이 내게 웬디가 자신을 두 번이나 기다리게 했다고 말했을 때 나는 뭔가 잘못되었다는 것을 알았다.
4 우리 이웃은 내가 휴가를 간 사이에 우리 개들에게 먹이를 주는 것을 잊었었다고 시인했다.
5 토드는 내가 켈로그 TV 광고에 출연했던 그 유명한 아역이었는지 물었다.

C

1 she would conduct interviews with people from all parts of the country
2 the body of the bee is divided into three parts: the head, thorax, and abdomen
3 he was the black sheep of the family, always getting into trouble
4 I had to get rid of my dog because pets weren't allowed in the building
5 they were prepared to cope with any kind of security threat their country faced
6 his knee hurt, but he couldn't afford to miss any more practices. He had missed too many already

해석

1 쉘리는 "나는 전국 각지의 사람들과의 인터뷰를 진행할 거야."라고 말했다.
  → 쉘리는 자기가 전국 각지의 사람들과의 인터뷰를 진행할 것이라고 말했다.
2 김 선생님은 "벌의 몸은 세 부분으로 나뉜다. 머리, 가슴, 그리고 배."라고 말씀하셨다.
  → 김 선생님은 벌의 몸은 머리, 가슴, 그리고 배의 세 부분으로 나뉜다고 말씀하셨다.
3 우리 부모님은 남동생에게 "너는 우리 집의 골칫거리이며 항상 문제를 일으켜."라고 말씀하셨다.
  → 우리 부모님은 남동생에게 그가 우리 집의 골칫거리이며 항상 문제를 일으킨다고 말씀하셨다.
4 우리 집주인은 나에게 "이 건물에는 애완동물이 허용 안 되니 개를 치우세요."라고 말했다.
  → 우리 집주인은 나에게 이 건물에는 애완동물이 허용 안 되니 개를 치우라고 말했다.
5 군인들은 "우리는 나라가 직면하고 있는 어떠한 안보 위협에도 대항할 준비가 되어 있다."라고 말했다.
  → 군인들은 자신들의 나라가 직면하고 있는 어떠한 안보 위협에도 대항할 준비가 되어 있다고 말했다.
6 존은 "무릎이 아프지만, 나는 더 이상 연습을 빠질 수가 없어. 나는 이미 연습을 너무 많이 빠졌어."라고 말했다.
  → 존은 자기 무릎이 아프지만, 더 이상 연습을 빠질 수가 없고 이미 연습을 너무 많이 빠졌다고 말했다.

D

1 The cashier said she is closing her register now. Let's use the self-service checkout machine over there.
2 Ms. Choi, the athletic coach, saw Stephen sitting on

the grass. He complained that he had been having leg cramps.

3 After Jeff confessed to me that he had started going out with Mary three month before. I spent a sleepless night wondering what to do.

4 Mrs. Smith asked Mark if[whether] he had seen her reading glasses around anywhere. She said she needed them to read the morning paper.

해석

1 출납원이 이제 금전등록기를 닫을 거라고 말했어. 저기 있는 셀프 서비스 체크아웃 기계를 사용하자.

2 운동 코치인 최 선생님은 스티븐이 잔디에 앉아 있는 것을 보았다. 그는 다리에 쥐가 났다고 불평했다.

3 제프가 나에게 석 달 전부터 메리와 사귀기 시작했다고 고백하자, 나는 어떻게 할지 고민하며 밤을 새웠다.

4 스미스 부인은 마크에게 주위에서 그녀의 돋보기를 보았냐고 물었다. 그녀는 아침 신문을 읽기 위해 그것이 필요하다고 말했다.

E

1 "What topics are you going to discuss today?"
2 "Do you have anything to share with us?"
3 "How do babies quickly develop such a large vocabulary?"
4 "You got the scholarship for the winter program at Berkeley."
5 "My daughter will no longer be allowed to go to your house unless I accompany her."

해석

1 실비아는 나에게 오늘 우리가 어떤 주제에 관해 논의할 것인지 나에게 물었다.
  → 실비아는 나에게 "오늘 어떤 주제에 관해 논의할 거니?"라고 물었다.

2 갑자기, 지도자는 나에게 그들과 나눌 이야기가 있는지 물었다.
  → 갑자기, 지도자는 나에게 "우리와 나눌 이야기가 있나요?"라고 물었다.

3 어느 날, 우리 아들은 나에게 어떻게 아기들은 빠르게 많은 단어를 습득하는지 물었다.
  → 어느 날, 우리 아들은 나에게 "어떻게 아기들은 빠르게 많은 단어를 습득하나요?"라고 물었다.

4 모르간 교수는 제니퍼에게 그녀가 버클리에서 겨울 프로그램 장학금을 받게 되었다고 말했다.
  → 모르간 교수는 제니퍼에게 "네가 버클리에서 겨울 프로그램 장학금을 받게 되었어."라고 말했다.

5 알리샤의 엄마는 나에게 자기 딸은 자기의 동행 없이는 더 이상 너의 집에 갈 수 없다고 말씀하셨다.
  → 알리샤의 엄마는 나에게 "우리 딸은 나의 동행 없이는 더 이상 너의 집에 갈 수 없어."라고 말씀하셨다.

1 ②   2 ④   3 ②

해설/해석

1 방금 말한 내용을 바로 다시 보고할 때는 명사절의 동사를 단순현재 시제로 쓸 수 있으므로 needs가 적절
  A: 너의 어머니가 너에게 방금 스페인어로 뭐라고 말씀하셨니?
  B: 어머니는 맛있는 식사를 대접해 주신 것에 대해 밀러 씨게 감사해야 한다고 하셨어요.

2 의문사 뒤에는 「주어+동사」 또는 to부정사가 올 수 있음. '언제 가야 할지'라는 의미가 되어야 하므로 when to go 또는 when I should go가 적절
  A: 라오스로 언제 떠날지 정했니?
  B: 사실, 문제는 언제 떠날지가 아니라 다섯 명의 어린아이들을 데리고 어떻게 가느냐야.

3 yesterday는 과거 시점을 나타내므로 과거시제 lost가 적절
  A: 왜 앨버트가 요즘 우울해 보이는지 궁금하네. 그에게 무슨 일 있니?
  B: 그는 내게 어제 휴대용 메모리 드라이브를 잃어버렸다고 말했어. 그 안에 그의 기말 프로젝트가 들어있었대.

1 ②   2 ④   3 ④

해설/해석

1 ② 의문사가 문장 중간에 연결된 경우 「의문사+주어+동사」의 어순이 되어야 하므로, what Dr. Hahn meant가 적절
  A: 꽤 흥미로운 인류학 강의였어, 그렇지 않니?
  B: 음, 솔직히, 나는 한 선생님이 말씀하신 "운동 습성"이 무슨 말인지 모르겠어.
  A: 운동은 인간이 개발한 기본적 생존 능력에 대해 많은 것을 알려준다는 의미였어.
  B: 그렇구나. 아, 알겠다! 이제 좀 이해가 되는 것 같아.

2 ④ 동사 ask 뒤에는 질문하려는 내용이 와야 하므로, '~인지 아닌지'의 의문문의 내용을 담을 수 있는 접속사 whether 또는 if를 쓰는 것이 적절
  A: 나는 더 작은 아파트에서 살고 싶어. 다음 달에 이사를 갈까 생각 중이야.
  B: 어디로 갈지 결정했어?
  A: 아니, 아직. 나는 하클리 힐만 쪽으로 마음이 기울고 있지만, 정보가 더 필요해. 네 삼촌께서는 아직도 부동산중개인으로 일하고 계시니?
  B: 응, 하고 계셔. 거기에 빈집이 있는지 물어볼게.

3 ④ say 다음에는 명사절이 오고, tell 다음에는 (대)명사 다음에 명사절이 나옴. me라는 대명사가 있으므로 said가 아니라 told나 said to가 적절
  A: 이번 학기에 책 비용이 얼마나 드는지 믿기지 않아! 나는 서점에서 이미 300달러를 넘게 썼어!
  B: 대학 서점에서 대부분 중고 교과서를 판다고 들었어. 거기 가볼까?
  A: 내가 필요한 수학책이 있는지 모르겠다. 나는 네 번째 개정판이 아닌 다섯 번째 개정판이 필요해.
  B: 우리 교수님이 나에게 말씀해주시기를 그 서점은 최신판만 가져다 놓는다고 하셨어.

1 ①　　**2** ④　　**3** ①

해설/해석

1 ① 의문사가 문장에서 명사절로 쓰일 때 명사절을 구성하기 위해서는 뒤에 「주어+동사」의 어순이 되어야 하므로 he was가 적절

어젯밤의 화재로 인한 대혼란 속에서, 대학생인 제레미는 기숙사에 있는 다른 이들을 구하기 위해 목숨을 걸었다. 인터뷰 도중 그는 얼마나 큰 위험 속에 있었는지 설명하려고 노력했다. 그는 공기가 별로 없었고 자신의 목과 폐가 타고 있었다고 말했다. 그는 충동적으로 행동했고 그의 본능이 앞섰다고 덧붙였다. 도움이 필요한 이들에게 도움을 주는 것이 그의 의무였다.

2 ④ 전달동사가 과거형인 경우, 뒤에 따라오는 명사절의 시제는 과거 또는 과거완료가 되어야 함, 말하는 시점에서 원하던 일이므로 과거형 wanted로 쓰는 것이 적절. 참고로, wants는 진행형이 불가능한 동사

데이비드 그가 마지막으로 농구를 석 달 쉰 것이 언제였는 지 기억이 나지 않았다. 하지만 그것이 이 대학교 2학년생 포워드 선수가 지난여름에 그의 집인 남부 캐롤라이나, 콜롬비아에 돌아가서 한 일이다. 가끔 옛 친구들과 가벼운 게임을 한 적 빼고는 데이비드가 가장 힘을 들여 한 일은 그의 엄마가 만들어 준 스파게티를 포크를 들어 그의 입으로 가져간 것이었다. 그는 잘 낫지 않는 그의 발목 부상을 낫게 하려고 쉰 것이라고 말했다.

3 ① 명사구 the origins of jazz가 복수이므로 is가 아니라 are가 적절

재즈의 기원은 그 음악만큼이나 풍부하게 짜여 있다. '재즈'라는 용어는 많은 다양한 종류의 음악을 포함한다. 19세기 말, 아프리카계 미국인들은 노예였던 선조들의 노래에 기원을 둔 블루스라고 알려진 새로운 음악 장르를 만들었다. 아프리카계 미국인들의 지역 사회 안에서, 블루스는 발전했고 상업적인 인기 있는 형태의 음악으로 성장했다. 전통적인 아프리카계 미국민요와 블루스의 만남인 재즈는 "미국의 고전 음악"으로 불려 왔다.

②

해설/해석

(A) 주어는 전치사구 with islands의 수식을 받는 The highest lake로 단수명사이므로 동사도 단수 형태인 is가 적절 (B) 주어가 Rain and melted snow로 복수 취급해야 하기 때문에 flow가 적절 (C) 관계사절의 동사 형태를 결정짓는 선행사가 four of which로 복수 취급해야 하므로 are가 적절

섬을 가지고 있는 가장 높은 호수는 티베트에 있는 오바코이다. 이 호수의 표면은 해발 5,209m이다. 티베트는 '세상의 지붕'으로도 알려져 있다. 이는 거칠고, 메마르며, 추운 히말라야 북부 고원이다. 이곳은 겨울에는 매우 춥고 일 년 내내 바람이 세차게 분다. 비와 녹은 눈은 수많은 호수로 흘러 들어 가며, 그중 4개는 지역 사람들에 의해 신성시되고 있다. 그 황량하고 돌투성이인 지형에는 식물이 거의 없다. 유일한 나무들이 가장 바람의 영향을 덜 받는 계곡에만 있으며, 그것들마저도 대부분 매우 작다. 하지만 이렇게 황량한 땅도 자비로울 때가 있다. 사람들은 이 호수 주변에 살면서 건강한 곡식들을 키운다.

④

해설/해석

④ think라는 동사 뒤에는 명사절이 와야 하며, 뒤에 완전한 문장이 왔기 때문에 접속사 that이 적절

내 친구의 가족이 길을 잃은 개 한 마리를 입양했다. 그 개의 전 주인을 찾을 수 없었기 때문에 그들은 그 개를 기르게 되었고 토비라고 이름을 붙여 주었다. 그 개의 과거에 대한 단서라고 할 수 있는 것은 누구든지 그의 주변에서 담배를 피우면 토비가 긴장한다는 사실이었다. 사람들이 땅에 담배 꽁초를 버리자마자 토비는 꽁초에 달려들어서 꽁초의 불이 다 꺼질 때까지 짓밟았다. 가족은 아마 불과 관련된 어떤 일 때문에 토비가 길을 잃었을 것이라고 생각했다. 토비는 담배가 불을 의미한다고 생각하는 것 같았고, 불을 끄는 방법을 배운 것이다.

1 I have no idea how a sugar pill can make sick people feel better.
2 Uncle Danny said that the doctors don't expect Angelina's mother to live more than six months.
3 When I came across Ian yesterday, he told me that he had not decided whether to subscribe to the new cable service yet.
4 I asked him to remember that both trust and respect are qualities that have to be earned, they cannot be demanded from anyone.

해석

1 나는 설탕 알약(위약)이 어떻게 아픈 사람을 낫게 하는지 전혀 모르겠다.
2 대니 삼촌은 의사들이 안젤리나의 엄마가 6개월 이상 살 것으로 보지 않는다고 말했다.
3 어제 이안을 만났을 때 그는 나에게 그가 새로운 케이블 서비스를 신청할지 말지 아직 결정 못했다고 말했다.
4 나는 그에게 믿음과 존경은 둘 다 얻어지는 것이라는 것을 기억하라고 했다.

1 an Air Force engineer
2 very important institutions in our economy
3 faint sunlight
4 repetitive strain injury

해석

1 공군 엔지니어인 엘리엇 힐은 항상 군사 전쟁 게임에서 악역을 한다.
2 우리 경제에 매우 중요한 기관인 은행은 돈을 빌려줄 뿐만 아니라 투자도 한다.
3 약한 햇빛인 "지구 반사광"은 지구에서 달로 반사되었다가 다시 돌아온 것이다.
4 반복성 긴장 장애인 RSI는 신체가 계속적으로 움직여서 생긴다. 예를 들어, 손을 쉼 없이 같은 방향으로 움직이는 것이다.

C

1 I think that my roommate tends to take a lot of things for granted.
2 I think that human adults everywhere in the world enjoy making their children laugh.
3 I think that you should follow a logical series of steps to complete your experiment.

해석

1 내 룸메이트는 많은 것들을 당연시하는 경향이 있다고 생각한다.
2 세계 어디에서나 어른들은 자신의 아이들을 웃게 하는 것을 즐긴다고 생각한다.
3 네 실험을 완수하려면 논리적인 단계들을 밟아야 한다고 생각한다.

D

1 Most people have great difficulty in balancing family life and work nowadays.
2 The Sanchez family has had great difficulty adapting to life in America.
3 All of my classmates had great difficulty in saying "goodbye" to each other on the last day of school.

해석

〈보기〉 나는 다른 사람들과 친해지는 데 큰 어려움이 있다.
1 대부분의 사람들은 요즘 가족생활과 일 사이에서 균형을 잡는데 많은 어려움을 겪는다.
2 산체스 가족은 미국에서의 삶에 적응하는 데 큰 어려움을 겪어왔다.
3 우리 반 모든 학생들은 학교 마지막 날 서로에게 작별 인사하는 데 큰 어려움을 겪었다.

E

1 shopping   2 know   3 had to
4 to do   5 approaching[to approach]

해석

1 A: 용돈을 전부 쇼핑몰에서 썼어? 너희 엄마 무진장 화나시겠는걸.
   B: 알아, 하지만 다시는 쇼핑 안 할 거라고 약속하면 돼.
2 A: 실례합니다. 이 사진에 있는 젊은 여성을 아시는지 여쭤보려고요.
   B: 그녀를 알지만, "친구"라고 할 정도는 아니에요.
3 A: 화학 프로젝트는 아직 안 끝냈니?
   B: 응. 좋은 생각을 떠올리는 데 어려움이 있네. 선생님이 창의적이어야 한다고 했거든.
4 A: 헨리와 캐런은 저녁 식사 중에 뭔가에 대해 싸웠어.
   B: 나도 거기에 있었기 때문에 알아. 그 순간, 어떻게 해야 할지 모르겠더라고.
5 A: 숲에서 곰을 만나면 어떻게 해야 하지?
   B: 너에게 해줄 수 있는 가장 좋은 조언은 새끼와 함께 있는 곰에게 절대로 다가가지 말라는 거야.

PART 8

 EXERCISES   p. 161~162

A

1 It was Mark who spilled grape juice all over the kitchen floor, not me!
2 What caused the crane to topple over was a combination of high winds and an excessively heavy load.
3 There are millions of tiny, invisible germs lurking on every surface of your home, just waiting to be picked up.
4 What woke me up early this morning was the noise from the fruit vendors hawking their wares outside my hotel window.
   또는 The noise from the fruit vendors hawking their wares outside my hotel window was what woke me up early this morning.

B

1 It is rice that[which] three billion humans eat as the main ingredient for their meals.
2 It was last week that[when] Daniel finally got in touch with me about starting a photography club.
3 It was on the ankle that[where] the tiny black dog wearing a red choke collar suddenly bit the passerby.

해석

〈보기〉 마크는 쇼핑몰에 있는 한국 식당에서 엄청 뜨겁고 영양가 많은 쇠고깃국을 주문했다.
   → 마크가 엄청 뜨겁고 영양가 많은 쇠고깃국을 주문한 곳은 쇼핑몰에 있는 한국 식당이었다.
1 30억의 사람들이 주식으로 쌀을 먹는다.
   → 30억의 사람들이 주식으로 먹는 것은 쌀이다.
2 다니엘이 사진 동아리를 여는 것에 대해 마침내 지난주에 나와 연락이 되었다.
   → 다니엘이 사진 동아리를 여는 것에 대해 마침내 나와 연락된 것은 지난주였다.
3 빨간색 개 목걸이를 하고 있던 작고 검은 개가 갑자기 지나가는 사람의 발목을 물었다.
   → 빨간색 개 목걸이를 하고 있던 작고 검은 개가 갑자기 지나가는 사람을 문 곳은 발목이었다.

C

1 had I got out of bed when the doorbell rang
2 does Samuel hear such words of praise from his teacher
3 did I understand the importance of what my mother was saying at the time
4 had I made a bowl of noodles for myself when my sister walked into the kitchen

5 had Ms. Park stepped into the classroom when her students jumped out of their seats and yelled, "Surprise!"

해석

〈보기〉 나는 이렇게 불쾌한 적이 없었다.

1 내가 침대에서 나오자마자 초인종이 울렸다.
2 새뮤얼은 선생님께 그런 칭찬을 거의 듣지 못한다.
3 그 당시에는 어머니가 나에게 한 말의 중요성을 몰랐다.
4 내가 먹을 국수 한 그릇 만들자마자 내 여동생이 부엌으로 걸어 들어왔다.
5 박 선생님이 교실에 들어서자마자 그녀의 학생들이 자리에서 뛰쳐나와 "서프라이즈!"라고 소리쳤다.

1 The Boston Red Sox are in first place.
2 Mr. Kim was so happy that he took us all out to celebrate.
3 It may be dry weather, but isn't it a nice change from all that rain?
4 The waves were so high that only the most experienced surfers dared to brave them.

해석

〈보기〉 네 남자 친구는 정말로 잘생겼구나!
1 보스턴 레드삭스 팀이 1위이다.
2 김 선생님은 매우 기뻐서 축하하려고 우리 모두를 데리고 나오셨다.
3 건조한 날씨이기는 하지만, 내내 비가 오다가 바뀌어서 좋지 않니?
4 파도가 너무 높아서 가장 숙련된 서퍼들만이 이에 도전했다.

Unit 32 EXERCISES

p. 166~167

1 Tina's homework is always both neat and accurate.
2 Jeff and I mowed the lawn, and Luke trimmed the hedges.
3 Grandpa is a slow walker, but[yet] he is still quite muscular for his age.
4 Ralph gave it all he could, but[yet] he kicked the ball barely twenty yards.
5 We didn't win the relay race at the track and field meet, but we didn't care.
6 The trip to Orlando and Tampa was a delight for us, for we had a great time.
7 The invitations will be sent tomorrow or the next day and will arrive in time for the event.
8 The principal and the teachers were shocked, but[yet] they soon calmed down and tried to come up with a solution.
9 The rabbit hopped and skipped about in the yard, and then it squeezed its body under the fence and disappeared forever.

1 티나의 숙제는 항상 깔끔하고 정확하다.
2 제프와 나는 잔디를 깎았고, 루크는 울타리들을 다듬었다.
3 할아버지는 걸음이 느리시지만, 연세보다 아직도 꽤 근육질이시다.
4 랄프는 최선을 다했지만, 공을 3야드도 차지 못했다.
5 우리는 육상경기 중 계주에서 이기지 못했지만, 신경쓰지 않았다.
6 우리는 즐거운 시간을 보냈기에 올란도와 탬파로의 여행은 우리에게 기쁨이었다.
7 초대권은 내일이나 그 다음 날 발송되어서 행사에 맞춰 도착할 것이다.
8 교장 선생님과 교사들은 너무 놀랐지만, 곧 안정을 찾고 해결책을 마련하기 위해 노력했다.
9 토끼는 마당을 깡충 뛰어다니다가, 담장 아래로 몸을 구겨 넣어 영원히 사라졌다.

B

1 The goalie stood in his net waving to the crowd.
2 Peter began separating the clothes piled up next to the washer.
3 It was announced earlier in the week that IBM and Sun have together donated almost $500 million to the Gates Foundation this year alone.
4 The woman who was carrying a French poodle and fiddling with her smartphone didn't even notice the taxi screech to a halt directly behind her.

해석

1 골키퍼는 골대 그물 안에 서서 관중을 향해 손을 흔들었다.
2 피터는 세탁기 옆에 쌓인 옷들을 분리하기 시작했다.
3 이번 주 초에 IBM과 Sun이 올해에만 게이츠 재단에 거의 5억 달러를 함께 기부했다는 발표가 있었다.
4 프렌치 푸들을 들고 자신의 스마트폰을 만지작거리던 여자는 그 여자 바로 뒤에서 택시가 끽하는 소리를 내며 멈춘 것을 알아차리지도 못했다.

C

1 Alexis exclaimed to everyone in earshot that her IQ was higher than Sue's.
2 Everyone in attendance agreed that the lecture was long and tedious.
3 Barbara and Jeanne whispered and giggled all night like schoolgirls on a sleepover.
4 In her freshman composition class, Mina learned to read poems critically and to appreciate good prose.
5 After the first week, the student dorms were filled with torn banners, broken bottles, and overflowing garbage bins.

해석

1 알렉시스는 모두가 들리는 데서 자기 아이큐가 수보다 높다고 소리쳤다.
2 참석한 모든 사람들이 강의가 길고 지루하다는 데에 동의했다.
3 바바라와 진은 둘이 같이 외박하는 여학생들처럼 밤새 속삭이고 깔깔 웃었다.
4 1학년 작문 시간에, 미나는 시를 비판적으로 읽는 법과 좋은 산문을 감상하는 법을 배웠다.
5 신입생들이 들어온 지 일주일 후, 학생기숙사는 찢어진 배너, 깨진 병, 넘치는 쓰레기통들로 가득했다.

A

1 After the long and exhausting journey, we were all so relieved to be finally home.
2 Unlike in the past, the people of India can now travel cheaply by rail, water, or air.
3 I love a meal of fresh garden salad, spaghetti and meat balls, and chocolate cake for dessert.
4 Steve Jobs, an alumnus of the college, spoke to the graduating class at the commencement ceremony.

해석

1 길고 지친 여행 후에 우리 모두는 드디어 집에 오게 되어서 매우 마음이 편했다.
2 과거와는 달리, 인도 사람들은 이제 철도, 수상 또는 항공으로 저렴하게 이동할 수 있다.
3 나는 신선한 야채 샐러드, 미트볼 스파게티, 그리고 디저트로 초콜릿 케이크를 먹는 것을 매우 좋아한다.
4 그 대학의 졸업생인, 스티브 잡스는 졸업식에서 졸업생들에게 연설을 했다.

B

1 There was a sudden silence in the classroom; everyone was shocked by the news.
2 My new girlfriend has three personality merits: optimism, cheerfulness, and consideration.
3 A: How lovely your Christmas decorations are!
   B: Do you like them? I made them myself.
4 A: I heard on the radio that tomorrow will be a sunny, warm day.
   B: Great! Shall we go to the pool?

해석

1 교실이 갑자기 조용해졌다. 모두가 그 소식에 충격을 받았다.
2 내 새로운 여자 친구는 성격적으로 장점이 세 가지 있다: 낙천주의, 쾌활함, 그리고 배려심.
3 A: 네 크리스마스 장식은 정말 아름답구나!
   B: 마음에 드니? 내가 직접 만들었어.
4 A: 내일은 화창하고 따뜻할 것이라고 라디오에서 들었어.
   B: 좋은데! 수영장에 갈까?

REVIEW

A

1 ②   2 ③   3 ①

해설/해석

1 앞의 문장과 뒤의 문장은 방문할 수 없는 두 가지 이유를 설명하고 있으므로, 문법적으로 동등한 종류의 내용을 연결하는 and가 적절
   A: 시간이 되면 부산에 간 김에 네 여동생 좀 보고 오렴.
   B: 스케줄이 꽤 빡빡한데다, 그룹 프로젝트도 있어요.

2 'If you don't mind(괜찮다면)'는 부탁 또는 요청을 할 때 관용어처럼 사용
   A: 저스틴, 내가 빌려준 골프 훈련 DVD 아직 가지고 있니?
   B: 응, 있어. 미안해. 괜찮다면 다음 주에 돌려줄게. 아직 못 봤어.

3 like는 to부정사 또는 동명사를 목적어로 취하는 동사이고, and는 등위접속사로, 동등한 문법적 역할을 하는 구와 절을 연결하기 때문에 to hang out and (to) watch movies 또는 hanging out and watching movies가 적절
   A: 네 친구 수진이는 여전히 이번 여름에 온다고 하니?
   B: 오면 좋겠어. 그녀는 대부분의 청소년들과 같아. 돌아다니고 영화 보는 것을 좋아해.

B

1 ①   2 ②   3 ②

해설/해석

1 ① To raise a pet ~ 부분의 의미상 주어는 일반인 you로 볼 수 있고, 주절의 주어를 부사구나 절에 일치시켜주는 것이 자연스러우므로, 주절을 능동태로 바꿈, 따라서 you need patience가 적절
   ① 공간이 귀한 도시에서 애완동물을 키우려면 인내가 필요하다.
   ② 천천히, 그리고 부지런히 바닥을 기어서, 캐리는 마침내 장난감에 도달했다.
   ③ 고양이 밥을 다 먹은 후, 막시는 더 달라고 야옹거렸다. 그녀는 정말 작은 돼지 같다.
   ④ 지난 5년간 매 학기 음운론을 가르친 다니엘은 구문론을 매우 가르치고 싶어한다.

2 ② 「both A and B」는 'A와 B 둘 다'라는 의미로 복수 주어 취급하고, 그에 따라 동사도 복수 동사인 want가 적절
   ① 낸시는 남자 친구가 그리워서 도쿄에 있는 그에게 전화했다.
   ② 존과 로저 둘 다 다음 주에 있을 역사 시험을 정말 잘 보고 싶어한다.
   ③ 대부분 스트레스와 관련된 질환들은 세로토닌 반응 억제로 치료될 수 있다.
   ④ 상급 학습자용 사전조차도 어려운 전문 용어가 들어 있지 않다. 하지만 언어를 공부하는 학생들에게 유용한 다른 정보가 많다.

3 ② 주절과 종속절의 주어가 서로 같지 않을 때는 종속절의 접속사 뒤 「주어+be동사」는 생략할 수 없음, 따라서 when절에 주어인 you로 시작하는 것이 적절
   ① 새로운 스포츠카를 세차한 후, 스티브는 왁스칠을 했다.
   ② 문법 퀴즈를 볼 때 집중력이 제일 중요하다.
   ③ 마감일까지 프로젝트를 완수하려면 너와 네 파트너는 지금 당장 시작해야 할 것이다.
   ④ 평생을 그 회사에서 일한 스튜어트는 자신이 해고되었다는 것을 알고 충격에 빠졌다.

REVIEW PLUS

p. 172~173

1 ③ **2** ④ **3** ②

해설/해석

1 ③ 두 개의 주절을 등위 접속사를 이용하지 않고, 콤마로만 연결할 수는 없음. 콤마(,) 다음에 and를 넣는 것이 적절

내 올케 "팻"은 항공사에서 일하며, 공짜로 비행하고 있어요. 결과적으로, 그녀는 최근에 우리를 자주 방문하고 있죠. 그녀는 우리 집에 머물면서, 차를 빌리지도 않고, 거의 온다고 알려주지도 않아요. 팻의 아버지는 우리 가까이 사시고, 점점 나이가 드셔서 그녀는 그를 자주 보고 싶어 해요. 문제는 나와 내 남편은 정말 바쁜 삶을 살고 있고, 아버지도 돌보고 있어요. 그리고 팻이 나타나 대접받기를 원해요. 저를 오해하지 마세요. 팻은 매우 사랑스럽지만, 어떻게 이렇게 모를 수가 있는지 이해할 수 없어요. 그녀에게 상처를 주지 않으면서 그녀가 우리에게 짐이 된다는 사실을 어떻게 알릴 수 있을까요?

2 ④ the government there(그곳의 정부)가 주어이므로 are가 아니라 is가 적절

세계 보건 기구는 최근에 전염병 경고를 단계 5에서 두 번째로 가장 높은 단계로 높였다. 이 조치는 세계가 돼지 독감의 확산 위험이 심각함을 보여주지만, 다른 이들은 나라들이 과하게 반응한다고 논쟁한다. 예를 들어, 이집트는 돼지가 질병을 퍼뜨렸다는 증거가 없음에도 불구하고 300,000마리 돼지 전부의 도살을 명령했다. 12명이 안 되는 발병 환자가 나타난 영국에서는, 보건 당국에서 3천 2백만 개의 마스크를 입수할 계획이다. 그리고 멕시코에서는 정부가 사람들에게 키스를 하지 말라고 권고하고 있다. 모순적이게도 세계 건강 전문가들은 이러한 많은 조치들이 질병의 확산을 막는 데 전혀 도움이 되지 않을지도 모른다고 한다.

3 ② A, B, and C의 병렬 구조를 이루고 있고, A, B가 모두 명사 형태인 것으로 보아, C부분도 to take를 뺀 medical care가 적절

극복하기에 너무 크거나, 힘들거나, 또는 너무 어렵다고 생각되는 도전에 직면한 적이 있나요? 항복하거나, 백기를 들기 전에 마뉴엘 우리베를 생각하세요. 그는 최근까지 세계에서 가장 무거운 사나이라는 기네스 기록을 가지고 있었습니다. 10월 26일 그는 수년간의 다이어트, 운동, 그리고 치료 후 오래된 연인과 결혼을 했습니다. 우리베는 한때 1,200파운드까지 무게가 나갔고, 결혼 전까지 550파운드 이상을 뺐습니다. 결혼식에서 눈물을 흘린 우리베와 그의 신부는 이후 결혼식 전통의 '첫 댄스'를 즐겼습니다. 하지만 그는 결혼 케이크에는 손도 대지 않고, 대신에 다이어트를 계속하기로 했습니다.

⑤

해설/해석

(A) look은 형용사를 보어로 취하는 불완전 자동사. 「look+형용사」는 '~하게 보이다' (B) '~하면서'의 의미를 갖는 동시 동작을 나타내는 분사구문이 and로 연결된 것으로, looking ~ and listening ~이 올바른 병렬 구조를 이루게 됨 (C) the old wizard가 주체가 되어 앉는 행동을 스스로 하는 것이므로 능동형 분사인 sitting이 적절

잠에서 깨어난 프로도는 자신이 침대에 누워 있음을 알게 되었다. 처음엔 여전히 기억의 가장자리에 맴돌고 있는 오랫동안의 불쾌한 꿈 때문에 늦게 일어났다고 생각했다. 아니면 아파서였을까? 그러나 천장이 이상해 보였다. 천장은 평평했고 화려하게 조각된 어두운색의 들보가 있었다. 그는 벽에 비치는 햇빛을 보고 폭포 소리를 들으면서 조금 더 누워 있었다. "여

기가 어디지? 지금이 몇 시지?" 하며 그는 천장에 대고 큰 소리로 말했다. "엘론드의 집 안이야. 그리고 아침 10시야."라는 목소리가 들렸다. 한 늙은 마법사가 열린 창문 옆의 의자에 앉아 있었다.

⑤

해설/해석

⑤ that절 안의 주어는 the removal로 단수 형태이므로, 동사도 단수형에 맞게 has pushed로 써야 함. of the barriers와 between child information and adult information은 모두 앞의 명사 the removal을 수식해주는 전치사구로 볼 수 있음

텔레비전이 아이들을 성인처럼 만드는 데 주된 역할을 해 왔다. 전자 시대 이전의 아동은 사회에 대한 정보 중 많은 부분을 읽은 책에서 얻었다. 아동은 자신의 이해 수준에 적절한 정보가 담긴 아동용 책을 읽었다. 성인을 위한 정보는 성인용 책에 담겨 있었고, 아동은 그러한 책들을 읽지 않았다. 오늘날, 아동은 텔레비전을 통해 성인용 정보를 접한다. 아동은 성인의 상황과 성인의 인생관에 노출된다. 많은 사회 과학자들은 아동용 정보와 성인용 정보 사이의 장벽을 없앤 것이 아동을 성인의 세계로 너무 일찍 밀어 넣었다고 주장한다.

WRITING PRACTICE

p. 174~175

1 I listened to almost the whole album. What I heard sounded great!
2 Because I am on a diet, I ate only one donut and ignored the other three on the table.
3 The faulty alarm system in my apartment complex went off nearly five times yesterday.
4 For homework, Professor Willis made us read three chapters that covered almost the entire history of the Art Deco movement.

해석

1 나는 거의 앨범 전체를 다 들었다. 내가 들은 것은 훌륭했다!
2 나는 다이어트 중이기 때문에 도넛을 한 개만 먹고 식탁 위에 있는 다른 세 개는 무시했다.
3 아파트에 있는 고장 난 경보 시스템은 어제 거의 다섯 번이나 울렸다.
4 윌리스 교수님은 숙제로 우리에게 아르 데코 운동에 관한 역사 전반을 다루는 3장을 읽어오라고 하셨다.

1 As Sue was running across the floor, the rug slipped, and she lost her balance and fell.
2 The hot sand burned my feet as I was walking along the beach on my way to get a massage.
또는 As I was walking along the beach, the hot sand burned my feet on my way to get a massage.
3 We watched the squirrels while they built their nests high up in the spruce trees that lined the street.
4 The nervous rookie pilot climbed into the cockpit, adjusted his view finder, attached his oxygen mask, and flashed a "thumbs-up" sign to the controller.

1 수는 마루를 가로질러 달려오고 있었다. 양탄자가 미끄러져서 그녀는 균형을 잃고 넘어졌다.
  → 수는 마루를 가로질러 달려오다가 양탄자가 미끄러져서 균형을 잃고 넘어졌다.
2 해변을 따라 걷고 있었다. 마사지를 받으러 가는 도중 뜨거운 모래에 발을 데었다.
  → 해변을 따라 걷고 있을 때 마사지를 받으러 가는 도중 뜨거운 모래에 발을 데었다.
3 우리는 다람쥐들을 지켜보았다. 그들은 길가에 늘어서 있는 전나무에 높이 둥지를 지었다.
  → 우리는 다람쥐들이 길가에 늘어서 있는 전나무에 높이 둥지를 짓는 것을 지켜보았다.
4 긴장한 신참 조종사는 조종실로 들어갔다. 그는 자신의 파인더를 조절하고, 산소 호흡기를 장착한 후, 관제사에게 엄지 손가락으로 승인 표시를 했다.
  → 긴장한 신참 조종사는 조종실로 들어가서, 자신의 파인더를 조절하고, 산소 호흡기를 장착한 후, 관제사에게 엄지 손가락으로 승인 표시를 했다.

C

1 It is learning English that I find most enjoyable nowadays.
2 What I like most about your brother, Jeremy, is his dry sense of humor.
3 Never have people been as well informed as they are now, thanks to the Internet.
4 What we have grown to love most about Korea is the endless supply and variety of fresh vegetables.

해석

1 요즘 내가 가장 즐겁게 느끼는 것은 영어를 배우는 것이다.
2 너의 오빠 제레미에 대해 내가 가장 좋아하는 건, 그의 무미건조한 유머 감각이야.
3 인터넷 덕분에 사람들은 어느 때보다도 정보에 밝아졌다.
4 한국에 대해 우리가 가장 사랑하게 된 것은 끝없이 제공되는 다양하고 신선한 채소들이다.

D

1 Older television sets had tubes; the newest models, which take less space, are digital.
2 My daughter, Jean, has solo backpacked throughout the world; for example, Australia, Brazil, Canada, and Russia.
3 Your first draft is really quite good. However, I might suggest that you add a few more specific details to your second paragraph.
4 The reason why so many young people go off to college is to gain knowledge, to prepare for a career, and to have a good time, but not necessarily in that order.

해석

1 옛날 TV에는 튜브(관)들이 있었지만, 공간을 덜 차지하는 최신 모델들은 디지털이다.
2 내 딸 진은 혼자 세계 배낭여행을 나섰다. 예를 들어, 호주, 브라질, 캐나다, 그리고 러시아.
3 네 초안은 정말 꽤 잘 썼다. 하지만 두 번째 단락에 좀 더 구체적인 설명을 더 해줄 것을 제안한다.
4 많은 젊은이들이 대학에 가는 이유는·지식을 얻기 위해서, 취업을 준비하기 위해, 그리고 좋은 시간을 보내기 위해서지만, 이 순서는 순위와는 상관없다.

MEMO

MEMO

MEMO

THIS IS GRAMMAR

이것이 진화하는 New This Is Grammar다!

· 판에 박힌 형식적인 표현보다 원어민이 실제 일상 생활에서 바로 쓰는 생활 영문법
· 문어체뿐만 아니라 **구어체 문법**을 강조한 회화, 독해, 영작을 위한 실용 영문법
· 현지에서 더는 사용하지 않는 낡은 영문법 대신 **시대의 흐름에 맞춘 현대 영문법**

이 책의 특징

★ 실생활에서 쓰는 문장과 대화, 지문으로 구성된 예문 수록
★ 핵심 문법 포인트를 보기 쉽게 도식화 · 도표화하여 구성
★ 다양하고 유용한 연습문제 및 리뷰, 리뷰 플러스 문제 수록
★ 중 · 고등 내신에 꼭 등장하는 어법 포인트의 철저한 분석 및 총정리
★ 회화 · 독해 · 영작 실력 향상의 토대인 문법 지식의 체계적 설명

This Is Grammar (최신개정판) 시리즈

초급 **기초 문법 강화 + 내신 대비**
1, 2 예비 중학생과 초급자를 위해 영어의 기본적 구조인 형태, 의미,
용법 등을 소개하고, 다양한 연습문제를 제공하고 있다. Key
Point에 문법의 핵심 사항을 한눈에 보기 쉽게 도식화·도표화하여
정리하였다.

중급 **문법 요(Key Point) + 체계적 설명**
1, 2 중·고등 내신에 꼭 등장하는 문법 포인트를 철저히 분석하여 이해
및 암기가 쉽도록 예문과 함께 문법을 요약해 놓았다. 중급자들이
체계적으로 영문법을 학습할 수 있도록 충분한 콘텐츠를 제공하고
있다.

고급 **핵심 문법 설명 + 각종 수험 대비**
1, 2 중·고급 영어 학습자들을 대상으로 내신, 토익, 토플, 텝스 등 각종
시험을 완벽 대비할 수 있도록 중요 문법 포인트를 분석, 정리하였다.
다양하고 진정성 있는 지문들을 통해 풍부한 배경지식을 함께 쌓을
수 있다.

www.nexusEDU.kr | **www.nexusbook.com**
넥서스 초·중·고등 사이트 | 넥서스 홈페이지

책에 대해 궁금한 사항은 넥서스에듀 홈페이지 1:1 **고객상담 게시판**을 이용하세요.

초1	초2	초3	초4	초5	초6	중1	중2	중3	고1	고2	고3

Writing

공감 영문법+쓰기
1~2

도전만점
중등내신 서술형 1~4

영어일기 영작패턴
1-A, B · 2-A, B

Smart Writing 1~2

Reading

Reading 101 1~3

Reading 공감 1~3

This Is Reading Starter 1~3

This Is Reading
전면 개정판 1~4

원서 술술 읽는
Smart Reading Basic 1~2

원서 술술 읽는
Smart Reading 1~2

[특급 단기 특강]
구문독해 · 독해유형

[앱솔루트 수능대비
영어독해 기출분석]
2019~2021학년도

Listening

Listening 공감 1~3

The Listening 1~4

After School Listening
1~3

도전! 만점
중학 영어듣기 모의고사
1~3

만점 적중
수능 듣기 모의고사
20회 · 35회

TEPS

NEW TEPS 입문편 실전 250⁺
청해 · 문법 · 독해

NEW TEPS 기본편 실전 300⁺
청해 · 문법 · 독해

NEW TEPS 실력편 실전 400⁺
청해 · 문법 · 독해

NEW TEPS 마스터편 실전 500⁺
청해 · 문법 · 독해